SECRET LIVES

OF THE

U.S. PRESIDENTS

★ ★

SECRET LIVES

OF THE

U.S. PRESIDENTS

STRANGE STORIES
AND
SHOCKING TRIVIA
FROM
INSIDE THE WHITE HOUSE

by Cormac O'Brien
Illustrations by Eugene Smith

QUIRK BOOKS
PHILADELPHIA

★ ★

Copyright © 2017 by Cormac O'Brien

Library of Congress Cataloging in Publication Number: 2016954045

ISBN: 978-1-59474-935-3

Printed in China

Typeset in Chronicle, Rift, and Vitesse

Designed by Andie Reid
Illustrations by Eugene Smith

Quirk Books
215 Church Street
Philadelphia, PA 19106
quirkbooks.com

10 9 8 7 6 5 4 3 2 1

CONTENTS

INTRODUCTION

"When I was a boy, I was told that anyone could be president. I'm beginning to believe it."

—CLARENCE DARROW

Chief Executive. Commander in Chief. Leader of the Free World. The Big Cheese. Whatever you want to call them, American presidents wield a fantastic amount of power. They keep the military at their beck and call. They can veto Congress's best efforts at the drop of a hat. They receive birthday cards from foreign heads of state. Their actions even affect the stock market, sometimes dramatically.

Like it or not, they're the closest thing we have to a monarch, a figure who encapsulates elements of celebrity and authority all at once. Little wonder, then, that the people who have held the title of "President" have become household names. (Except William Henry Harrison and Chester Arthur. Oh, and Benjamin Harrison.) George Washington was the Father of Our Country, Abraham Lincoln led the nation through its greatest trial, Franklin Roosevelt took on the Great Depression and fascist aggression, and John Kennedy stared down the Soviets during the Cuban Missile Crisis. Yadda, yadda, yadda.

At least, that's what you read in the textbooks. And some of it is actually true. But what were these fellas really like? Here's what the Constitution has to say: "No person except a natural born Citizen . . . shall be eligible to the Office of President; neither shall any person be eligible to that Office who shall not have attained to the Age of thirty five Years, and been fourteen Years a Resident within the United States."

These prerequisites don't narrow the field by much. Of course, we all know there are a few more unspecified requirements—anyone who wants to be president should probably have enormous piles of cash and close contacts in big business. And until quite recently, having white skin and a penis were pretty important, too. But compared with the situation in most other countries on Earth, eligibility for the highest office in this land is still pretty wide open. And if there's any doubt in your mind about that, consider all the ninnies who have managed to get there.

Take Zachary Taylor. He dressed like an old shoe, never voted before becoming president, spat tobacco juice all over the Executive Mansion, and died from an overdose of bad cherries. Then there's Warren Harding. Bad enough that his middle name was Gamaliel. But this was a man who liked to screw his mistresses in White House closets, lived in fear of his wife, and was a devout believer in his own outstanding incompetence. Rutherford Hayes held sing-alongs every night in the White House, William Taft was too big to fit in an ordinary bathtub, Lyndon Johnson drank Scotch out of a paper cup while driving, and Gerald Ford farted. A lot.

The giants of the presidential pantheon are just as colorful, from George Washington (who had a notoriously short temper) to Jack Kennedy (who had a notoriously long list of mistresses). Remember Ulysses S. Grant, whose generalship during the Civil War led to some of the most gruesome slaughters in American history? He hated the sight of blood. And how about Teddy Roosevelt, whose progressive politics brought him into conflict with some of the nation's richest robber barons? He loved the sight of blood.

Not that we shouldn't continue to revere these folks for their accomplishments or thank them for their devotion. After all, they have one of the hardest jobs in the world. But through more than two centuries of war, legislation, and diplomacy, this country's highest leaders have displayed the consistent ability to remind us that they're not only presidents but also human beings—flawed, neurotic, hapless, bizarre, frightened, and sometimes depraved.

And thank goodness. Because if they weren't, this would have to be a book about Hollywood celebs or corporate tycoons. And who wants another one of those?

GEORGE WASHINGTON

| BORN February 22, 1732 | NICKNAMES |
| DIED December 14, 1799 | "Father of Our Country," "The Old Fox" |

ASTROLOGICAL SIGN	PARTY	AGE UPON TAKING OFFICE
Pisces	N/A *(first term)* Federalist *(second term)*	57

RAN AGAINST	VICE PRESIDENT
John Adams, John Jay *(first term)* John Adams, George Clinton *(second term)*	★ John Adams ★

HEIGHT	SOUND BITE	TERM OF PRESIDENCY
6′ 2″ ↑	*"My movements to the chair of government will be accompanied by feelings not unlike those of a culprit who is going to the place of his execution."*	1789 – TO – 1797

alk about a warm welcome. When General George Washington visited New York City at the end of the Revolutionary War, one local newspaper cheered, "He comes! 'Tis mighty Washington! Words fail to tell all he has done!"

These sentiments were shared by virtually every American. Having defeated the mightiest nation on earth (with a healthy dose of French help), the tall, stately Virginian had achieved the stature of a demigod in the freshly minted United States. It's no wonder he became the fledgling nation's first chief executive; in fact, the office was created by the founding fathers with old George in mind.

Washington was a minor Virginia aristocrat born of humble means whose career in surveying, land speculation, and militia service blossomed into immortality. Over the course of the American Revolution, he managed to avoid losing an army of underfed, underpaid, and often underwhelming rebels to the fierce predation of the British Empire and went on to assume the role of patriarch to an embryonic country. Above all, he resisted the impulse to become king over a people willing to make him one—no small feat.

As president, Washington established many of the customs that today we take for granted. The inaugural address was his idea (although his speech was written primarily by James Madison). He also liked to be called "Mr. President," which (when you consider that the Senate wanted to call him "His Highness the President of the United States of America, and the Protector of Their Liberties") shows good judgment. During his two terms, he put down a serious insurrection (the Whiskey Rebellion) and, by acting as referee in their many heated disputes, prevented Thomas Jefferson and Alexander Hamilton from tearing each other to pieces.

It's stuff like this that gets your face on a quarter, but there's another side of the coin. The Father of Our Country had just as many flaws as any other dysfunctional dad. Here are some of the highlights.

DREAMS OF WEEMS

Chopping down the cherry tree. "I cannot tell a lie." Throwing a dollar across the Rappahannock River. These are the myths that come to mind when we think of George Washington, and they've been standard fare in textbooks for years. But why? Where did they come from? Blame it all on Mason Locke Weems, a parson who, almost immediately after Washington died, published a book of the man's (alleged) exploits. *A History of the Life and Death, Virtues and Exploits of General George Washington* says a great deal about how the young nation viewed its late patriarch. People wanted to remember him as something more than human, and that's just how Parson Weems portrayed him.

AN ODD COUPLE

For most of his life, Washington was in love with a woman named Sally Fairfax, the wife of George William Fairfax—Washington's neighbor and best friend. Although his passions for the worldly and beautiful Sally probably never waned, Washington settled for a much more practical match: the widow Martha Custis, whose considerable holdings made him the wealthy gentleman he longed to be. The two were married in January 1759 and made a very odd couple indeed. George, a giant for the time at about 6′2″, towered over his portly bride, whose head didn't even reach his shoulders.

WOODEN TEETH?

Hardly. You try keeping wood in your mouth without ending up with a maw full of rotting pulp. Washington did have to endure numerous sets of dentures, however, many of which were painfully inadequate. He even had one pair constructed out of hippopotamus bone, a particularly porous material that absorbed much of the first president's port, staining the dentures black. No wonder he never smiled.

PITCHING A FIT

You could say George Washington was all the rage—in more ways than one. At the Battle of Kip's Bay, when Connecticut militia retreated from British soldiers without firing a shot, the general exploded in apopleptic fury, hurling his hat to the ground, swearing himself blue in the face, and cane-whipping everyone within reach.

A few years later Thomas Jefferson, while serving on Washington's cabinet, had this to say about the president's reaction to a bit of particularly

← George Washington's salary was around a million dollars in today's money—and he indulged in such luxuries as leopard-skin robes for all of his horses.

bad press: "The President was much inflamed. [He] got into one of those passions when he cannot control himself . . . [yelling] that BY GOD he had rather be in his grave than in his present situation."

IT'S A LIVING

According to historian Willard Randall, "the first president of the United States, George Washington, needed the job." The Revolutionary War had put Washington in serious financial straits, and accepting the highest office in the land—a responsibility he was somewhat loath to assume—was the answer to his money troubles. He soon proved just how big a spender a chief executive could be. His salary was $25,000 (equivalent to about a million dollars today), of which an incredible 7 percent was spent on alcohol. He even splurged on such luxuries as leopard-skin robes for his stable of matched horses.

SEMINAL ISSUE

Was the Father of Our Country sterile? It's possible. Although he enthusiastically embraced the role of stepfather (Martha had children from a previous marriage), he never sired any offspring of his own. Some speculate that he'd been rendered sterile by sickness. He had contracted malaria and smallpox simultaneously when he was just seventeen years old, a double affliction that could've done the trick.

Interestingly enough, it was Washington's lack of a blood heir that allowed the founding fathers to imbue the office of president with real power. Because the framers of the Constitution created the position of chief executive with Washington in mind, any fears that the first president would have delusions of kingly grandeur could be put to rest. After all, what's a monarch without an heir? For his part, Washington consistently denied having any such notions. In fact, he made no secret that all he really wanted to do was get back to Mount Vernon and spend his golden years growing tobacco and drinking Madeira by the fire.

BAD MEDICINE

George Washington, who spent the vast majority of his life outdoors, who reveled in horse riding and swordsmanship, who had a physique remarkable for its size and strength, and who managed to avoid getting killed through two savage wars, appears to have died of a cold.

Or pneumonia.

Or was it strep throat?

It's unclear from contemporary accounts what sent Washington to the beyond, but we do know that his throat was sore and constricted and that the men attempting to cure him, like most eighteenth-century physicians, were quacks. They bled him four times, despite Martha's protests. They made him drink a concoction of molasses, vinegar, and butter. And they filled him full of laxatives in an attempt to purge his foundering system but succeeded only in forcing the poor geezer to spend many of his last hours on a chamber pot. With medicine like that, who needs sickness?

★ ★ ★ ★ ★

BORN October 30, 1735 DIED July 4, 1826	NICKNAMES "His Rotundity," "Colossus of Independence," "Duke of Braintree"

ASTROLOGICAL SIGN	PARTY	AGE UPON TAKING OFFICE
Scorpio	Federalist	61

RAN AGAINST	VICE PRESIDENT
Thomas Jefferson, Thomas Pinckney, Aaron Burr	★ Thomas Jefferson ★

HEIGHT	SOUND BITE	TERM OF PRESIDENCY
5′ 7″ ↑	*"No man who ever held the office of president would congratulate a friend on obtaining it."*	1797 – TO – 1801

I t was John Adams's great misfortune to be the one man who had to fill the shoes of George Washington. But someone had to do it, and Adams had everything to recommend him to the position.

Born and raised in the Massachusetts hamlet of Braintree, Adams was a consummate thinker, a gifted writer, and an indispensable part of the revolutionary cause. He made a name for himself by eloquently defending in court the British soldiers accused of killing colonists in the infamous Boston Massacre, a task well suited to a man who believed that laws applied equally to all. The constitution of the Commonwealth of Massachusetts—one of the oldest such documents still operating in the world—was his creation. And his diplomatic postings to France, the

Netherlands, and England made him the most experienced and widely traveled American ambassador of his time.

Then again, he was also a pigheaded, intemperate prima donna who constantly wrestled with his own insecurity. Indeed, many historians still aren't sure how the fragile new country managed to survive its second chief executive.

When Washington finished his term as president in 1797, he urged his successors to avoid party politics—a request they completely ignored. The emerging partisanship of Federalists and Democratic-Republicans was so pervasive, it makes today's arguments between Democrats and Republicans seem like child's play. Though a Federalist, Adams tended to avoid party preferences and made decisions based on his own opinions, a habit that earned him enemies in both factions.

Complicating matters was that Adams's vice president, Thomas Jefferson, was a *Democratic-Republican*. Until the electoral system was modified in 1804, the position of vice president was filled by whichever presidential candidate came in second. As you might expect, Adams and Jefferson got along poorly; Jefferson used every available opportunity to fuel opposition to his boss in the press.

Dissension, name-calling, and mudslinging dominated their entire term. Even foreign nations threw decency to the wind. In a scandal that would come to be known as the XYZ Affair, the French foreign minister tried to bribe a group of American envoys. The incident caused Adams to wonder if his VP was secretly aiding French spies, and it led to the president's biggest blunder, the Alien and Sedition Acts, which made it a crime to speak or print libelous opinions about the government. Though he didn't originate the acts, Adams signed them into law, thereby feeding the widespread belief that he had delusions of kingship. (Jefferson would later scrap them when he became president.)

In the end, Adams's rocky term reflected qualities that one can't help but associate with the man himself. For John Adams was a complex and difficult man indeed . . .

TALK ABOUT A HEARTY BREAKFAST

Whenever his governmental responsibilities allowed, John Adams spent as much time as possible at his farm in Quincy, Massachusetts. While there, he rose with the sun and began nearly every day by downing a "gill" of hard cider (a *gill* being roughly equivalent to half a pint).

MR. POPULARITY

John Adams once described his principal attributes as "candor, probity, and decision." His contemporaries probably would have added four more: irritability, vanity, vanity, and irritability. Adams was headstrong, perhaps to a fault; he was convinced of his own genius and ability, and his temper blew with alarming frequency. Those around him took note, including

Thomas Jefferson: *"He is vain, irritable, and a bad calculator of the force and probable effect of the motives which govern men."*

Ben Franklin: *"[Adams is] sometimes absolutely mad."*

Abigail Adams (his devoted wife): *"[You have] a certain irritability which has sometimes thrown you off your guard."*

James McHenry (secretary of war, noisily fired by Adams): *"Actually insane."*

HIS ROTUNDITY

As vice president under George Washington, Adams was president of the Senate, which empowered him to cast the deciding vote whenever the Senate was equally divided. Aside from this power, it was understood that his role was mostly passive and that he would essentially keep his mouth shut.

→ Adams's wife, Abigail, used the East Room of the White House for hanging wet laundry—a practice that may have increased her husband's grouchiness.

When it came to the subject of how to address the president, however, Adams voiced his opinion with every opportunity: "Whether I should say, 'Mr. Washington,' 'Mr. President,' 'Sir,' 'may it please your Excellency,' or what else?" Adams believed that noble-sounding titles bestowed dignity on an office; his opponents accused him of being pompous. Neither side would let the issue die, and the debate turned really nasty when Adams's opponents began referring to him as "His Rotundity."

PEN PALS

Nothing but mutual love and respect was evident when John Adams and Thomas Jefferson first met. Their backgrounds could not have been more different. Adams, a Yankee lawyer who abhorred slavery, almost never went into debt and had a modest farm that would never make him rich; Jefferson, a Virginia gentleman, depended on slavery, lived his life grandly, and always owed money to someone. Despite these differences, they instantly impressed each other and put their extraordinary heads together to create a nation. While serving as diplomatic envoys in Europe, they grew even closer, each finding fascination in the other's company and ideas.

In time such mutual admiration would disappear, a casualty of their vehement, often vicious disagreements over the French Revolution, states' rights, the limits of executive power, and other issues that typically divided Democratic-Republicans and Federalists. During Adams's presidency, their communication essentially ceased, and a silence endured for years until a mutual friend, Benjamin Rush, got them to start writing to each other again. In their final years, Adams and Jefferson kept up a correspondence that remains one of the most extraordinary in the English language, reflecting the thoughts, fears, ideals, and geniuses of two of history's most outstanding intellects.

They died on the same day—July 4, 1826—the fiftieth anniversary of the Declaration of Independence.

★ ★ ★ ★ ★

3 | THOMAS JEFFERSON

BORN April 13, 1743
DIED July 4, 1826

NICKNAMES
"Sage of Monticello,"
"Philosopher of Democracy"

ASTROLOGICAL SIGN
Aries

PARTY
Democratic-
Republican

AGE UPON
TAKING OFFICE

57

RAN AGAINST
Aaron Burr, John Adams,
Charles Cotesworth Pinckney
(first term)
Charles Cotesworth Pinckney
(second term)

VICE PRESIDENT
★ Aaron Burr ★
(first term)
★ George Clinton ★
(second term)

HEIGHT
6' 2"

SOUND BITE
*"I wish to see this beverage
[beer] become common instead
of the whiskey which kills one-
third of our citizens and ruins
their families."*

TERM OF
PRESIDENCY

1801
– TO –
1809

I n 1962, when President John F. Kennedy entertained a group of Nobel Prize winners in the White House, he heralded the event as the most distinguished gathering of intellectual talent that had ever graced the Executive Mansion—except for when Thomas Jefferson dined there alone.

JFK wasn't far off the mark. Thomas Jefferson was the walking, talking embodiment of the Enlightenment, a polymath whose list of achievements is as long as it is varied. As if penning the Declaration of

Independence, sitting as governor of Virginia during the Revolution, and serving as secretary of state in George Washington's first term weren't enough, he went on to do much more—architecture, linguistics, agriculture, philosophy, music, prose, you name it. While others dabbled, Jefferson mastered.

He left behind a vast collection of essays and correspondence, which reveal a mind of stunning complexity and apparent contradictions. Jefferson was an avowed abolitionist whose fortune relied on a large population of slaves; a forward-thinking humanist whose opinions on minorities such as Native Americans could be truly alarming; a man whose awkwardness around women stood in stark contrast to his legendary romances.

Since this was an era before candidates chose their running mates, Jefferson was free to challenge his boss, John Adams, in the election of 1800. His victory marked the first time his new party, the Democratic-Republicans, held the office of chief executive, and they looked upon the triumph as a second revolution. Jefferson used the opportunity to make a clean break with his Federalist predecessors. If they had cloaked the chief executive in a mantle of aristocratic solemnity, he brought it back down to earth. While they embraced the British model of government, he was a Francophile. And while they believed that the masses needed to be led by a class of educated gentlemen, he put his faith in the ordinary man.

Despite his preference for a less active federal government, his two terms were eventful ones. After purchasing the Louisiana Territory from Napoleon for $15 million (thereby doubling the size of the United States), he sent Lewis and Clark to discover just how big a bargain he'd really made. He worked ceaselessly to retire the national debt that the Federalists had worked so hard to maintain. He aggressively promoted westward expansion. And although he mostly managed to avoid the labyrinth of European hostilities, he did endure one nasty run-in with Britain (when the British ship *Leopard* fired on the American *Chesapeake*, drawing the

← Thomas Jefferson was fond of greeting ambassadors in his pajamas, a practice that most of them found appalling.

two nations perilously close to war). He also took on the Barbary States of North Africa, whose piracy on American ships threatened to make a mockery of the new nation. Through it all, Jefferson endured an endless barrage of acrimony from the Federalist press, which fanned whatever flames his detractors were eager to spark.

Revolutionary, leader, inventor, romantic—the Sage of Monticello was all of these and more. How much more, you ask? Well, let's see . . .

CHILLIN' CHIEF

Jefferson believed that both Washington and Adams had acted a bit too much like kings during their terms as president. And few things irritated him more than kings. To Jefferson, the Revolution had done away with tyranny and all its trappings—a new age had dawned, and it had no room for fancy titles, powdered wigs, elaborate regalia, or any other aristocratic mumbo jumbo. As far as Jefferson was concerned, the president was just another voting member of the Republic, and he was proud to act like one.

Not everyone agreed, of course, and there were countless ways to offend foreign dignitaries back in the early nineteenth century. One of which was to greet them in your pajamas. As Andrew Merry, British minister to the United States, fumed, "I, in my official costume, found myself at the hour of reception he had himself appointed, introduced to a man as president of the United States, not merely in an undress, but ACTUALLY STANDING IN SLIPPERS DOWN TO THE HEELS, and both pantaloons, coat, and under-clothes indicative of utter slovenliness and indifference to appearances, and in a state of negligence actually studied."

PROMISES, PROMISES . . .

Jefferson's original draft of the Declaration of Independence included a fiery condemnation of slavery, but the Continental Congress struck it from the document. That Jefferson had taken the opportunity to shed light on the issue is no surprise. He was a devout opponent of slavery, and he lobbied against it virtually his entire life.

Of course, we would be more inclined to applaud his efforts were it not for the fact that *he owned so many slaves.* His home was one of the largest slave-operated estates in the country. That he often endeavored to make their lives easier is true—he gave as many as possible household duty, sparing them the hardship of working in the fields. And he freed them when he could, although bestowing liberty upon a person who had known nothing but servitude had its share of complications. When Jefferson freed his chef, James Hemings, the poor guy didn't know what to do with himself, begged to be taken back, became an alcoholic, and ended up committing suicide.

Despite Jefferson's reliance on enslaved labor, he was unable to avoid serious financial woes. For a while, he even had a manufacturing enterprise in which he subjected young African men and boys to the monotonous routine of producing nails—as many as a ton per month. All for naught. By the time of his death, Jefferson was $107,000 in debt—a deficit that his heirs partially alleviated by sending most of his enslaved servants to the auction block.

TOM FOOLERY

By all accounts, Jefferson was devoted and faithful to his wife, Martha, during the ten years of their marriage before her death. But that didn't stop him from walking all over *other* people's marriage vows.

Consider Betsey Walker, the wife of Jefferson's close friend John Walker. In 1768 John ventured to New York to negotiate a treaty and asked Jefferson to keep an eye on Betsey. Jefferson promptly proceeded to do more than just that. Their indiscretions didn't come to light until years later, at which time John Walker's opinion of both his spouse and his "trusted" friend took a precipitous nosedive.

Or consider Maria Cosway, the wife of portraitist Richard Cosway. In 1786 Jefferson—then a widower—was minister to France, where he met and fell hard for Maria, a beautiful, talented musician and artist. While walking with her through the countryside, in an apparent fit of romantic zeal, Jefferson attempted to leap a fence and fractured his wrist. It isn't clear whether the couple consummated their attraction.

However, Maria—a devout Catholic who'd considered entering a convent in her youth—probably wasn't as crazy about the idea as was Jefferson, whose firm belief in natural philosophy included a conviction that sex was perfectly right and normal for lovers (even those cheating on their husbands).

FOREIGN FELON

Jefferson's knowledge of and passion for all things agricultural were truly extraordinary (the man even had a family of plants named after him, *Jeffersonia diphylla*). Driven by a desire to see the South freed from its reliance on cotton, he was always on the lookout for crops that could replace it.

While touring the south of France in 1787, Jefferson discovered that Italian rice was preferred to the American import grown in the Carolinas. Intent on discovering why, he took a detour into the Italian region of Lombardy on a mission of rice reconnaissance (a journey that, because it required crossing the Alps, was extremely dangerous at the time). He discovered that the good folks of Lombardy were growing a superior strain—one whose export outside of Italy was a crime punishable by death. Undaunted, Jefferson proceeded to literally stuff his pockets with seeds. He even went so far as to bribe his mule driver into smuggling some and keeping his mouth shut. The stolen strain of rice is grown in parts of the United States to this day.

WHEN TOMMY MET SALLY

In September 1802, James Thomson Callender, a onetime supporter of Thomas Jefferson who had taken a beating in the press and was bent on revenge, printed the scandalous accusation that President Jefferson "keeps, and for many years past has kept, as his concubine, one of his own slaves. Her name is SALLY." And so began the American preoccupation with Thomas Jefferson and Sally Hemings—what historian Joseph J. Ellis says "may be described as the longest-running miniseries in American history."

Sally Hemings wasn't just one of Jefferson's enslaved servants—she was also the half sister of Jefferson's late wife, Martha. Their romance began when Hemings was seventeen and Jefferson was forty-eight and continued on and off until Jefferson's death at age eighty-three. Recent DNA evidence confirmed that they had at least one child together and perhaps as many as five. The kicker? Jefferson was known to abhor interracial relationships, and the propagation of children by such a match made his hair stand on end.

Go figure.

For all that, Jefferson didn't even give Sally Hemings her freedom. In his will, he provided for the manumission of only five of his slaves. Sally was later given "unofficial" freedom by Jefferson's daughter Martha Randolph.

THE GOSPEL ACCORDING TO TOM

"The Life and Morals of Jesus of Nazareth," a written work begun by Jefferson during his first term as president and concluded in 1820, was a sincere expression of his understanding of what Jesus Christ contributed to Western notions of morality. It was also, from a dyed-in-the-wool Christian standpoint, a work of outright blasphemy. In effect, Jefferson had gone through the Gospels, removed anything remotely supernatural, rearranged the wording to suit his own humanist tastes, and produced a work that revealed Jesus Christ as a really neat fellow with ideas worthy of the greatest ancient thinkers but devoid of the otherworldly qualities that made him the center of Christianity. No wonder Jefferson kept the project a secret (it was discovered by his daughter after his death).

A MASTER TINKERER

Among Jefferson's numerous talents was the art of invention. Monticello, his elegant Virginia manor, was peppered with bizarre and often amusing creations of its master's vast imagination. These include a copying machine that allowed its user to write two identical letters at once; "magical" sets of doors (as one pair is opened or closed, the following pair does so automatically); and dumbwaiters (that's right, Jefferson invented them).

One of his most celebrated "conveniences" was a closet in which he had installed a "turning machine"—a sort of rotating set of clothes hangers that could be turned with a stick.

COLD FEET

In a time when people were lucky to make it into their fifties, Thomas Jefferson lived to the ripe old age of eighty-three. His secret? According to him, cold foot baths. For sixty years, he would soak his feet every morning in chilly water.

A MINOR OMISSION

Jefferson left behind specific instructions for the design of his tombstone. On it, he insisted, should be inscribed the following:

HERE WAS BURIED
THOMAS JEFFERSON
AUTHOR OF THE DECLARATION OF AMERICAN INDEPENDENCE
OF THE STATUTE OF VIRGINIA FOR RELIGIOUS FREEDOM
& FATHER OF THE UNIVERSITY OF VIRGINIA

Notice anything missing? Yep—our third president didn't think his two terms as chief executive were worth mentioning. Makes you wonder, doesn't it?

4

JAMES MADISON

BORN March 16, 1751	NICKNAME
DIED June 28, 1836	"Father of the Constitution"

ASTROLOGICAL SIGN	PARTY	AGE UPON TAKING OFFICE
Pisces	Democratic-Republican	57

RAN AGAINST	VICE PRESIDENT
Charles Cotesworth Pinckney, George Clinton *(first term)*	★ George Clinton ★ *(first term)*
DeWitt Clinton *(second term)*	★ Elbridge Gerry ★ *(second term)*

HEIGHT	SOUND BITE	TERM OF PRESIDENCY
5' 4" ↑	*"Nothing more than a change of mind."* *(spoken just before he expired)*	1809 – TO – 1817

No man had more to do with the writing of the American Constitution than James Madison. His "Virginia Plan" was adopted as its basis, and his considerable intellect was instrumental during the months of debate that created a new government. Indeed, his career reads like the early history of the very Republic he helped create.

A devoted patriot from the moment war broke out in 1775, Madison helped create the independent government of his native Virginia. In 1779 he was appointed to the Continental Congress, where he argued persuasively for a strong central government. Along with Alexander Hamilton and John Jay, he composed the Federalist Papers, which persuaded many reluctant Americans of the need for a potent federal government with the power to tax.

Madison was extremely learned, wise beyond his years, and even-tempered, and he became a compassionate supporter of an America capable of exerting great influence in the world. He even had the good sense to marry Dolley Payne Todd, who would go on to become one of the country's most beloved first ladies. Thomas Jefferson, a close friend in whose administration Madison served as secretary of state, hailed him as "the greatest man in the world."

Now for the bad press. As invaluable to the founding of the United States as Madison was, things turned ugly when he was elected president. His administration has been slammed by contemporaries and historians alike—and you can't really blame them. After all, Washington, D.C., was sacked and burned by the British on his watch (ouch). It seems that matters of international diplomacy and war weren't Madison's strong suits.

Nevertheless, by the time he'd finished his stint as president, the economy was booming and the country was on its way to international respect. So things could have been a whole lot worse . . .

SIZE ISN'T EVERYTHING

George Washington and Thomas Jefferson were both quite tall. Even John Adams had size (albeit width, not height). Compared with his predecessors, James Madison was virtually a prawn, and he still holds the distinction of being the shortest chief executive in the nation's history. Standing just 5′4″ tall, he hardly made a presidential impression. At his inauguration, Louisa Catherine Adams, the wife of future president John Quincy Adams, described the new president as "a very small man in his

→ At 5′4″, James Madison has the distinction of being the shortest president in U.S. history.

person, with a very large head." (She was referring to his intellectual capacity, by the way, not the size of his cranium—just in case you were envisioning the fourth president as some sort of extraterrestrial.)

FRAIL THE CHIEF

James Madison was without a doubt the sickliest president in American history. The man's life reads like the index to a medical textbook. Influenza, dysentery, rheumatism, hemorrhoids—you name it, he had it. He suffered frequent bouts of illness from a young age and abstained from serving in the Continental Army during the Revolution on account of them. In accordance with a common eighteenth-century belief that avoiding outdoor activities could weaken a man's constitution, his sorry state of health was blamed on his love of books and studying. Doctors actually told him to lay off the excessive scholarship. (Fortunately for us, he didn't listen.)

The location of the founded capital—Washington, D.C.—didn't help. The area's proximity to a swamp meant summers there could be infernally humid and plagued by fetid, unhealthy air. Unpleasant for most people, it was downright crippling for Madison, whose "bilious indispositions," as he called them, usually forced him to flee during the hot months. In March 1807, when hostilities between France and Britain started posing a dire threat to American commerce overseas, then–Secretary of State Madison, weak with fever, could barely make it to his office. It was a sorry state of affairs when you consider that during the same period, President Thomas Jefferson was suffering one of his notorious migraines, requiring him to seek seclusion in a dark room by as early as nine o'clock in the morning.

STIFF ONE

According to one observer who met Madison in Philadelphia during the first Continental Congress, the diminutive Virginian was "the most unsociable creature in existence." Another fan of Madison's observed in 1809 that he was "a very small thin pale-visaged man of rather a sour, reserved and forbidding contenance. He seems to be incapable of smiling." Yet more fawning praise from one who'd met the president-elect on his inauguration night: "Mr. Madison ... is a small man quite devoid of dignity in his appearance—he bows very low and never looks at the person to whom he is bowing but keeps his eyes on the ground. His skin is like parchment."

If you haven't figured it out yet, James Madison was no charmer. Yet his wife would go down in history as one of the capital's most beloved and respected hostesses. No event more clearly emphasized the differences between them than Madison's inauguration party. While the president-elect showed up looking more like an undertaker than a politician (he even told one reveler that he'd rather be home in bed), Dolley was the focus of much attention, an intelligent and eager hostess whose natural gift for gab and wit shone in such an environment. "She was all dignity, grace and affability," hailed one partygoer. Unfortunately, the first lady's graces couldn't completely compensate for the huge crowd—4,000 visitors jostled and elbowed one another, and windows were broken to let in air. As John Quincy Adams observed, "The crowd was excessive, the heat oppressive, and the entertainment bad."

JEMMY GET YER GUN

When James and Dolley Madison arrived at the White House in 1809, the building was mostly barren—the majority of the furnishings had been Thomas Jefferson's, and he took them back to Monticello. As a result, Congress appropriated $26,000 for Dolley and an extravagant architect named Benjamin Henry Latrobe to overhaul the place. Within just a few years, virtually all their hard work would be in ashes. War can make a mess of things.

The War of 1812 lies at the heart of the controversy surrounding James Madison's administration. The central cause of the conflict can be summed up neatly in one word, *impressment*, which was the British navy's nasty habit of boarding American vessels and stealing their sailors. Madison handled the crisis by attempting to play the British and the French off each other with threats of commercial boycotts. Unfortunately, neither nation took him very seriously, New England merchants went berserk when their shipping interests were threatened, hawks in Congress started calling him a wuss, and the impressments continued apace. After settling on a more aggressive path and getting Congress to declare war against the British, Madison faced an even worse problem. The army and the navy were laughably unprepared, a condition for which his own antimilitary policies were mostly to blame. As defeat followed defeat, the conflict—soon mockingly referred to as "Mr. Madison's War"—was leading many Americans to hate their own president more than the British.

Then things went from awful to horrid. In August 1814, the British landed on the coast, sent the American militia scurrying like mice, and captured Washington, D.C.—which they proceeded to torch. All Dolley Madison could save before fleeing the Executive Mansion was the household silver, a clock, some exorbitant red velvet curtains, bundles of state papers, and—last but not least—the famous portrait of George Washington by Gilbert Stuart. Dinner was set and still waiting to be eaten when, at around 7:30 on the evening of August 24, British Rear Admiral Sir George Cockburn and company entered the evacuated building.

The British sat down to dine on the spread before them, and the admiral toasted Madison (whom he always referred to as "Jemmy"). Then they trashed the place and set it aflame. Before leaving, Cockburn snatched two souvenirs: one of Madison's hats and a chair cushion belonging to the first lady—with which, the admiral was heard to say, he would remember her seat (wink, wink).

By the next day, a hurricane had rolled in, hastening the British back to their ships and extinguishing much of the conflagration they'd left behind. It was a harbinger of things to come. Within the next five months, the Treaty of Ghent would end the war, and James Madison—his incompetence seemingly forgotten—would be a hero for winning America's second war of independence. How's that for a comeback?

★ ★ ★ ★ ★

5

JAMES MONROE

BORN April 28, 1758	NICKNAME
DIED July 4, 1831	"Last Cocked Hat"

ASTROLOGICAL SIGN	PARTY	AGE UPON TAKING OFFICE
Taurus	Democratic-Republican	**58**

RAN AGAINST	VICE PRESIDENT
Rufus King *(first term)*	★ Daniel D. Tompkins ★
John Quincy Adams *(second term)*	

HEIGHT	SOUND BITE	TERM OF PRESIDENCY
6′ ↑	*"Mrs. Monroe hath added a daughter to our society who, tho' noisy, contributes greatly to its amusement."*	**1817** — TO — **1825**

James Monroe was the last president to hail from the revolutionary generation, and he was the last of the Virginia dynasty that included Washington, Jefferson, and Madison. As a junior officer during the Revolution, he had been with Washington at the Battle of Trenton, where he received a musket ball in the shoulder for his efforts. Elected to the Virginia legislature, he was later sent as a delegate from that state to the convention that ratified the Constitution. He went on to represent the United States as a diplomat to both Britain and France, was elected a senator, and served as Madison's secretary of state and acting secretary of war.

Jefferson once remarked that his friend Monroe was "a man whose soul might be turned wrong side outwards without discovering a blemish to the world." Such opinions of Monroe were common, and his stint as president would, for the most part, mirror his hardworking, good-natured qualities. The period became known as the "Era of Good Feelings," during which the country's pride in defeating the British for a second time in the War of 1812 went hand-in-hand with growing industry and declining partisanship in government. The result was a nationwide warm and fuzzy feeling.

Isn't that nice? Of course, all was not sweetness and light. Monroe's two terms would witness the acquisition of Florida (thanks to a reckless brute named Andrew Jackson, who went crashing into Spanish Florida looking for Seminole Indians and proceeded to turn a bloody international incident into a real estate opportunity), a frightening recession called the Panic of 1819, the extension of the Louisiana Purchase all the way to the Pacific Ocean, an ominous struggle over the admission of Missouri into the Union as a slave state, and—most famously—the Monroe Doctrine. This last, though shaped and worded mostly by Secretary of State John Quincy Adams, would forever be attached to the president and let the predatory European powers know that their cutthroat colonizing days in the Western Hemisphere were over. Simply put, the United States was saying, "Hear me roar."

THAT'S SOOO LAST CENTURY

Everybody knew Monroe was a member of the old revolutionary gang, but he felt obliged to remind people anyway by dressing the part—right down to his britches and buffcoat that were already out of style. He even wore an old-fashioned wig and one of those eighteenth-century cocked hats. The effect was odd and disquieting. (Imagine George W. Bush appearing in public dressed like Mike Brady from *The Brady Bunch*.)

← In the middle of a heated argument, James Monroe chased his secretary of the treasury out of the White House with a pair of fire tongs.

"ERA OF GOOD FEELINGS"?!

Despite Monroe's administration being remembered for its relative tranquillity, his White House bore witness to a few moments that were anything but serene, notably:

Era of Good Feelings Personal Foul #1: Secretary of the Treasury William Crawford once came calling on the president with a stack of patronage recommendations, all of which Monroe rejected. Enraged, Crawford threw a temper tantrum and demanded to know whom Monroe intended to appoint; the president replied that it was none of Crawford's damn business. Crawford snapped and advanced on the chief executive with his cane raised, calling Monroe a "damned infernal old scoundrel." Monroe then stepped to the fireplace, seized a pair of fire tongs, and chased Crawford from the Executive Mansion.

Era of Good Feelings Personal Foul #2: At a White House dinner for foreign dignitaries, British minister Sir Charles Vaughan and French minister the Count de Sérurier drew swords following an exchange of insults. The two may well have mixed it up had the president not drawn his own blade and stepped between them. Today, one can't help wondering why nineteenth-century society considered it acceptable for high-ranking, excitable officials to dine together at the American president's home armed with deadly rapiers.

ESPRIT DÉCOR

James Monroe was the only U.S. president to inherit a White House completely devoid of furnishings (everything had been burned by the British, remember), and he took the redesign very seriously—so seriously, in fact, that he persuaded Congress to give him a hefty $50,000 for the project. Being an inveterate Francophile, he relied heavily on Parisian style, lavishing the mansion with all manner of extravagant furniture and knickknacks. It didn't take long for the price tag to spin out of control; in addition, and unbeknownst to Monroe, the man in charge of handling the funds, Samuel Lane, was cooking the books. Years later, when Congress discovered that some $20,000 was unaccounted for, a legislative inquiry determined that Monroe had sold some of his own White House furniture to the government for more than $9,000. (Monroe was always strapped for cash.) He reasoned that, because many of the furnishings had been paid for out of his own pocket, the money was rightfully his. Though seemingly unrelated to the connivings of Lane (who by this time was dead), the transaction raised more than a few eyebrows and compelled Monroe to allow Congress complete access to all financial transactions, public and private, that he'd made during his terms as a government official. Congress backed off.

But Monroe's financial troubles were far from over. When he ran into more later in life, he proceeded to barrage Congress with letters demanding reimbursement for funds paid out of his own pocket while in the office. Congress's limited compliance to his request wasn't enough, and Monroe was forced to abandon his failing Virginia estate for his daughter's digs in New York City. He died there in 1831, a virtual pauper.

IT'S GETTING OLD, GUYS

Unoriginal to the end, James Monroe died on the auspicious date of July 4—the third president to do so.

6

JOHN QUINCY ADAMS

BORN **July 11, 1767** DIED **February 23, 1848**	NICKNAMES "Accidental President," "Old Man Eloquent"

ASTROLOGICAL SIGN	PARTY	AGE UPON TAKING OFFICE
Cancer 	Democratic- Republican 	57

RAN AGAINST	VICE PRESIDENT
Andrew Jackson, William Harris Crawford, Henry Clay	★ John C. Calhoun ★

HEIGHT	SOUND BITE	TERM OF PRESIDENCY
5' 7" ↑	*"The four most miserable years of my life were my four years in the presidency."*	1825 – TO – 1829

John Quincy Adams was the first son of a previous president to also become president. It was a role he was destined to play from an early age when, accompanied by his mother, Abigail, he witnessed the Battle of Bunker Hill from the crest near his childhood home. His father, John Adams, second president of the United States, went out of his way to cultivate in John Quincy the pursuit of excellence and public service. When you're an Adams, you'd better do things.

And JQA did lots of things. At age fourteen, he proved indispensable to the American legation in Russia, where he spent a lot of his time translating French (the official language of the Russian court) for the American minister Francis Dana. He would go on to become his nation's most esteemed diplomat, holding posts not only in St. Petersburg but in Berlin and London. (He would spend more than twenty years overseas.) He spoke seven languages, was a published poet, and remains the only president to serve in the House of Representatives after leaving the White House. Indeed, it was in Congress—where he earned the nickname "Old Man Eloquent"—that he made perhaps his greatest contribution: the repeal of the official gag rule that prevented representatives from raising the issue of slavery for debate. His passion for the subject would earn him the right to successfully defend the freedom of Africans from the slave ship *Amistad*, another notable success.

But such laurels came after his term as president. His mother, despite her belief in public service, once said that she'd rather see JQA "thrown as a log on the fire than see him president of the United States." These were ominous words, for John Quincy's years as chief executive turned out to be a living hell. The election of 1824 was a fiasco in which none of the four candidates won a large enough margin in the Electoral College. Despite Andrew Jackson winning the popular vote, Congress proceeded to elect Adams president, largely because of his buddying up to Henry Clay, whose influence swung the balance. (When the popular vote threw Clay out of the race, he decided to back Adams over Jackson.) When the new president then appointed Clay secretary of state, Jackson and his cronies cried foul and vowed to do everything in their power to make Adams's administration impotent. They succeeded. Virtually everything the president attempted to accomplish—including an ambitious public works program that called for the building of everything from roads and canals to national observatories—became utterly stymied by a hostile Congress. The result was one of the most ineffectual administrations in American history.

By 1828 Jackson had done everything possible to ensure an easy victory over Adams, whose elitist dislike of political campaigning only sealed his fate. JQA then had to endure the sort of humiliation that, until then, only his father had faced: getting voted out of a second presidential term.

But then, virtually nothing about being JQA was easy...

AQUATIC NEUROTIC

John Quincy Adams's obsession with self-improvement often left him soaking wet. He believed in ice-cold baths, in which he scrubbed himself raw with a mitten made of horsehair. In addition to taking long walks (sometimes six miles a day), he was an avid swimmer, especially fond of doing so in the nude—until he discovered that swimming with his clothes on was much more difficult and, therefore, more therapeutic. While president, he set aside time virtually every day for a swim in the Potomac—a preoccupation that nearly killed him one day when, upon rowing with a servant to the far shore with the intent of swimming back, a storm began to brew. After their flimsy canoe filled with water and sank, the two barely made it to the far shore. The servant set off in search of clothing while Adams waited patiently, sitting naked on the riverbank, until the man returned.

HIGH-OFFICE HIGHBROW

John Quincy Adams was no man of the people. Haughty, arrogant, and incapable of small talk, he had an icy effect on everyone around him. It didn't help that he was thin-lipped and spoke in a shrill, high-pitched voice. He was confrontational, quick to anger, and scornful of indulgences of every sort. While negotiating the Treaty of Ghent (which ended the War of 1812), he insulted the rest of the American contingent by insisting on dining alone and galvanized his unsociable reputation by scolding Henry Clay for his smoky late-night card games. To be fair, JQA was the first to admit to his glaring lack of interpersonal skills. Writing from Ghent to his wife, Louisa, he went on about his "dogmatic, overbearing manner" and "forgetfulness of the courtesies of society."

→   John Quincy Adams loved to skinny-dip in the Potomac River.

CLOSE CALL

While serving in London as minister to England, JQA attempted to instruct his sons in the proper use of firearms. Taking pistol in hand, he showed the eager young students how to load a gun, ignoring that it had already been loaded. The thing fired off in his face. He suffered damage to an eye and was treated by the finest ocular doctor in London. Fortunately, the wound healed.

SINS OF THE FATHER

It could not have been easy being the son of a wound-up perfectionist like John Quincy Adams. Unfortunately, JQA had three—George, John, and Charles. To make matters worse, none of the boys had JQA's zest for extraordinary achievement. Their lack of academic excellence was particularly troubling to Dad, whose attempts to inspire could be borderline sadistic. Upon discovering that John ranked only 45th in a class of 85 at Harvard, JQA forbade him from visiting his family in the capital until he ranked among the school's ten best students. "I would feel nothing but sorrow and shame in your presence," was his response to his son's desperate appeal. In the end, JQA's efforts—both good and bad—were tragically in vain. Both George and John became alcoholics. George committed suicide by jumping off a ship bound for a meeting with his father, and John died of an illness fed by obesity and liquor. Only Charles lived to an old age.

RED, WHITE, AND BLUES

If antidepressants had been available in the early nineteenth century, John Quincy Adams would have benefited from them. His diary entries abound with doom and gloom. "I have no plausible motive for wishing to live," he wrote upon losing the election to Jackson in 1828. Another typical entry went on about his "uncontrollable dejection of spirits . . . a sluggish carelessness of life, an imaginary wish that it were terminated." Although he engaged in various activities to brighten his mood (particularly gardening), he remained depressed until the end of his life.

BILLIARDS AND OTHER DEADLY VICES

JQA's honesty and attention to detail got him into trouble in 1826, when he listed a billiard table he'd purchased in Europe within his lengthy report of expenses. He paid for the "gaming furniture" himself and sought no governmental reimbursement, but such details were lost on his notoriously scrappy Jacksonian opponents, who saw in this otherwise insignificant factoid an opportunity to smear the president as a depraved gambler. (Apparently, billiards was seen by contemporary Americans as a "gateway" game: One moment you're chalking up a cue stick and, before you know it, you're whoring and betting your way into debtors' prison.) Despite that JQA was a New England Puritan who didn't go a day without his Bible fix, the accusation stuck, becoming part of the cavalcade of bad press that helped Jackson boot him out of the White House in 1828.

FALLING CLOSE TO THE TREE

JQA had a lot in common with his dear ol' dad, John Adams. Both were believers in a strong central government, and as a result both were accused of being monarchists. They both made a point of leaving Washington, D.C., on the night before their successors' inauguration (sour grapes, anyone?) Both were as inwardly repulsed by political campaigning as they were preoccupied with their own ambition and achievements. They were both accused of putting on airs and being stubborn and needlessly confrontational. And, perhaps most tellingly, they were the only two of the first seven presidents to be summarily kicked out of the presidency after only one term.

★ ★ ★ ★ ★

FOUNDING FODDER

They never made it into the Oval Office—but each of these Founding Fathers played a role in the birth of our nation.

JOHN HANCOCK, first signer of the Declaration of Independence, had one of the largest fortunes in New England and an even larger taste for rum punch—he kept a huge bowl of it by his bedside at all times.

BEN FRANKLIN's list of accomplishments is breathtaking, from inventing the Franklin stove and "taming the lightning" to setting Paris society ablaze with his scorching wit and wisdom. A shameless bon vivant, he freely and enthusiastically proffered advice on matters of the heart . . . and the bedroom. He even had an illegitimate son who went on to become royal governor of New Jersey (and, unfortunately for their once-close relationship, an inveterate Loyalist). Ol' Ben wrote plenty of books and pamphlets, too—including one little-known gem called *Fart Proudly*, in which he pondered, among other things, the possibility of sweetening the smell of people's gastrointestinal expulsions.

ALEXANDER HAMILTON knew a lot about money. We have the country's first secretary of the treasury to thank for much of the centralized economic system we take for granted today. Which is why we know that he must have appreciated the market forces at work when one James Reynolds demanded money to keep quiet about Hamilton's affair with his wife, Maria Reynolds. The Democratic-Republicans, eager to seize on anything to discredit the Federalists in general (and Hamilton in particular), used the whole sordid mess to besmirch Hamilton's character, creating what was the first sexual scandal in American political history.

SAMUEL ADAMS, often called the Father of the Revolution, was America's first professional revolutionary—which was fortunate for him, because he failed at everything else. He had no business sense, went through money as if he had a hole in his pocket, and couldn't even succeed at tax collecting. When he went to the First Continental Congress in 1774, his constituents felt obliged to remedy his notoriously shabby appearance by buying him a new suit.

AARON BURR is in a class by himself. As if shooting and killing Alexander Hamilton in a duel weren't enough, he did it *while serving as vice president of the United States* (under Jefferson, in 1804). After both New York (where Hamilton died of his wounds) and New Jersey (where the duel took place) issued charges of murder, Burr merely fled their jurisdiction by going back to Washington, D.C., to serve out his term. Burr would go on to bigger and better things—namely, treason. With the help of sixty followers, he hatched a plot to create an empire beyond the Appalachian Mountains that would entail stealing territory from the United States and waging war on Mexico. When one of his cronies betrayed him to President Jefferson, Burr was tried for treason and acquitted. Not surprisingly, he fled to Europe.

7

ANDREW JACKSON

BORN March 15, 1767	NICKNAMES
DIED June 8, 1845	"Old Hickory," "Sharp Knife," "King Andrew the First"

ASTROLOGICAL SIGN	PARTY	AGE UPON TAKING OFFICE
Pisces	Democratic	61

RAN AGAINST	VICE PRESIDENT
John Quincy Adams *(first term)*	★ John C. Calhoun ★ *(first term)*
Henry Clay *(second term)*	★ Martin Van Buren ★ *(second term)*

HEIGHT	SOUND BITE	TERM OF PRESIDENCY
6′	*"If you have a job in your department that can't be done by a Democrat, then abolish the job."*	1829 – TO – 1837

It is fitting that the earliest surviving letter we have from Andrew Jackson is a demand for "satisfaction": "Sir: When a man's feelings and charector are injured he ought to seek a speedy redress. . . . My charector you have injured; and further you have Insulted me in the presence of a court and larg audianc. I therefore call upon you as a gentleman to give me satisfaction for the Same; and I further call upon you to give Me an answer immediately without Equivocation and I hope you can do without dinner until the business done."

This letter tells us several important things about its author: that he was wrathful and argumentative, that nothing was as important as the settling of matters of honor through dueling, and that he couldn't spell.

Andrew Jackson grew up in the Waxhaws, a region that straddled North and South Carolina and was populated by folks who tried, mostly in vain, to scratch a living out of the soil. His limited education didn't make nearly as big an impression on him as his experiences in the American Revolution. By the time he was thirteen, he'd been captured by the British, barely survived smallpox, and lost his mother and two brothers to the conflict. Such trials forged his appreciation for tenacity, vengeance, and force.

After distinguishing himself in a legal career, Jackson served in Tennessee's Constitutional Convention, then briefly in both the U.S. House of Representatives and the Senate. He then went back to practicing law until finagling an officer's commission in the Tennessee militia, beginning the military career that would make him a national hero. By the time of the War of 1812, he'd already made a name for himself as "Old Hickory" the Indian fighter, and in January 1815 he beat back a British invasion of New Orleans that remains one of the most one-sided victories (read "slaughter") in American history.

It was Jackson's reputation as an audacious battlefield commander that would carry him to the White House. But first he had to suffer defeat at the hands of John Quincy Adams in the controversial election of 1824, a debacle that galvanized Jackson's belief that Washington was run by a bunch of dandified, overeducated crooks. Fortunately for him, plenty of Americans agreed, and he waltzed into the presidency in 1828 on a populist platform that would come to be known as Jacksonian democracy. It was high time, he believed, for the "virtuous majority" to reclaim the principles of the American Revolution. He co-opted Jefferson's Democratic-Republican Party, renamed it the Democratic Party, and declared war on government corruption.

Which, naturally, was a farce since his primary solution—a "rotation" of Washington bureaucrats that would replace old appointees with his own choices—suggests that he was merely rewarding his lackeys. He also unleashed an attack on the Bank of the United States, the sort of influential centralized institution he opposed on principle, and forced South

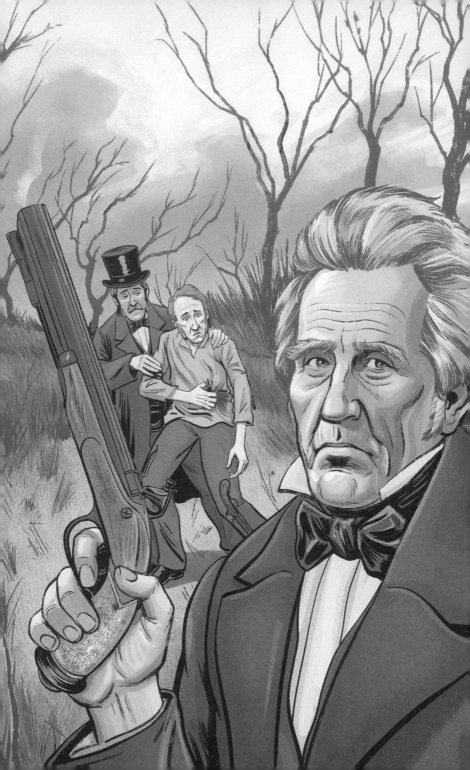

Carolina to revoke its nullification of a national tariff in a conflict that presaged the coming strife over states' rights. These kinds of measures earned Jackson the nickname "King Andrew the First" from opponents convinced that he was overstretching executive authority. They responded by forming the Whig party, named after the old opponents of monarchy during the Revolution.

All this, however, is less notable than the fact that the man whose visage graces the $20 bill got into the White House in the first place. For Andrew Jackson was essentially a madman...

HARD STUDY

As a young man, Andrew Jackson "studied law" in Salisbury, North Carolina, adopting a curriculum of reading, clerking, fighting, drinking, and vandalism. Stories of his besotted hooliganism abound. When asked to organize the local dancing school's Christmas ball, he secretly invited two of the town's most experienced prostitutes, causing a scandal. On another occasion, he and his fellow miscreants, in an advanced and increasingly rampageous state of drunkenness, demolished a local tavern—beginning with the glassware, advancing to the furniture, and concluding their soirée by setting the building ablaze. (Boys will be boys!) Jackson was also known to complete many of his wild nights with a practical joke or two. His favorite: moving outhouses to places they couldn't be found.

UNNECESSARY ROUGHNESS, EXHIBIT A

Andrew Jackson was a hard and driven man, ever willing to resort to cruelty in pursuit of his interests. While practicing law as a Tennessee prosecutor, he once coldcocked a stubborn tax dodger with a piece of

← Jackson is rumored to have fought in more than 100 duels.

wood. As a military commander, he frequently executed those who disobeyed orders or displayed mutinous behavior. During the Creek War in 1813, an entire brigade of his soldiers—officers included—threatened to march back north to Tennessee; they were exhausted by the campaigning and nearly starving for lack of provisions. Jackson promptly rode his horse to the head of the column, leveled his musket, and threatened to shoot the first man who a moved in the wrong direction. It worked. You didn't call Andrew Jackson's bluff.

UNNECESSARY ROUGHNESS, EXHIBIT B

Jackson displayed a similar lack of delicacy with his slaves. Here's an ad he placed in the *Tennessee Gazette* in September 1804:

> *STOP THE RUNAWAY*
> *Fifty Dollars Reward.*
> *Eloped from the subscriber, living near Nashville, on the 25th of June last, a Mulatto Man Slave. . . . The above reward will be given any person that will take him, and deliver him to me, or secure him to jail, so that I can get him. If taken out of the state, the above reward, and all reasonable expenses paid—and ten dollars extra, for every hundred lashes any person will give him, to the amount of three hundred.*

At least it featured correct spelling, no doubt thanks to the paper's editor.

STICKING TO HIS GUNS

Everyone has a hobby, and presidents are no different. Take Andrew Jackson: He liked to unwind by shooting at people. Whether because of his frontier environment, a tragic childhood, or some unknown frontal lobe damage, Old Hickory was overly fond of dueling. Here are the details surrounding three of the one hundred or so duels he was rumored to have fought.

His first known duel occurred in 1788 with a fellow attorney named

Waightstill Avery, who had insulted Jackson in court. (The letter calling out Avery includes the passage mentioned earlier in this chapter.) Avery was no marksman, but it didn't matter—both parties ended up intentionally firing into the air, thereby affirming their honor without shedding blood.

An 1806 duel with Charles Dickinson was much bloodier. The two men faced each other at roughly twenty-four feet, but Dickinson got off the first shot—it thumped dead center into Jackson's chest. Incredibly, Jackson merely staunched the blood flow with his left hand while calmly proceeding to take aim with his right. Dickinson found himself in the unenviable position of having to stand perfectly still and receive the bullet of a man he'd just shot. Jackson fired, hitting his mark below the ribs and killing Dickinson. The bullet that had struck Jackson lodged close to his heart and would remain there the rest of his life.

In 1813 two of General Jackson's officers entered a duel that left them both wounded. Jackson had witnessed the duel as a "second," which means he was there as an impartial witness on one of the parties' behalf. When one of the wounded men's older brother, Thomas Benton, discovered that Jackson had been irresponsible enough to allow this sort of reckless thing to happen, he publicly lambasted Jackson. The situation exploded when Jackson and two friends ran into Benton and his brother in the streets of Nashville. Jackson assaulted them with his whip, and the scuffle quickly erupted into a running gun and knife fight that engulfed much of the ground floor of the City Hotel. For his trouble, Jackson was rewarded with two gunshot wounds in the arm and shoulder, very nearly requiring doctors to amputate his arm. He would have the bullets removed twenty years later.

OLD SICKERY

Jackson was always rail thin, a man whose six-foot frame rarely carried more than 145 pounds. Though he was robust in his youth, years of hard living on the frontier and in military campaigns took their toll. (Once, during the Creek War of 1813, Jackson narrowly escaped starvation by eating acorns.) The bullet he'd taken in the duel with Charles Dickinson remained lodged near his heart and regularly led to inflammation, breathing problems, and other unpleasantries. By the time he was president, his battered body was falling apart. He suffered from persistent headaches and painful diarrhea. Afflicted with severe bronchial problems, he was often seized with coughing spells that produced frightful amounts of ugly, viscous sludge. His legs and feet swelled up, preventing him from getting around without difficulty. And his teeth were rotting out of his head. He only exacerbated his condition with alcoholic "tonics" and by chewing and smoking as much tobacco as he could lay his hands on.

BEATING THE ODDS

In January 1835, while walking through the rotunda of the Capitol, Andrew Jackson very nearly met his maker at the hands of a would-be assassin. Richard Lawrence, who somehow had convinced himself that he was the rightful heir to the British throne and that Jackson was preventing him from assuming it, approached the president and leveled a pistol at him. It misfired. By that time, Jackson was advancing on his assailant with cane raised. Lawrence produced another pistol, which *also* misfired. Old Hickory pummeled his assistant with his walking stick until witnesses were able to take Lawrence into custody. He was acquitted of his crime on account of insanity.

Both of Lawrence's pistols were subsequently fired. The odds of two consecutive misfires were later estimated to be 1 in 125,000.

★ ★ ★ ★ ★

8 | # MARTIN VAN BUREN

BORN December 5, 1782	NICKNAMES
DIED July 24, 1862	"The Little Magician," "Little Van," "Martin Van Ruin"

ASTROLOGICAL SIGN	PARTY	AGE UPON TAKING OFFICE
Sagittarius	Democratic	**55**

RAN AGAINST	VICE PRESIDENT
William Henry Harrison	★ Richard M. Johnson ★

HEIGHT	SOUND BITE	TERM OF PRESIDENCY
5′ 6″	*"As to the presidency, the two happiest days of my life were those of my entrance upon the office and my surrender of it."*	**1837** – TO – **1841**

Martin Van Buren was a new kind of president. To begin with, he was the first to be born after the Declaration of Independence. But more important, he was a party man, an organizer who felt more at home pulling strings behind the scenes than giving speeches before the masses.

A protégé of Andrew Jackson, Van Buren was largely responsible for creating the Democratic party that Old Hickory came to symbolize. The two had a great admiration for each other, despite having virtually nothing in common. Jackson was a frontier legend who fit the image of charismatic hero, whereas Van Buren, an easterner from Kinderhook, New York, aspired to aristocracy and hated crowds. Together, however, they were more than a match for Jackson's opponents, and Van Buren was handpicked by the general to succeed him in 1837.

"Little Van" fashioned the first statewide political machine in American history, the Bucktails of New York. He went on to work the same magic on a national scale with the Democratic Party, earning him all manner of nicknames referring to conjuring and sorcery. He was sharp, imaginative, driven, and adept at bringing together unlikely coalitions, which earned him such positions as secretary of state, minister to Great Britain, and vice president.

But backroom etiquette and a silver tongue do not a president make (at least they didn't in 1838), and the little magician found his hat woefully empty of rabbits while in the White House. The financial panic of 1837, though largely the result of Jackson's emasculation of the Bank of the United States, hit the country with its economic pants down, and blame fell immediately on the new president. It was the worst economic crisis yet in American history, and Van Buren—convinced, like his predecessor, that government shouldn't interfere with such things—embraced a policy of inactivity. Doing so worsened both the economy and his popularity. When the economy took another hit in 1839, Van Buren, having learned his lesson, took action by creating a strong and independent treasury. But by then it was too late—known popularly as "Martin Van Ruin," he failed to win reelection in 1840.

His single term as chief executive also witnessed the continued resettlement of American Indians, resulting in the infamous "Trail of Tears" that decimated the Cherokee people. To his credit, Van Buren managed to avoid a war with Great Britain (yes, the British again!) that was sparked by a rebellion in Canada.

In the end, his necromantic nicknames could not have been more apt. For there was more to Martin Van Buren than meets the eye . . .

→   Van Buren soothed his chronically upset stomach by drinking water mixed with charcoal and soot.

COATS, SOOTHES, RELIEVES . . .

Van Buren's angst over the Panic of 1837 gave him a chronic upset stomach. His remedy: a concoction of soot and charcoal mixed in water. Granted, this was long before the days of modern medicine, but still—*the poor fool dumped soot, charcoal, and water into his agitated stomach.*

COMMITTED WAFFLER

Martin Van Buren was renowned for not taking a stand. One story, which Van Buren admits to in his autobiography, tells how a senator once accepted a bet that he could make Van Buren admit to something with finality. "It's been rumored that the sun rises in the east," said the senator to Van Buren. "Do you believe it?" "Well, Senator," came the reply, "I understand that's the common acceptance, but as I never get up till after dawn, I can't really say."

LOONY SPOONS

There is a paradox about Martin Van Buren: though born of middle-class means and a champion of populist politics, he aspired to the aristocracy his whole life. Even before becoming president, he was widely accused of putting on airs and throwing lavish, decidedly unrepublican parties and dinners. He wore clothes that other Democrats thought effete, and he generally avoided the bustling public gatherings that other presidents—particularly Andrew Jackson—used to congregate with voters. (Van Buren was the first president not to hold a Fourth of July reception, deciding instead to join a garish parade in his native New York.) Such behavior eventually was his undoing.

The man who would most effectively use Little Van's reputation against him was Pennsylvania congressman Charles Ogle. During the election of 1840, Ogle, a longtime opponent of Van Buren, gave a lengthy speech on the alleged extravagance of the president's lifestyle. According to Ogle, the White House had become "a *palace* as splendid as that of the Caesars, and as richly adorned as the proudest Asiatic mansion." It would go down in history as the "gold spoons" speech, for Ogle referred to the gold utensils that Van Buren held in his gloved hands to daintily sip rich food. Though mostly hogwash, it made an impression—Ogle's speech was even distributed as a pamphlet. As a result, voters had "golden spoons" dancing in their heads when they cast their ballots for contender William Henry Harrison, who went on to win the election.

Most of Ogle's speech was inaccurate (in fact, much of the White House furniture was old and falling apart), but the chief executive's residence did indeed possess a set of golden spoons. It had been purchased twenty years earlier by James Monroe.

HANNAH WHO?

Martin Van Buren wrote an autobiography that is notable for two reasons:
1. It is as dry as unbuttered toast.
2. It fails to mention, even once, his wife, Hannah Hoes Van Buren.

★ ★ ★ ★ ★

BORN February 9, 1773	NICKNAMES
DIED April 4, 1841	"Tippecanoe," "Old Granny"

ASTROLOGICAL SIGN	PARTY	AGE UPON TAKING OFFICE
Aquarius	Whig	
		68

RAN AGAINST	VICE PRESIDENT
Martin Van Buren	★ John Tyler ★

HEIGHT	SOUND BITE	TERM OF PRESIDENCY
5′ 8″ ↑	*"Some folks are silly enough to have formed a plan to make a president of the U.S. out of this Clerk and Clod Hopper."* (referring to himself)	**1841**

O ne of William Henry Harrison's campaign promises was to forgo seeking a second term if elected president. It was the only part of his platform he carried out. One month after taking office, he was dead.

Harrison was the last American president born as an English subject. Though his father (a signer of the Declaration of Independence) had hoped he would become a physician, army life beckoned and Harrison became an officer, making a name for himself on the northwestern frontier as an Indian fighter and territorial governor. In 1811 he fought an Indian alliance at the junction of the Tippecanoe and Wabash Rivers, beginning his rise as a war hero. His reputation would be enhanced during the War of 1812 at the Battle of the Thames, where troops led by Harrison defeated a British and Indian force that included Tecumseh, who was killed. Aside from bloodstained credentials like these, he had little to recommend him to the presidency besides a stint in the Senate (which took him several tries to win) and a posting as ambassador to Colombia (where he was almost thrown in jail for supporting an uprising against the government).

But if Harrison was no dream candidate, his campaign for president was one of the most important in American history. Before 1840, active campaigning for office was considered as crass as writing a blurb for your own book. Candidates were supposed to maintain an air of ambivalence while others did their stumping for them. Harrison changed all that by personally jumping into the fray with earnest, smiling enthusiasm, and his Whig Party cohorts turned the campaign into a circus. They dismissed opponent Martin Van Buren as a snob and a dandy, claiming their boy Harrison was the real man of the people. There were parties, bands, garish banners. It worked.

Unfortunately, prominent Whigs like Henry Clay expected Harrison to be the sort of president they could dominate. They'd pulled out all the stops to get him into the White House, and he was supposed to return the favor by letting them run his administration. Alas, Harrison—in his sixties and unaccustomed to being treated like a child—chafed under the party's collar and began telling Clay and company where they could stick their "suggestions."

The conflict was resolved not by compromise or negotiation but by what was probably pneumonia. Harrison caught it, and the Whigs ended up getting President John Tyler—who would prove even tougher to dominate than Harrison had been. But that's another story.

LET THIS BE A LESSON TO US ALL: KEEP IT SHORT!

If William Henry Harrison is remembered for having the shortest term of office, he's also famous for having the longest inaugural speech on record— an insufferable one hour and forty-five minutes. To make matters worse, he delivered it on a day that was remarkably cold and blustery. His audience had dressed for the occasion, but Harrison insisted on delivering his epic

sans coat or gloves. He fell sick the next day, and though he recovered after only a few days, the illness may have weakened his system. Just weeks later, on March 27, he started having chills that forced him to skip a cabinet meeting and head straight for his bed.

Doctors soon descended and for the next week besieged him with "remedies" that were old-fashioned even for 1841. After a regimen of castor oil, calomel, ipecac, opium, camphor, and brandy, it is perhaps little wonder that his condition worsened; from chills, his affliction diversified into colitis, vomiting, and hepatitis. Mercifully, the man died on April 4, 1841.

← Harrison's 105-minute inaugural speech—made on a cold and blustery day in March—would ultimately cost the new president his life.

BORN **March 29, 1790**	NICKNAME
DIED **January 18, 1862**	**"His Accidency"**

ASTROLOGICAL SIGN	PARTY	AGE UPON TAKING OFFICE
Aries	Whig *and* Democratic	**51**

RAN AGAINST	VICE PRESIDENT
N/A	★ None ★

HEIGHT	SOUND BITE	TERM OF PRESIDENCY
6′	*"Popularity, I have always thought, may aptly be compared to a coquette—the more you woo her, the more apt is she to elude your embrace."*	**1841** – TO – **1845**

William Henry Harrison was the first president to kick the bucket while in office, a situation that posed a particularly thorny problem for Vice President John Tyler. Was he now the president of the United States or merely the *sitting* president of the United States?

The Constitution was a bit vague on the issue, but Tyler didn't hesitate to give his opinion: he was the chief executive, fully vested with the office's powers, and he accepted no arguments to the contrary. Indeed, for the first few months of his administration, whenever he received official mail addressed to the "Acting President of the United States," he promptly returned it marked "addressee unknown."

Tyler was a Virginian who had served as governor of his home state as well as in both houses of the U.S. Congress. He had received the vice presidential nod because of his support for big Whig Henry Clay, and now he found himself in the same pickle that Old Man Harrison had been in: Clay and the rest of the Whig Party would govern the country, and Tyler—already dubbed "His Accidency"—would have to play along nicely or there'd be trouble.

There was trouble. The Whig-run Congress wanted to reestablish the powerful Bank of the United States that had been destroyed by Jackson and Van Buren. Tyler, a devout states' rights man, feared what such a bank could be capable of; he broke party lines and vetoed the idea. The Whigs went berserk, banishing him from the party. Five of his six cabinet members resigned. It was a disaster.

Because Tyler had once betrayed the Democrats as well, he now found himself openly loathed by both parties. It was a gloomy four years as he and Congress battled (Tyler cast an unprecedented nine vetoes in his one term), and threats against his life seemed to arrive daily at the White House. As if that weren't enough, his first wife, Letitia, who'd been wasting away in her bedroom for months, died from a stroke in 1842.

Despite all that, Tyler's administration managed two triumphs: the settlement with England of firm boundaries between Maine and Canada and—in the eleventh hour of his term—beginning the annexation of Texas (which the president considered his greatest accomplishment). Perhaps more important, Tyler also took another bride: Julia Gardiner, a vivacious, intelligent beauty who was thirty years his junior. She would be the brightest star of his failed presidency.

OCCUPATIONAL HAZARD

Tyler's estrangement from the Whig Party was no joke. Angry mobs made a habit of showing up at the White House—some even burned him in effigy. There were also plenty of bomb threats. Once, when an unmarked package arrived at the White House, a staff member was called to look at it. While Tyler hid behind a marble column, the servant proceeded to hack the parcel to pieces with a meat cleaver, only to reveal a dilapidated toy.

In a unique act of pity, Congress passed "Tyler's Bill," which provided for the first federally funded White House security. The force consisted of four men—they would be in plain clothes and referred to officially as "doormen." And, no, they didn't wear dark glasses.

GARNERING GARDINER

In 1842 John Tyler's son, John Jr., fell for a bright and flirtatious young woman from East Hampton, New York, named Julia Gardiner. She and her sister had been brought by their father to fish for husbands in Washington high society. But it wasn't John Jr. who would find a marital hook in his mouth, for John Sr. had his eye on the irresistible Julia, too. And, well, *he* was the president of the United States.

Having gone through a rather hasty mourning for his deceased first wife, Letitia, President Tyler set about winning Julia's heart with impressive tenacity. But though the young lady was captivated by Tyler, she didn't say yes to the big question.

At least, that is, until her father was blown to pieces by a defective cannon. The tragedy happened on February 28, 1844. On that day the new steam frigate *Princeton*, jewel of the American navy, was making its maiden cruise down the Potomac. Aboard were many of Washington's elite and powerful, including the president and the Gardiners (now regularly seen in Tyler's company at social events). Also aboard was a giant monstrosity called, ironically, Peacemaker—a new cannon of prodigious proportions, the largest in the world. As the vessel made its way down the river, the *Princeton*'s crew, delighted with their new toy and eager to show it off, fired Peacemaker twice, to everyone's delight. When upon passing Mount Vernon someone suggested firing it one last time in honor of George Washington, the crew enthusiastically complied.

That was unfortunate because the big beast was flawed. It exploded, turning the *Princeton*'s deck into a killing ground. Among the instantly

→ John Tyler had more children than any other president in U.S. history—fifteen in all!

slain were Secretary of State Abel Upshur, Secretary of the Navy Thomas Gilmer, and Julia Gardiner's father.

Upon hearing of her father's demise, Julia fainted. When the ship later docked at Alexandria, she was carried ashore in the arms of the president. According to Julia, the death of her father occasioned a change in her feelings for the president. She agreed to marry him, and the two were wed in a secret ceremony in New York City on June 26, 1844.

PRESIDENTIAL PROGENY

"My children are my principal treasure," John Tyler was once heard to say. If we are to take him at his word, he was a wealthy man indeed. Tyler had more children than any other president in American history: eight by Letitia and seven by Julia. When he married the latter, his eldest daughter was five years older than her stepmother. Someone once asked Tyler if he weren't a trifle old to be marrying a woman as young as his second wife, who was twenty-three. "Pooh," he replied. "Why, my dear sir, I am just full in my prime." And here's a mind-bender: Tyler had been born when George Washington was president, and his youngest daughter, Mary—born when Tyler was seventy years old—died during Harry Truman's administration. That's a span of thiry-two presidents—more than 150 years!

★ ★ ★ ★ ★

11 | JAMES KNOX POLK

BORN November 2, 1795 DIED June 15, 1849	**NICKNAMES** "Young Hickory," "Napoleon of the Stump"

ASTROLOGICAL SIGN	PARTY	AGE UPON TAKING OFFICE
Scorpio	Democratic	**49**

RAN AGAINST	VICE PRESIDENT
Henry Clay	★ George M. Dallas ★

HEIGHT	SOUND BITE	TERM OF PRESIDENCY
5′8″ ↑	*"No president who performs his duties faithfully and conscientiously can have any leisure."*	**1845** – TO – **1849**

ames Knox Polk, a stern-faced man whose hair looked like an early nineteenth-century version of the mullet, was the original dark horse candidate. Martin Van Buren was the Democratic favorite for the election of 1844, and the Whigs were pinning their hopes on the incomparable Henry Clay, who ran Congress as if it were his personal fiefdom. But both Van Buren and Clay had spoken out against what had become the issue of the day: annexing Texas. Polk wanted to gobble up all the territory he could, and he let everybody know it. For this reason, Andrew Jackson—philosopher-king of the Democratic party and an ardent fan of annexation—supported Polk, and Polk went on to win the election. Though John Tyler had laid all the groundwork to make Texas part of the United States,

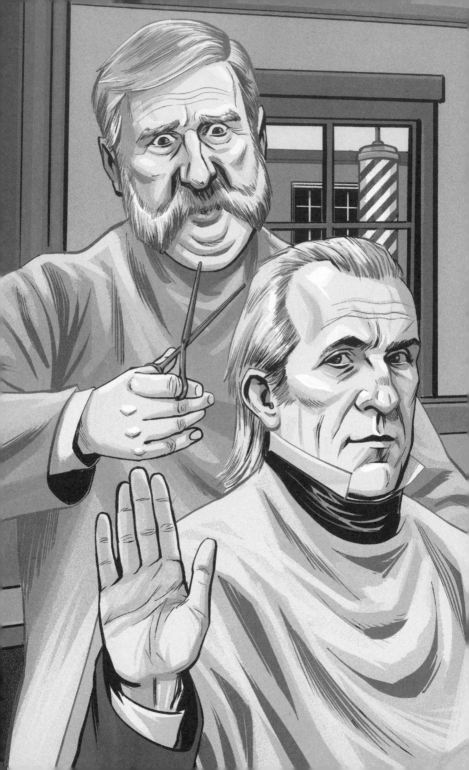

Polk rode into the White House for supporting it. And stealing land from Mexico would become his administration's legacy.

Sweeping the country was a belief in Manifest Destiny, which envisioned the United States expanding its borders all the way to the Pacific Ocean. The concept had become so popular that most Americans didn't give a darn who or what stood in the way of their pancontinental ambitions. In such an environment, Polk was the man of the hour, a leader convinced of his nation's destiny and its right to exercise force to make it happen.

The new president eyed California the way a glutton ogles a buffet, and he was determined to get it at any cost. That cost would ultimately be war—California, after all, was Mexican territory. After bullying, bribing, and berating Mexico to no effect, Polk settled on naked force. Texas would be the spark. While Mexico believed that its boundary with Texas ran along the Nueces River, Polk insisted that the Rio Grande, farther south, was the true border. It was a dubious claim at best, but that didn't stop him. (Plenty of congressmen saw through the ruse and protested loudly, to no avail.) General Zachary Taylor was sent to keep an eye on the Mexicans, and he was ordered *south* of the Nueces, to the Rio Grande. When Mexican forces reacted with force to foreign troops on their territory, Polk had the *cojones* to accuse them of shedding "American blood on American soil" and convinced Congress to pass a declaration of war.

In 1848, after two years of bloody fighting, a beaten Mexico was forced to give away a hell of a lot more than the land between the Nueces and the Rio Grande. To the victor go the spoils, and America secured a stretch of territory that includes much of present-day California, Nevada, New Mexico, Colorado, and Arizona.

That Manifest Destiny thing is something else, ain't it?

← Polk's distinctive mullet hairstyle would later influence generations of heavy metal bands and country western singers.

CHUCKLES THE BUSY BEE

James Knox Polk was an utterly humorless workaholic who believed that public servants, especially the president, had no business indulging in anything as frivolous as private time. He kept preposterously long hours, his sense of fun was notoriously lacking, and he was by all accounts incapable of discussing subjects that didn't relate to politics. Vacations were simply not an option. He and his wife, Sarah, were the first presidential couple to spend their summers in the Executive Mansion. Indeed, Polk would be absent from the capital for just six weeks throughout his four years in office.

AND NOW, THE MOST BORING DIARY ENTRY YOU'LL EVER READ

Polk viewed handshaking as a labor to be endured and once wrote a lengthy essay in his diary that relegated the act to an academic subject: "If a man surrendered his arm to be shaken, by some horizontally, by others perpendicularly, and by others again with a strong grip, he could not fail to suffer severely from it, but that if he would shake and not be shaken, grip and not be gripped, taking care always to squeeze the hand of his adversary as hard as he squeezed his, that he suffered no inconvenience from it . . ." blah, blah, blah.

THE PRICE OF POWER

Polk may have been proud of his devotion to his duty, but that devotion would ultimately be his undoing. At age forty-nine, he was the youngest president yet to take office. Only three months after his term ended, Polk died. The immediate cause was some sort of intestinal disorder, though most historians agree that the poor guy weakened his system by literally working himself to death.

★ ★ ★ ★ ★

12 | ZACHARY TAYLOR

BORN November 24, 1784 DIED July 9, 1850	NICKNAME "Old Rough and Ready"

ASTROLOGICAL SIGN	PARTY	AGE UPON TAKING OFFICE
Sagittarius 	Whig 	**64**

RAN AGAINST	VICE PRESIDENT
Lewis Cass	★ Millard Fillmore ★

HEIGHT	SOUND BITE	TERM OF PRESIDENCY
5′8″ 	*"Tell him to go to hell."* *(in response to Mexican general* *Santa Anna's demand to surrender)*	**1849** – TO – **1850**

When someone asked General Zachary Taylor during the war with Mexico whether he would run for the highest office in the land, he replied that "such an idea never entered my head. Nor is it likely to enter the head of any sane person." Less than two years later, the American people—crazy or not—made him their twelfth president.

Taylor was a simple man. Despite being a career officer, he conspicuously disliked formal military attire. His run-down look became legendary, as did his willingness to share in his troops' hardships. His unimpressive appearance, however, belied a gift for martial leadership. Having made a name for himself in the War of 1812, the Black Hawk War, and the Seminole War, "Old Rough and Ready" became a national hero in the conflict with Mexico following a series of stunning victories.

But Taylor was as ignorant of politics as he was knowledgeable of battlefield tactics. A political naïf who openly admitted to having never voted(!), he was nevertheless vigorously courted by both parties to run for president. He eventually settled on the Whigs and went on to defeat Democratic opponent Lewis Cass in the election of 1848.

Unfortunately, this political amateur took the reins of government at a time that would've challenged a president with ten times the political acumen. The problem, of course, was slavery, a subject that was threatening to tear the country apart. After the discovery of gold at Sutter's Mill, California, settlers began swarming west to make their fortunes, and soon the territory was petitioning the government for admission as a state—a free state. The ensuing controversy would ignite regional tensions and paralyze Congress as men such as Henry Clay, Daniel Webster, and John C. Calhoun fed the flames with some of the most eloquent oratory in American history. When Clay introduced a bill offering all kinds of concessions to Southern slaveholders in compensation for a slave-free California, Taylor—the last president to own slaves—surprised everybody by insisting that the admission of California shouldn't hinge on placating a bunch of whining Southerners. Indeed, not only did Taylor oppose the expansion of slavery, he also noisily vowed to personally lead the army against anyone so treasonous as to secede from the Union, which many Southerners were threatening to do.

Called the Compromise of 1850, Clay's bill and the rancor it caused were an ominous sign of things to come. But Taylor wouldn't live long enough to witness the Civil War. Stricken with a nasty intestinal affliction brought on by the searing heat and some bad cherries, Old Rough and Ready died on July 9, 1850, leaving lackluster veep Millard Fillmore to handle America's fiercest sectional conflict to date.

He may not have been the most gifted president we've ever had, but

→   Some combination of bad milk, bad water, and bad cherries led to Zachary Taylor's untimely death.

Taylor exemplifies how even the simplest, weirdest, and downright funniest-looking men can attain the White House.

UGLY AMERICAN

With all due respect to our twelfth president, Taylor was one strange-looking dude. Given his thick trunk, long spindly arms, and a face like shoe leather, he bore an unsettling resemblance to an orangutan. Old Rough and Ready may have been at home in the saddle, but he needed help getting into it—his legs were too short and bow shaped to do it alone. His hat of choice was a broad-rimmed, floppy thing woven of palmetto leaves, which—along with the mismatched set of rags that he frequently passed off as clothes—led some people to mistake their general and president for a farmer. Though he never drank or smoked, he did chew tobacco and was known as a sure shot when spitting—which he was willing to do on the White House carpet when a proper vessel wasn't within range.

MAIL DROP

Even after the Whig Party had nominated Taylor as their candidate, he almost lost his chance to accept. They had sent him word by mail that wasn't prepaid—a common practice at that time. The ever-frugal Taylor had instructed his post office not to deliver mail that wasn't already paid for, and the letter notifying him of his candidacy sat unopened for weeks. By the time he learned of it, the Whigs had almost given up on him.

LONG SHOT

You have got to respect Taylor's presidential victory, if only because so many people didn't think he had it in him. Including Taylor himself.

His wife wasn't hot on the idea, either. Peggy Taylor had spent her adult life as the spouse of a career officer (living in tents in remote garrisons, churning butter and gathering firewood, raising colicky brats without the comforts of civilization, and so on), but she drew the line at being a first lady. Afraid that the presidency would steal the last years of their marriage, she prayed every day for her husband's defeat during the electoral campaign of 1848. Apparently she didn't pray hard enough.

As for those in government—well, James Polk called Taylor "narrow-minded," "bigoted," and "exceedingly ignorant of public affairs." And here's what Congressman Horace Mann had to say: "[Taylor] talks artlessly as a child about affairs of State, and does not pretend to a knowledge of anything of which he is ignorant. He is a remarkable man in some respects and it is remarkable that such a man should be President of the United States."

AN UNDIGNIFIED CONCLUSION

On the Fourth of July, 1850, Washington was in the midst of one of its infamous heat waves. But that didn't stop ol' Zach Taylor from attending the festivities being held on the newly designated grounds of the future Washington Monument. Cholera had broken out in the city, and people were warned not to eat raw fruit or drink water without knowing where it came from. Taylor, having endured the usual round of interminable speeches in the scorching sun, stumbled back to the White House, where he proceeded to quench his thirst with as much water as he could pour down his parched throat. Still unsatisfied, he wolfed down a bowl of cherries. Then he moved on to iced milk.

Whether the culprit was the water, the milk, or the cherries, nobody knows for sure. But the president soon became sicker than a dog. By July 6, his system had succumbed to severe dehydration from constant diarrhea and vomiting, despite his doctors' efforts. He was dead by 10:30 p.m. on July 9.

★ ★ ★ ★ ★

13 | MILLARD FILLMORE

BORN January 7, 1800 DIED March 8, 1874	NICKNAME "His Accidency"

ASTROLOGICAL SIGN	PARTY	AGE UPON TAKING OFFICE
Capricorn	Whig	**50**

RAN AGAINST	VICE PRESIDENT
N/A	★ None ★

HEIGHT	SOUND BITE	TERM OF PRESIDENCY
5′ 9″	*"It is a national disgrace that our presidents, after having occupied the highest position in the country, should be cast adrift, and, perhaps, be compelled to keep a corner grocery for subsistence."*	**1850** – TO – **1853**

Millard Fillmore was the second American vice president to be unceremoniously yanked from the comfortable obscurity of his office by the untimely death of his boss. And the situation he inherited must've made him curse Zachary Taylor's love of fruit.

Fillmore was a self-made, self-educated man who rose from meager beginnings to occupy public office in Buffalo, New York. He served in Congress and distinguished himself as an accomplished comptroller of his home state. But this experience failed to prepare him for the challenges of the presidency. When contemporary historians look back and rank the residents of the White House, Fillmore almost always ends up in the bottom ten.

Of course, his presidency had its fair share of challenges. The question of slavery's extension into the new territories was inflammatory enough, and the new president had also inherited a border dispute between Texas and New Mexico that promised to ignite into all-out war. Henry Clay's Compromise of 1850, stalled by Taylor before he died, was now given the go-ahead by Fillmore, who saw it as the only hope of keeping the nation from blowing apart. California was brought into the Union as a free state, and—to placate Southerners—a new fugitive slave act was passed, requiring greater, more aggressive action against runaway slaves in free states. In the end, it accomplished little, except to delay the inevitable Civil War. Many Southerners looked at the Compromise as a sellout, while in the North, mobs of abolitionists forcibly rescued runaway slaves taken back into custody.

By 1852, Fillmore's own party had abandoned him—they gave their nomination to Winfield Scott, another hero from the Mexican War. But Fillmore wasn't ready to quit. In 1856, he staged a comeback as the presidential candidate of the notorious American Party, an anti-Catholic, anti-immigrant, anti-all-sorts-of-things group that sought somehow to heal the nation's growing rift by fostering a lot of others. He carried only Maryland. Too bad.

GOLDEN GUANO

The Compromise of 1850 wasn't Millard Fillmore's only legacy. He also sent a fleet of ships under Commodore Mathew C. Perry to open Japan to American trade (though the initiative wouldn't bear fruit until the next administration). Last but not least, he also negotiated a treaty with Peru that was literally for the birds.

Peru maintained a giant bird reserve offshore for the harvesting of droppings. (Back then, bird excrement was a cheap and abundant fertilizer.) Thanks to Fillmore's administration, American businessmen secured access to it, ensuring a steady stream of, well, filthy lucre.

ROYAL FAVORITE

Unlike his predecessor, Millard Fillmore cut quite a figure. He was well built, a natty dresser, and a generally good-looking guy. We have corroboration from no less distinguished a source than Queen Victoria, who, upon receiving the former president in 1855, called him the handsomest man she'd ever met.

A DEGREE OF HUMILITY

Though he achieved the highest office in the land, Millard Fillmore never had a high opinion of himself. He had come from a humble background and never forgot it. In 1855, during Fillmore's visit to Great Britain, Oxford University offered him an honorary degree. He turned it down, claiming that "no man should, in my judgment, accept a degree he cannot read."

★ ★ ★ ★ ★

← Is Millard Fillmore the handsomest man you've ever seen?
Queen Victoria thought so.

BORN November 23, 1804 DIED October 8, 1869	NICKNAME "Young Hickory of the Granite Hills"

ASTROLOGICAL SIGN	PARTY	AGE UPON TAKING OFFICE
Sagittarius 	Democratic 	48

RAN AGAINST	VICE PRESIDENT
Winfield Scott	★ William Rufus King ★

HEIGHT	SOUND BITE	TERM OF PRESIDENCY
5′10″ 	*"There's nothing left . . . but to get drunk."* (on his plans after losing a second nomination in 1856)	1853 – TO – 1857

F ranklin Pierce was such a dark horse that his own party had trouble seeing him. At the Democratic convention, his name didn't appear until the thirty-fifth ballot. Stuck over the issues that typically divided pro- and antislavery elements, the party finally settled on Pierce because he was a "doughface," a Northerner with Southern sympathies. He would prove a calamitous choice.

Son of a two-time governor of New Hampshire, Pierce went to school at Bowdoin College, where he rubbed shoulders with Nathaniel Hawthorne and Henry Wadsworth Longfellow. Though he served in the Senate and fought in the war with Mexico, it was his militant devotion to the Democratic party and its core principles that put him on the organization's radar. Indeed, his states' rights rhetoric nearly out-Jacksoned Jackson, earning Pierce the nickname "Young Hickory of the Granite Hills." His Whig opponent in the election of 1852 was Mexican War hero Winfield Scott, who was widely believed to be a haughty uniformed bandit bent on stealing power from the people. Pierce won the election by a landslide.

By now, the reader can probably guess which explosive national issue threatened to bedevil the new president. But if his predecessors managed to stumble their way through slavery's minefield, Pierce's footing wasn't nearly as lucky, and he blew his administration to pieces. The problems began when Senator Stephen Douglas, a fellow Democrat, sought to organize the land beyond Iowa and Missouri into a federal territory. At stake were vast chunks of real estate, a potential transcontinental railroad, and plenty of money. The proposal became known as the Kansas-Nebraska Act.

Right on cue, powerful Southerners saw an opportunity to extend the rights of slaveholders. They convinced Douglas that the act should include legislation undoing the Missouri Compromise of 1820 (which set the geographical boundaries of slavery at a latitude of 36°30′). Douglas agreed to the notion of "Popular Sovereignty"; in other words, he felt the citizens of Kansas and Nebraska had the right to vote for slavery if they wanted it. Pierce gave Douglas his support, the act was passed, and the Missouri Compromise was trashed.

The results were catastrophic. Outrage against the Democratic Party ignited, costing them dearly in the elections. Worst of all, settlers in Kansas and Nebraska—empowered to decide the slavery issue themselves—set about casting their ballots with bullets and bowie knives. "Bloody Kansas" descended into a fierce guerrilla conflict that gave the nation some idea of what the future would be like.

And Pierce? Unable to stop the horror that was unfolding in the American interior, he was accused of impotence. To make matters worse, he showed just as little tact in foreign policy. After demanding that Spain offer to sell Cuba or suffer military consequences, he was reviled as a reckless blusterer. His own party's slogan for the upcoming 1856 convention had become "Anybody but Pierce." Oh, what a mess.

The lesson here is obvious: The next time you feel like life is getting the better of you, thank your lucky stars you aren't Franklin Pierce.

IN A GLASS BY HIMSELF

Pierce struggled with alcoholism all his life. His years as a senator had been darkened by rumors of excessive drinking—indeed, his opponents called him "a hero of many a well-fought bottle." He did manage to fight the bottle successfully on occasion and even joined the Temperance League in Concord, New Hampshire, after leaving the Senate to practice law. He seems not to have had a drinking problem while serving as an officer in the Mexican War, either.

But then he was elected president.

And his son's head was crushed in a train accident.

And his marriage fell apart.

And he was surrounded by congressmen who'd left their spouses back home and loved to get together and act like frat boys.

So he started drinking again, relying on liquid encouragement (and solace) to carry him through four years of strife, suspicion, loneliness, bloodshed, and criticism. It only worsened once he left the White House. By 1869, alcohol had gotten the better of him, and he died of stomach inflammation.

INAUSPICIOUS BEGINNING

"You have summoned me in my weakness," Franklin Pierce said in his inaugural address. "You must sustain me by your strength." Given in the middle of a snowstorm, without the presence of his wife, Pierce's speech was nothing if not grim. The cause of his sorrow was a tragedy that had occurred just two months prior to his swearing-in. Shortly after boarding a train in Boston, the president-elect and his family found themselves stuck in a derailed car that was rolling down an embankment. The accident had just one fatality: Pierce's only child, eleven-year-old Bennie.

→ When Pierce's own party changed its campaign slogan to "Anybody but Pierce," our fourteenth president abandoned his hopes for reelection.

The tragedy would've been hard going for anyone. But Franklin and Jane Pierce were extremely religious people who'd already lost two sons before Bennie's death. They tortured themselves with Calvinist self-examination, scouring their faith for an answer. Jane, a withdrawn, dour, borderline fanatic who'd always hated Washington and dreaded spending another four years there, came to the conclusion that God had taken their last child so that her husband would be free to concentrate on his presidential responsibilities—a notion that didn't cast God or her husband in a very rosy light. Overwhelmed by emotions on the train to Washington, she eventually disembarked, leaving her husband to be sworn in without her.

SECURITY BREACH

When you're president of a country with its knickers in a twist over something as contentious as slavery, you take precautions. Crowds at the White House—which had always been open to the public—had grown over the years, and many feared that someone might take a shot at Pierce. Which is why he became the first U.S. president to have a full-time bodyguard on the government's tab. The man's name was Thomas O'Neil, an officer who had served with Pierce in the Mexican War, and he was charged with accompanying the president wherever he went.

Unfortunately, O'Neil was nowhere in sight when, in 1855, someone finally *did* take a shot at Pierce—with a hard-boiled egg. After being taken into custody, the assailant attempted suicide with a pocketknife. The president took pity on the poor bastard and dropped the charges.

RECKLESS DRIVER

One night, while returning from a friend's house, President Pierce struck an old woman with his carriage in the streets of Washington. He was arrested, but after the officers discovered his identity, they let him go.

PRESIDENT WHAT'S-HIS-NAME

After James Buchanan was chosen as Pierce's successor in the 1856 election, both presidents were supposed to ride in the inaugural parade. The event was half over before somebody noticed that Pierce wasn't there. The committee had forgotten to get him.

If Pierce's lackluster performance makes his presidency hard to remember, his pro-Southern sentiments would never be forgotten. He was a critic of Abraham Lincoln during the Civil War, a stance that didn't go over so well with his neighbors in New Hampshire, who accused him of being a traitor to the Northern cause. When word of Lincoln's assassination reached Concord, a mob marched on Pierce's property, angered that he wasn't displaying a flag. He quickly snatched one up and talked the rabble down, but it was a narrow escape. Franklin Pierce remains the only New Hampshire native to have become president of the United States. Yet fifty years would pass after his death before citizens of the state could bring themselves to honor him with a statue.

SECRET LIVES OF THE U.S. FREEMASONS

You have only to look at the back of a one-dollar bill to see the influence of Freemasonry on American history. See that pyramid with a giant glowing eye over it? It's a Mason's symbol, and you can find others in the Washington Monument, on the Capitol Building, and in other official places if you look hard enough.

The origins of Freemasonry may go back to the craftsmen guilds of medieval Europe, but by the seventeenth century the society had traded in its trowels and mortarboards for quills and philosophy books. Organized to improve the lot of humankind through the cultivation of democracy and virtue, the Masons' secretive lodges offered an opportunity for men of middling birth to better themselves and climb the social ladder. Many of America's founding fathers were Freemasons, and their influence is everywhere, from the Declaration of Independence to the Constitution itself.

In upstate New York in 1826, a disillusioned Mason named William Morgan threatened to publish the details of the society's secret rituals. He soon disappeared, and though his body was never found, nobody doubts that the Masons had murdered him. Much of America was soured on the organization, which, despite having played a fundamental role in creating American democracy, now seemed to threaten it. In the 1850s, they transformed themselves into a sort of charitable men's club, which they remain to this day. As for whether or not they're still sworn to secrecy upon pain of death, well… you'll have to ask one.

So which presidents were Masons? George Washington, James Monroe, Andrew Jackson, James Polk, James Buchanan, Andrew Johnson, James Garfield, William McKinley, Theodore Roosevelt, William Taft, Warren Harding, Franklin Roosevelt, Harry Truman, Lyndon Johnson, and Gerald Ford.

JAMES BUCHANAN

BORN April 23, 1791
DIED June 1, 1868

NICKNAMES
"Ten-Cent Jimmy," "Bachelor President," "Old Buck"

ASTROLOGICAL SIGN
Taurus

PARTY
Democratic

AGE UPON TAKING OFFICE
65

RAN AGAINST
John C. Frémont

VICE PRESIDENT
★ John C. Breckenridge ★

HEIGHT
6'

SOUND BITE
"My dear sir, if you are as happy on entering the White House as I on leaving it, you are a very happy man indeed."
(to Lincoln in 1861)

TERM OF PRESIDENCY
1857
– TO –
1861

And so we come to the last president who would attempt to deal with the growing conflict over slavery without force. James Buchanan was as unimaginative and ineffective as his predecessors, leaving a rough-hewn, flappy-eared comedian from Illinois named Abe Lincoln to carry a fractured nation through its bloodiest trial.

Buchanan was a tireless and clever Pennsylvania lawyer whose courtroom gifts earned him a fortune that supported him till the end of his days. His greatest asset in the election of 1856, however, was his absence from the country. Having been appointed ambassador to Great Britain by President Pierce, he was untainted by the turmoil over the Kansas-Nebraska Act, which had largely gutted the Democratic Party.

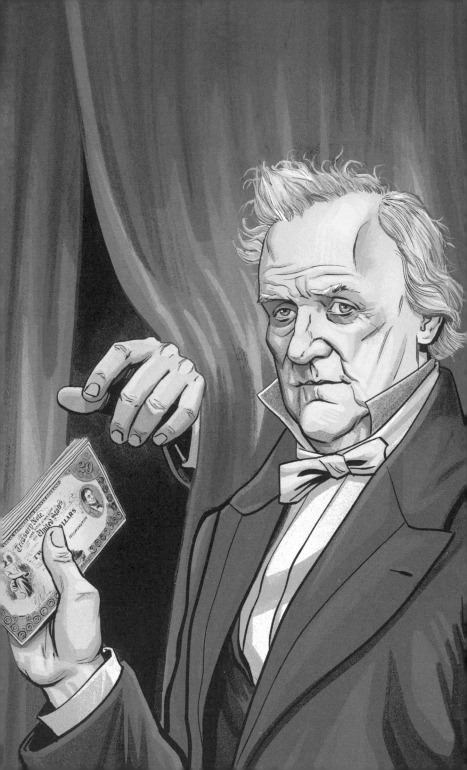

The new antislavery Republican Party performed surprisingly well in the election, but not quite well enough. Buchanan prevailed and became the country's fifteenth president.

The same absence from controversy that won him the White House would also doom him to failure. Buchanan had no grasp whatsoever of how enormous an issue slavery had become. "What is right and what is practicable are two different things," he once said. Though personally disgusted by the institution of slavery, he considered abolitionists to be a noisy, treasonous lot who'd thrown all reason to the wind. When the Supreme Court handed down its ruling in the infamous Dred Scott case, claiming that Congress had no right to outlaw slavery, Buchanan thought the matter settled. Northern outrage proved him woefully wrong.

Another imbroglio over the new Kansas Constitution made matters worse. Buchanan gave his support to a first draft (called the Lecompton Constitution, after its town of origin) that allowed slavery, but it was boycotted by most of Kansas and eventually rejected by Congress. The president was out of touch, losing allies, and looking like a real bozo.

All of which merely strengthened the first political party in American history to take on slavery: the Republicans. Their man Lincoln was considered the Antichrist by agitated Southerners, the vast majority of whom started planning their secession rather than just thinking about it. When Lincoln won the election of 1860, Southern states started hightailing it out of the Union like drunkards from a dry county, and Buchanan did . . . nothing. Nothing at all. Held captive by a legalistic belief that stopping secession was unconstitutional, he embraced his lame-duck status and waited till Lincoln took the reins.

To his dying day, James Buchanan insisted that posterity would vindicate his troubled decisions (or lack thereof). As most historians now agree, he was wrong.

← Buying votes was the least of Buchanan's offenses. He's mostly remembered for doing nothing as the entire nation unraveled.

FUSSBUDGET BLUES

By all accounts, James Buchanan was a pedantic meddler who needed things to be just so. James Polk once claimed that he acted "like an old maid." Campaign manager John Forney called him "a sort of masculine Miss Fibble." Buchanan once rejected a payment for more than $15,000 because it was off by ten cents. On another occasion, he discovered that he'd underpaid a food bill by three cents—which he promptly forwarded to the merchant in question. Even his niece Harriet Lane, who functioned as White House hostess, had a run-in with the president's nitpicking. Incapable of keeping his nose out of her affairs, Buchanan insisted on intercepting her mail before she received it. Letters were resealed and forwarded on to her with the message "opened by mistake" scrawled on them. Harriet resorted to hiding her correspondence in empty butter jugs that her friends carried in and out of the White House kitchen. Uncle Jimmy never caught on.

A LIFELONG BACHELOR

Buchanan remains the only president in American history never to have married. But at the age of twenty-eight, he was briefly engaged. His fiancée was Anne Coleman, daughter of one of the wealthiest men in Pennsylvania. After a whirlwind courtship, it looked as if the two had a rosy future together.

But Buchanan's legal responsibilities took up all of his time, and Anne was not the most emotionally stable of women. She began to feel slighted. Her parents, already concerned that Anne was about to marry beneath her station, filled her head with the notion that young Buchanan was only after her money. Things gradually worsened until Anne finally broke off the engagement. Buchanan was crushed but responded more with polite indignation than fiery passion. Anne went to visit her sister in Philadelphia, where she soon became terribly ill and died. The doctor who treated her until her death was incredulous, claiming he'd never seen a person expire from "sheer hysteria" before. Rumors persist to this day that she may have committed suicide.

Buchanan, for his part, wrote a heartfelt letter to Anne's father in which he pleaded to be allowed to follow her coffin in the mourning procession. It was returned unopened.

MISS NANCY AND AUNT FANCY

Buchanan never again became involved with a woman, though flirtations seemed to surround him for the rest of his life, most notably with Dolley Madison's niece Anna Payne. Others have speculated that Buchanan may have been gay. From the moment they first met in Congress, Buchanan and William Rufus King (who served as vice president in Pierce's administration) were virtually inseparable, earning them the nicknames "Miss Nancy and Aunt Fancy" and "Mr. Buchanan and his wife."

PARTY POLITICS

In contrast to the dreary days of Pierce's administration, Buchanan's stay at the White House was one long party. He entertained lavishly, and large, garish gatherings were the norm. Buchanan loved his liquor, and he had legendary stamina. He spent many a long night in the company of fellow lushes yet never seemed to get drunk. He once chided a merchant for providing champagne in pint bottles (which were common back then); they simply weren't big enough. But Buchanan craved whiskey most of all. His carriage ride to church on Sunday often went by way of Jacob Baer's distillery, where he would buy himself a ten-gallon cask of "Old J.B."

NOSE JOB

While serving as secretary of state under James Polk, Buchanan developed a large nasal tumor that required some two years of treatment and surgery to remove.

MEN OF STEAL

In addition to sitting back and watching his nation come apart at the seams, Buchanan presided over an administration that remains one of the most corrupt in American history. During the contentious fight over passage of the Lecompton Constitution, Buchanan and his supporters offered cash to those who voted their way. One estimate puts the total price of "incentives" at more than $30,000, though of course this figure includes diversion of government funds to Democratic candidates, juicy kickbacks from government contracts, etc., etc.

In 1860, as the secession crisis picked up speed, a relative of Secretary of War John Floyd was found to have stolen a staggering $870,000 in federal bonds. Floyd was clearly implicated, and the president asked for his resignation. The whole administration was so corrupt that Congress even turned down a plan to give the president money to buy Cuba—they feared his cabinet would pilfer the funds.

BORN February 12, 1809
DIED April 15, 1865

NICKNAMES
"Honest Abe," "The Railsplitter,"
"The Great Emancipator"

ASTROLOGICAL SIGN
Aquarius

PARTY
Republican

AGE UPON
TAKING OFFICE
52

RAN AGAINST
Stephen Douglas,
John C. Breckinridge
(first term)

George B. McClellan
(second term)

VICE PRESIDENT
★ Hannibal Hamlin ★
(first term)

★ Andrew Johnson ★
(second term)

HEIGHT
6' 4"

SOUND BITE
*"Whenever I hear anyone
arguing for slavery, I feel a
strong impulse to see it tried
on him personally."*

TERM OF
PRESIDENCY
1861
– TO –
1865

I t was 1862, the Civil War was raging, and President Abraham Lincoln had had enough. Union General George McClellan, wary of engaging the Confederate army full-on, had allowed caution to degenerate into lethargy, and Lincoln's patience had run out. "My dear McClellan," the president wired to his sluggish commander. "If you are not using the army, I should like to borrow it for a while."

Abraham Lincoln had a vibrant sense of humor. And he needed it. If he is the only American president to have successfully brought a broken nation back together again, it is perhaps no coincidence that he was also one of the funniest men ever to occupy the White House. His story and accomplishments may well stand as history's greatest testament to the power of laughter.

Born in Kentucky, Lincoln combined a single year of formal education with an insatiable love of reading to become a successful lawyer and politician. He was an Illinois Whig but joined the new Republican Party on account of his stand against slavery. In a run for Senate against Stephen Douglas in 1858, he more than confirmed his reputation as an eloquent and persuasive opponent of the hated institution. Though he lost, he challenged Douglas again in 1860—this time for president. To Southerners, Lincoln's name was emblematic of the sentiment rising in the North against everything they held dear.

The truth was hardly that simple. Voted into the White House by a growing opposition to slavery, Lincoln was a moderate more concerned with healing national divisions than with freeing slaves. Despite the vociferous cries of radical Republicans to bring a complete and utter end to slavery, Lincoln wanted union at any price. His inaugural address even included a commitment to enforce the hated fugitive slave laws, which were intended to return runaway slaves to their owners (even those who had fled to free states). Years of bloody warfare would change his mind.

As would the miserable fortunes of Northern armies. Outnumbered and outproduced, the Southern forces nevertheless displayed a galling capacity to defeat one federal army after another. Lincoln, groping for a general who could deliver him victories, went through a slew of incompetents before finally settling on Ulysses Grant. The Emancipation Proclamation—the executive freeing of the slaves, and the one act with which Lincoln's name is most often associated—was a tactical maneuver: it not only threatened to deny the South its major labor force but also promised to swell Northern armies with freed blacks. That it imbued the Northern

→ When one of Lincoln's supporters was attacked during an Illinois political rally, Lincoln himself waded through the crowd, lifted the attacker, and literally threw him out of the building.

cause with a feeling of indisputable morality didn't hurt, either, especially when nations like England and France were itching to join the fight on the side of the Confederacy. And so Lincoln—who had wanted only to contain slavery in the South—became known as the Great Emancipator.

Through it all, this unrefined country boy would run fast and loose with the Constitution. He suspended the writ of habeas corpus, which protected every citizen from government search; he blockaded Southern ports from all commerce, an act accepted by the international community only during declared wars against foreign powers; and he called up and nationalized state militias to create an army. His actions, despite outcries from the other two branches of the federal government, were justified in his eyes by the issue of time: The very existence of the nation was at stake, and wasting time to follow correct procedure only strengthened those who had seceded from the Union.

For his troubles, Lincoln would receive a bullet in the back of the head. It's hardly surprising. No sitting president has ever been so vilified. If the South despised him for opposing slavery and answering its challenge with unrestricted force, many in the North looked upon him as a reckless tyrant, a comedic baboon, a latecomer to emancipation, or all of the above. Nevertheless, one is hard pressed to find an American president with more eloquence, humility, compassion, or decisiveness. And let's not forget humor. Lincoln is as great as they come. So who had the last laugh?

A ZOOLOGICAL CURIOSITY

He had charm, insight, a way with words, and—eventually—greatness. But Abraham Lincoln didn't have looks. "Barnum should buy and exhibit him as a zoological curiosity," said one New York newspaper. True to form, Lincoln was the first to admit his shortcomings. During the famous debates of 1858, Stephen Douglas accused him of being two-faced. "I leave it to my audience," replied Lincoln. "If I had another face, do you think I would wear this one?"

THE SIDE-SPLITTER

Lincoln once referred to laughter as "the joyous, beautiful, universal evergreen of life." No great man of politics has ever done more to spread the mirth. Here's a small taste:

Lincoln found himself cornered at a party by Robert Dale Owen, a devotee of spiritualism. After patiently hearing Owen read from a lengthy manuscript on the subject, Lincoln was asked his opinion. "Well," he offered, "for those who like that sort of thing, I should think that is just about the sort of thing they would like."

Back in Illinois, Lincoln observed an old woman, garishly dressed in finery and a plumed hat, attempt to cross the street, only to slip and fall in a puddle. "Reminds me of a duck," he said to a friend. "Feathers on her head and down on her behind."

While practicing law in Illinois, Lincoln once rented a horse from the local stable to take a case out of town. Upon his return several days later, he asked the owner if he kept this particular horse for funerals. "Certainly not," said the owner. "That's good," replied Lincoln, "because the corpse wouldn't get there in time for the resurrection."

A TOUGH AS NAILS

At 6'4", Abe Lincoln towered over his contemporaries. And until the trials of the presidency wrecked his health, he weighed more than two hundred pounds. If there's any doubt that he was a tough son-of-a-gun, consider this: as a child, he was kicked in the forehead by a horse and lived to tell the tale. His wrestling skill was legendary—as a shopkeeper on the frontier, he won the undying support of a local gang of ruffians by accepting their leader's challenge to a wrestling match. The details concerning who won remain sketchy and have long since become legend. One thing's is for sure: afterward, the gang showed up at every one of Lincoln's debates to show their rather persuasive support.

The sentiment went both ways: on seeing a supporter being attacked at an Illinois political rally, Abe waded through the crowd, lifted the attacker by the head and seat, and threw him some twelve feet out of the building.

WORSE OFF GENERALLY

While hurrying off on some errand, an officer in the War Department once ran right into President Lincoln. Upon realizing whom he'd bumped into, the soldier offered "ten thousand pardons." Lincoln merely smiled. "One is enough. I wish the whole army would charge like that!"

And he wasn't kidding. Northern armies during the Civil War were led by a long succession of hesitant, myopic, or just plain unimaginative generals whose poor efforts, along with Confederate resourcefulness, allowed the Civil War to drag on for years. When asked by a journalist how large the Confederate army was reported to be, Lincoln replied with the staggering figure, "1,200,000 men." Seeing the astonished look on his questioner's face, he went on to explain that every time one of his generals got whipped, he claimed to have been outnumbered at least three or four to one. "And we have 400,000 men," Lincoln noted.

PARDON ME, MR. PRESIDENT

Desertion, treachery, cowardice—crimes like these were commonplace in the armies of the day, and the punishment was always the same: death. But the commander in chief was no harsh disciplinarian—if anything, he was a big softy. He loved to issue pardons. When one appeal for mercy turned up on his desk without the usual supporting letters from influential people, Lincoln asked the adjutant if this man had no friends. "No sir, not one," came the reply. "Then I will be his friend," Lincoln said, and pardoned him.

TOO MANY PIGS FOR THE TEATS!

Patronage, the appointing of applicants to positions in the new administration, is something that has plagued presidents since George Washington. During the nineteenth century, when the White House was essentially open to the public, office-seekers would besiege the president with their appeals daily. It could be time-consuming and contentious—as Lincoln once exclaimed, "There are too many pigs for the teats!" But he managed the hordes with his usual aplomb and became famous for finding imaginative ways to dismiss persistent applicants.

"My grandfather fought at Lexington, my father fought at New Orleans, and my husband was killed at Monterey," claimed one woman intent on getting the president to appoint her son a colonel. Lincoln promptly replied that her family had clearly done enough already and that it was time to give somebody else a chance. When a group of men beseeched Lincoln to make their applicant commissioner to Hawaii (then called the Sandwich Islands), they made mention of the man's delicate health, for which such an appointment would be ideal. "Gentlemen," replied Lincoln, "I am sorry to say that there are eight other applicants for that place, and they are all sicker than your man."

MASS EXECUTION

It is a little-known fact that Abraham Lincoln authorized the largest mass hanging in American history. In 1862, Sioux Indians on the verge of starvation attacked white settlements in Minnesota, killing more than eight hundred men, women, and children. Union troops eventually subdued the Indians, tried them, and condemned 307 of them to hang. Alarmed by rumors that justice had been a little too swift, Lincoln personally reviewed all 307 convictions. All but thirty-eight sentences were commuted. Four thousand spectators were on hand to watch the thirty-eight hang on December 26 in Mankato, Minnesota.

A WAY WITH WORDS

Lincoln suffered fools badly and had a gift for fending them off with grace and humor. In the midst of the Civil War, he received a written request for a personally autographed "sentiment." He sent off the following reply: "Dear Madam: When you ask of a stranger that which is of interest only to yourself, always enclose a stamp. There's your sentiment, and here's my autograph. A. Lincoln." On another occasion, Peter Harvey, the associate and biographer of the late Daniel Webster, went to see Lincoln. After fill-ing the president's ears with the advice that he, as Webster's closest living friend, knew the great Webster would've given were he alive, Harvey expected to make quite an impression on his listener. But Lincoln, having sat quietly and attentively for two solid hours, merely reached over, grabbed Harvey's leg, and exclaimed, "Mr. Harvey, what tremendous great calves you've got!" No more was said.

DRUTHERS OF INVENTION

Abraham Lincoln was a tinkerer. He even patented an invention of his own, a device to lift steamships over dangerous shoals that employed a series of inflatable chambers. He was always on the lookout for innovations in weaponry that might give Union armies an advantage and was sometimes seen testing new creations on the back lawn of the White House. Among the inventions he reviewed were a primitive machine gun; a method for predicting the weather; and a steel cuirass, or breastplate, that proved far too bulky for troops to wear in combat.

FEARLESS LEADER

President Lincoln had no shortage of enemies—he kept all the written death threats he received in a file at his desk marked "Assassinations." That he lived as long as he did is something of a miracle, for his murder at the hands of John Wilkes Booth was only the last in a series of attempts on his life.

Consider the time Mary Todd Lincoln was injured in a carriage accident. It was discovered afterward that the bolts holding the driver's seat to the vehicle had been loosened, almost certainly with the intention of harming the president. Lincoln was alarmingly cavalier about his safety, a fact that drove those in his immediate circle crazy. Ward Lamon, marshal of the District of Columbia, took the president's protection very seriously, often to his own frustration. He once threatened to resign upon discovering that the president had up and gone to the theater attended only by radical Republican Charles Sumner and Baron Gerolt, the aged minister from Prussia, "neither of whom," Lamon fumed, "could defend himself against an assault from any able-bodied woman." Despite the precautions taken to protect Lincoln, there were a few close shaves—including a gunshot that would've killed him were it not that his horse reared up in fright (the bullet pierced the crown of his hat). It wasn't until 1864 that Lincoln was assigned protection: four plainclothes agents.

But they weren't there to protect him on April 14, 1865, when actor and Confederate sympathizer John Wilkes Booth casually walked into Lincoln's box at Ford's Theatre and shot him in the back of the head.

MOURNING HAS BROKEN

In the weeks following Lincoln's assassination, an already shattered nation went into mourning. Many also went into the White House—specifically, to run away with whatever they could get their hands on. With Mary Todd Lincoln upstairs in hysterics and President Andrew Johnson still making preparations to move in, the White House became fair game for enterprising souvenir seekers. The lost china alone was worth a staggering $22,000.

★ ★ ★ ★ ★

BORN December 29, 1808	NICKNAMES
DIED July 31, 1875	"King Andy," "Sir Veto"

ASTROLOGICAL SIGN	PARTY	AGE UPON TAKING OFFICE
Capricorn	Democratic	**56**

RAN AGAINST	VICE PRESIDENT
N/A	★ None ★

HEIGHT	SOUND BITE	TERM OF PRESIDENCY
5′ 10″ ↑	*"Of all the dangers which our nation has yet encountered, none are equal to those which must result from success of the current effort to Africanize the southern half of the country."* (on the subject of black suffrage)	**1865** – TO – **1869**

A ndrew Johnson was the only Southern member of Congress who didn't quit his post in Washington at the beginning of the Civil War. That took grit. Though a devoted Tennessean, he was staunchly, militantly devoted to the Union—and when he was elected vice president under Lincoln, his name became synonymous with treason throughout the Confederacy. After Lincoln's assassination, Johnson inherited one of the toughest situations faced by any president—and his grit merely got in the way. His administration would be a failure, and he would be the first president impeached by Congress.

Johnson rose from painfully humble means to become a tailor. Though he never spent a day in school, he taught himself to read and write (with the help of his wife, who'd had some schooling) and soon developed a talent for political debate that would take him to the Senate and the House of Representatives. He also served two terms as governor of Tennessee.

Johnson was a rare bird, a Southerner opposed to both emancipation and the landed, wealthy slave owners of the South. He saw himself as a champion of the common man—the common white man—who'd suffered too much at the hands of a bloated aristocracy. But in 1864, it was his Southern Democratic background that attracted the attention of Lincoln, who sought a running mate who could shatter the image that the Civil War was strictly a Republican cause.

After the Union took Nashville in 1862, Lincoln appointed Johnson military governor of Tennessee. In this post, Johnson would show his love of discipline and a seething hatred of treason. This is why many in the North, especially the radical Republicans, were thrilled when Johnson assumed the presidency in 1865. The South would be remade, they thought, with a real reformer like Johnson at the helm.

Boy, were they off the mark. Claiming that he was only doing what Lincoln would've done if he were alive, Johnson carried through a plan that was anything but ambitious. Hampered by his own racism and a suspicion of vigorous federal involvement, he left much of Reconstruction up to individual Southern states. The result was a return to power of the old landed aristocracy and the creation of laws and institutions that sought to turn African Americans into a perpetual underclass.

Radical Republicans, who controlled Congress, were appalled. Empowered by their voting numbers to put through their own Reconstruction agenda, they decided to rely on the army under Secretary of War Edwin Stanton, who was sympathetic to their cause. They strengthened their hand by passing the Tenure of Office Act, which prevented the president from firing a cabinet member (i.e., Stanton) who'd already been approved by the Senate. Johnson, convinced that the act was unconstitutional, sacked Stanton anyway—and was promptly impeached by the House. The Senate failed to convict him by a single vote, but the damage had been done; neither party wanted to risk the White House on Andy Johnson in 1868.

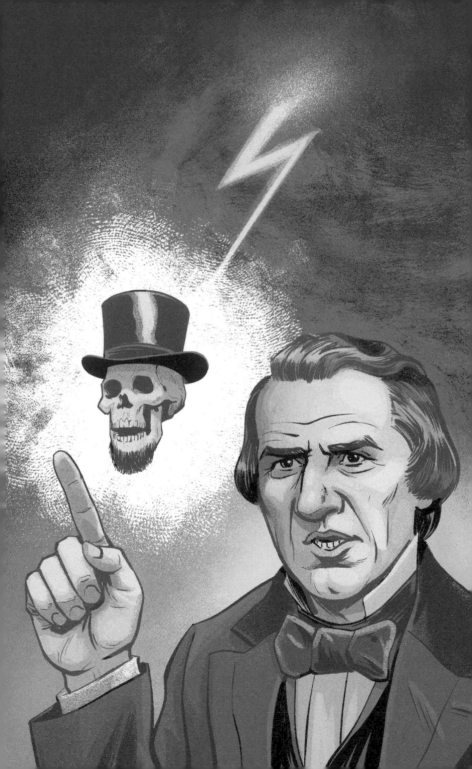

The Senate that had almost kicked Johnson's keister out of office made nice with him in 1875, when he was elected to that body once again (he was the only former president to serve in the Senate). They even gave him a bouquet of flowers. Isn't that precious?

YOU'VE COME A LONG WAY, BABY

No president has ever risen from such meager beginnings as Andrew Johnson. Born in North Carolina to a landless laborer and a washerwoman, Johnson lived in abject poverty until, at age fourteen, he was apprenticed to a tailor. After two years of hard work, he fled and lived on the lam while authorities hunted him down for breaking his indentured servitude. He eventually returned to his former employer to fulfill his tenure but was rebuffed. Johnson then gathered up what was left of his family (his father had died when Andrew was three) and crossed the mountains into Tennessee—everything they owned fit into a two-wheeled cart hauled by a blind pony. Shortly thereafter, Johnson met Eliza McCardle, made her his wife (she was sixteen when they were married), and opened his own tailor shop. The rest is history.

CLOTHES MAKE THE MAN

Andrew Johnson is the only tailor to have become president of the United States. He loved his trade and couldn't pass a tailor's shop without stopping in to talk, even while he was serving his term. As governor of Tennessee, he once made a suit for the governor of Kentucky—who, as a blacksmith, returned the favor by giving Johnson a shovel and tongs.

← Johnson's campaign efforts did little to help the Democratic cause—especially when he compared himself to Jesus Christ, claiming that God had deliberately struck down Lincoln so that Johnson could be president.

INAUGURAL SCREECH

At Lincoln's inauguration in 1865, Johnson was slated to precede the president's appearance by giving his own speech as vice president. He wasn't up to the job. Having fallen ill, he wanted to skip the address altogether, but Lincoln insisted. So Johnson did the only thing he could under the circumstances: he downed a few stiff drinks. Intoxicated and unprepared, he proceeded to deliver one of the most meandering, slurred, bizarre speeches in American history to a crowd that could only stare in stupefaction. The fiasco would've continued indefinitely had it not been for Lincoln's outgoing veep, Hannibal Hamlin, who took it upon himself to tug on Johnson's sleeve. Andy got the hint and walked off the podium in disgrace.

LIQUOR-LADEN LEGACY

In truth, Johnson was a responsible drinker who (aside from the incident described above) almost never became inebriated. His three sons were another matter. Andrew Jr. exacerbated his tuberculosis with a love of booze and died at age twenty-seven. Charles was spared a death from his own alcoholism by getting killed fighting the Confederates during the Civil War. And Robert, who liked to mix booze with prostitutes at his legendary White House soirées, was finally banished to Africa as an ambassador. He died of alcoholism at the age of thirty-five.

NARROW ESCAPE

Abraham Lincoln was killed in a conspiracy that had been intended to take out more than just the president. As soon as Lincoln was shot, a friend of Johnson's ran to the hotel on Pennsylvania Avenue in which Johnson slept. Secretary of War Edwin Stanton soon arrived and ordered guards to protect the vice president. They eventually discovered, in the room directly above Johnson's, a pistol, a knife, and a bankbook in John Wilkes Booth's name. They had been in the possession of one George Atzerodt, ordered by Booth to assassinate Johnson. However, Atzerodt, was nowhere to be found. He'd apparently thought twice about his mission and fled.

GO AHEAD, MAKE HIS DAY

When you're the only Southern congressman to oppose secession on the eve of the Civil War, you've got chutzpah. When you go to your secessionist constituents to try to talk them out of it, well, you've got some serious balls. And Andrew Johnson did. Never one to back away from a fight, he made a trip home to Tennessee at the height of the secession crisis that can only be described as suicidal. As his train made its way through Virginia, he had to force a mob off his car with a pistol. Another Virginia crowd made better headway—they dragged him off the train, beat the daylights out of him, and stopped short of hanging him only because they believed that folks in his native state of Tennessee should have the honor. Once home, he took to placing a revolver on the lectern before giving Unionist speeches.

DIVINE INTERVENTION?

Sometimes Johnson's scrappiness went too far. While president, he made a campaign tour for the 1866 congressional elections, hoping to garner votes for men sympathetic to his lackluster Reconstruction policies. His eagerness to respond to hecklers—of which there were many—resulted in one ugly shouting match after another. In a fit of pique, he once rashly compared himself to Jesus Christ, claiming that God had deliberately struck down Lincoln so that he, Johnson, could be president. Little wonder the ranks of his opponents swelled.

18 | ULYSSES S. GRANT

BORN April 27, 1822 DIED July 23, 1885	NICKNAMES "Useless," "Hero of Appomattox," "Unconditional Surrender"

ASTROLOGICAL SIGN	PARTY	AGE UPON TAKING OFFICE
Taurus 	Republican 	46

RAN AGAINST	VICE PRESIDENT
Horatio Seymour *(first term)* Horace Greeley *(second term)*	★ Schuyler Colfax ★ *(first term)* ★ Henry Wilson ★ *(second term)*

HEIGHT	SOUND BITE	TERM OF PRESIDENCY
5′8″ ↑	*"Labor disgraces no man; unfortunately you occasionally find men disgrace labor."*	1869 – TO – 1877

N o man so ordinary has ever done so much for his country as Ulysses S. Grant. The fun lies in watching how an understated, retiring pauper quickly became the most important soldier of his day and the first American president since Andrew Jackson to serve two full terms.

Grant had three natural gifts: riding horses, sketching pictures, and winning battles. Sadly, he attempted to do many other things and failed at nearly all of them. Even his father, Jesse, noticed his extraordinary ordinariness and nicknamed him "Useless" as a boy. When Jesse insisted that his son leave Ohio to make something of himself at West Point, young

Useless wanted nothing to do with it. Jesse insisted, and off his son went. Though he proved an unremarkable student who seemed utterly bored by all things military, Ulysses did win awards for his equestrian skills. He went on to serve with distinction in the Mexican War (to which he was morally opposed) and then suffered through a string of monotonous postings on the northwestern frontier that drove him to drink.

And drink. And drink some more. Even in a frontier military whose officer corps was known for its reliance on inebriation, Grant's boozing began to turn some high-ranking heads, and he was forced to resign. Glad to be reunited with his wife and children, he tried to provide for them and fell flat on his face. He had no business sense whatsoever and eventually found himself scratching out a living by peddling firewood on the streets of St. Louis. The Civil War rescued him.

After getting the army to overlook his drunken past, Grant was given command of troops again. He assumed a very unassuming manner, complete with rumpled civilian clothes and an aversion to martial pageantry. In outstanding victories such as Fort Donelson, Shiloh, and Vicksburg, Grant earned the nickname "Unconditional Surrender" and proved that Northern armies could win—even if the cost in lives was appalling. Lincoln latched onto him, made him the first lieutenant general since George Washington, and gave him whatever men and supplies he needed to cream Robert E. Lee in Virginia. Grant did just that, but at an ungodly cost. Though an American hero, he never could shake the association of his name with butchery.

His presidency has become something of a conundrum for historians, who can't seem to decide whether it was a flawed success or an abject failure. The truth probably lies in between: though his administration was beset by a level of corruption unprecedented in American history, Grant's commitment to empowering freed African Americans and making peace with the Plains Indians makes him stand out as a courageous national leader. His foreign policy was mostly a success (particularly in patching things up with Great Britain after the Civil War, which had strained the two nations' relationship), and he masterfully thwarted an attempt by financial buccaneers to corner the gold market. The powers arrayed against him, however, were formidable; by the time he left office, the

South had been returned to the grip of white supremacists. Overly trusting of those beneath him and unable to compensate fully for his lack of political experience, Grant presided over a government and a nation whose darker forces found room to prosper.

After deciding against running for a third term, Grant and his wife, Julia, embarked on a world tour, and they were received like royalty wherever they went. But financial woes would return to haunt the ex-president. Dying of throat cancer, he worried about providing for Julia after his death. The result was perhaps Grant's greatest gift to posterity: his memoirs, which earned Julia a fat royalty check after her husband's death and which remain to this day one of the finest accounts of the Civil War ever written.

WHAT'S IN A NAME?

The eighteenth president of the United States was originally christened Hiram Ulysses Grant. He didn't like Hiram, and so he didn't mind when the congressman who recommended him to West Point couldn't remember his full name. The military academy came to know him as Ulysses Simpson (after his mother's maiden name) Grant, and it stuck.

U(NBELIEVABLY) S(OUSED) GRANT

Grant wrestled with the bottle virtually all of his life, and he usually won. But when he lost, he tended to lose spectacularly. He was a binge drinker whose slight, 5′8″ frame succumbed quickly to booze. His troubles began after the war with Mexico, when he was posted to the faraway Pacific Northwest. Unable to pay for his family to join him, he longed to see his wife and young children, who were growing up without him while he wasted away in flea-ridden outposts that might as well have been on the moon.

→   Grant's name is often associated with the mass slaughters of the Civil War, but
    the mere sight of blood nauseated him.

He took to the bottle and soon could be relied upon to show up for duty half in the bag. His superior officer eventually asked for his resignation, and Grant complied.

It's interesting to note that while in the company of his family, Grant stayed on the wagon, despite years of destitution after leaving the army. Once he was back in the army, however, the urge overcame him again. During the monotony of the Vicksburg campaign, in which his forces were involved in a two-month siege of that famous city on the Mississippi, the usual triggers (boredom, separation from family, frustration) pushed him over the line. He began commandeering a riverboat for notorious all-night drinking binges. On one such excursion, Assistant Secretary of War Charles Dana saw the general get "as stupidly drunk as the immortal nature of man would allow." Fortunately, Grant's time in the White House was spent with his wife, who made sure his administration was mostly a sober one.

10,000 BOXES OF CIGARS

For all the talk about alcohol, it was Grant's smoking that eventually killed him. He smoked a preposterous number of cigars each day (he was almost never seen without one) and always reeked of tobacco. The public fed his habit—after his brilliant victory at Fort Donelson, a nation of well-wishers and admirers sent him more than ten thousand boxes of cigars. He no doubt smoked them all in short order. Grant would pay the piper years later by dying from throat cancer.

THANK GOODNESS FOR CIVIL WARS

In the years before the outbreak of the Civil War, Grant tried his hand at farming, rent collecting, working as a customshouse clerk, and cutting and selling firewood on the street. All of these ventures were failures. Desperate for work, he finally turned to his father, who got him a job clerking in a harness shop run by Grant's younger brothers.

Years later, when Grant's presidency ended, things were right back to business as usual. He borrowed enough money from William Vanderbilt to buy himself into a Wall Street brokerage firm. His partner was soon accused of illegal practices, the firm went belly-up, and Grant had to repay Vanderbilt with old war trophies and gifts given to him by foreign dignitaries while he was president.

WELL DONE

It is one of the paradoxes of the Civil War that the general most often called a butcher was acutely sickened by the sight of blood. When Grant was a boy, his father ran a tannery, whose blood-soaked hides always sent young Ulysses running in terror. While serving in Mexico, he once attended a bullfight—only to depart early, sickened by the gore and sadism. The man who sent countless soldiers to their grisly deaths had a hard time stomaching army hospitals, where the amputated limbs piled up like cordwood. Grant even took his hatred of blood to the dinner table—he couldn't tolerate meat that wasn't charred.

RUNNING RINGS AROUND HIM

The Whiskey Ring. The Gold Ring. The Indian Ring. Schemes and scandals like these rocked the Grant administration. Though the president was above most of it, the corruption of those years stained his administration and ruined his good name for posterity. The bottom line is, he should've known better. But Grant had a penchant for appointing anyone and everyone who'd ever done him a favor, and his trusting nature came back to haunt him—and the nation. Here are some of the uglier details:

When Erie Railroad "entrepreneurs" Jay Gould and Jim Fisk came close to cornering the gold market (the notorious Gold Ring), they did so with the aid of Daniel Butterfield, assistant secretary of the treasury, and Abel Corbin, President Grant's brother-in-law. Though Corbin was ignorant of the Gold Ring's true intentions, he did manage to get Gould and Fisk plenty of face time with the president, whose frequent visits with the two scoundrels did much for their credibility in New York's financial community. Grant headed off Fisk and Gould at the pass with the help of Secretary of the Treasury George Boutwell, but the result of their bold venture was widespread economic chaos that would last for years.

The Whiskey Ring was an attempt by distillers to avoid taxes by paying off government officials. Among those accused of participating was Orville Babcock, Grant's private secretary. Despite the overwhelming evidence against him, Babcock was acquitted mainly because of his boss's written deposition in his defense.

Secretary of the Interior Columbus Delano and Secretary of War William Belknap were both felled by participation in the Indian Ring, which involved kickbacks from profits slated to help Native Americans.

19 | RUTHERFORD B. HAYES

BORN October 4, 1822 DIED January 17, 1893	NICKNAMES "Rutherfraud Hayes," "His Fraudulency," "Granny Hayes"

ASTROLOGICAL SIGN	PARTY	AGE UPON TAKING OFFICE
Libra 	Republican 	54

RAN AGAINST	VICE PRESIDENT
Samuel Tilden	★ William A. Wheeler ★

HEIGHT	SOUND BITE	TERM OF PRESIDENCY
5′ 8″ 	*"I am heartily tired of this life of bondage, responsibility, and toil."*	1877 – TO – 1881

I f you think the election of 2000 was a debacle, you should've been a voter in 1876. By the time Rutherford Hayes made it to the White House, he'd received more than his fair share of death threats, barely escaped a bullet that shattered a window in his home, and was secretly sworn in to avoid revolution. Secret Service agents kept their eye out for assassins at his inauguration, and even the outgoing president, Ulysses Grant, found it prudent to walk Hayes to the podium on his arm. Why all the fuss? Because Hayes had *lost* to Democratic candidate Samuel Tilden by a mere 250,000 votes.

Rutherford B. Hayes had been a talented lawyer, Union army officer, congressman, and Ohio governor. The Republicans made him their

candidate for what he lacked—particularly his lack of a corrupt past and his lack of radical ideas that could alienate voters. He was up against a Democratic candidate who'd broken the corrupt Boss Tweed political machine in New York, and with the resurgence of the Democratic party throughout the country, everybody was expecting a close race.

They weren't disappointed. Corruption marked the election process clear across the country, but it was especially messy in three states: South Carolina, Louisiana, and—would you believe?—*Florida* each submitted two conflicting sets of electoral votes. Though the popular vote went to Tilden, each pair of returns included one favoring each candidate, and the insanity was on. To sort everything out, Congress appointed a committee that ended up splitting along party lines—eight Republicans, seven Democrats. Hayes was president.

Acutely cognizant of his situation, the new chief executive bent over backward to assure the nation that he would serve only one term and that he would avoid partisan choices. Such safe, inoffensive leadership became Hayes's modus operandi. Compared to the corruption and excess of the Johnson and Grant years, the Hayes administration was like a tall glass of milk. A religious, teetotaling family man, Hayes ran his presidency like a prayer meeting, and reforms, especially of the civil service, were pushed through with thoroughness and zeal. His good intentions could go a little too far, though. He reached out to the Democrats at every opportunity to prove his love of harmony, especially in the South; military occupation was brought to an end, thereby ending Reconstruction and leaving African Americans to their fate. A believer in the power of knowledge to defuse conflict, Hayes was a great promoter of education—especially when it came to American Indians, whose children were hurried off to Christian schools where their native heritage could be systematically expunged.

Hey, it could've been worse. After all, what can you expect from a guy who wasn't supposed to be president in the first place?

← The Hayes family banished alcohol from the White House and spent every night—yes, every night—singing gospel hymns.

GLORY HAYES

In his twilight years, Hayes was always prouder of his Civil War record than of his presidency. And little wonder: he began the conflict as a major and was eventually promoted all the way to major general. Having participated in dozens of battles, he was wounded on numerous occasions and had his horse shot from under him no fewer than four times. Even General Grant was impressed and praised Hayes for "conspicuous gallantry." Sure beats getting into the White House on a scam.

HOW DRY HE WAS

On August 19, 1877, the White House held a formal dinner in honor of Grand Duke Alexis of Russia, who was visiting the United States at the time. It was an appropriately sumptuous affair, and wine was served with every course. Given that American presidents entertain foreign dignitaries all the time, this hardly seems worth mentioning. What makes the evening worthy of note, however, is that it was the only White House function that featured alcohol of any sort during the entirety of the Hayes administration.

Several of Hayes's predecessors had banned hard liquor from the White House. But never before had a president banned every kind of alcohol, including wine and beer. The first lady, Lucy, was behind the moratorium. Nicknamed "Lemonade Lucy" by a Washington society fond of tippling, she endeared herself to the burgeoning temperance movement by forbidding anything but water at state dinners. Most visitors, especially foreigners, were simply appalled.

THE CABINET THAT PRAYS TOGETHER STAYS TOGETHER

The Hayes presidency reached new heights of puritanism. The family could be found every morning on their knees at prayer, and every night—*every night*—was spent singing gospel hymns. The rest of the administration often got in on the action. Vice President William Wheeler was fond of showing up with a copy of *The Presbyterian Hymn and Tune Book*, while Secretary of the Interior Carl Schurz played piano. Oh, the crazy times they had!

BORN November 19, 1831	**NICKNAMES**
DIED September 19, 1881	"The Preacher," "The Teacher President," "Martyr President"

ASTROLOGICAL SIGN	PARTY	AGE UPON TAKING OFFICE
Scorpio	Republican	49

RAN AGAINST	VICE PRESIDENT
Winfield Scott Hancock	★ Chester A. Arthur ★

HEIGHT	SOUND BITE	TERM OF PRESIDENCY
6′ ↑	*"My God! What is there in this place that a man should ever want to get into it?"*	1881

By 1880, there were still plenty of Republicans who wanted Ulysses Grant to return to the White House. Calling themselves "Stalwarts," they were opposed by the "Half-Breeds," the majority of whom were backing Senator James Blaine from Maine. The resulting stalemate at the Republican convention produced a dark horse: James A. Garfield, who, like so many before him, hadn't sought the presidency but acquiesced to his party's calling.

Garfield hailed from Ohio and was a close friend of Rutherford Hayes, with whose policies he generally agreed. (Garfield was a member of the controversial fifteen-man commission that elected Hayes in 1876.) Republicans saw Garfield as a compromiser who could breach the longstanding gap that had developed between the Capitol Building and the White House. Though implicated in some of the scandals that had rocked the Grant years, he was widely respected as a brilliant orator and man of letters, and most believed that his tainted past had more to do with naïveté than any lack of scruples. He was something of a prodigy: Elected to Congress at only thirty-two years of age, he'd already been a professor of ancient languages, the president of Hiram College, and a major general in the Union army. The guy had potential written all over him.

But few presidents can show the world what they're made of in four months, which is about how long Garfield lasted. A lunatic named Charles Guiteau would see to that with a couple of .44-caliber bullets. Guiteau was a particularly nasty manifestation of an issue that would plague Garfield throughout his brief stint as president: patronage. Legions of office-seekers were constantly hounding the new president, and he once observed, "These people would take my very brain, flesh, and blood if they could." Guiteau was among the most persistent—and when the president denied his petitions to become consul general of Paris, Guiteau flew into a murderous rage. The assassination shocked the country and jolted the government into overhauling the patronage system; the result was the Pendleton Act of 1883, which based appointments to the civil service strictly on talent and seniority.

After such a brief and uneventful administration, poor Garfield is mostly remembered—when he's remembered at all—for being the first left-handed president and the last one born in a log cabin. What a waste.

TOO MUCH MAN FOR ONE WOMAN

Garfield was considered a looker in his time, and his wife ... well, was not. Her name was Lucretia, but hubby James called her Crete for short. While an officer during the war, he had an affair with a woman known to history only as "Mrs. Calhoun." Though little is known about the latter, we do know that Crete learned of the relationship. Her reaction was interesting: She sent Garfield back for one last meeting with Mrs. Calhoun in New York City, where he was careful to reclaim every love letter he'd sent her and to destroy the evidence for posterity. The Garfields remained extremely close for the rest of their lives.

NUMBERS GAME

During the Grant administration, many in Congress had been implicated in a scam run by Crédit Mobilier, a corrupt organization that funded and oversaw the building of the Union Pacific Railroad. One of those implicated was James Garfield. The evidence revealed that he may have accepted a bribe in the amount of $329, acquired through stock dividends. Though the case against him was inconclusive, Garfield's connection with the scandal came back to haunt him during the election of 1880. Thanks to his opponents, the number 329 was scrawled on everything from barns and street corners to the steps of Garfield's own home.

WHEN LIGHTNING STRIKES

As President Garfield once said, "Assassination can no more be guarded against than can death by lightning." Perhaps not; but when you're president of the United States, the likelihood of the former becomes a hell of a lot greater than the latter.

Charles Guiteau didn't look like a nut when he came calling on the president for a position as consul general at Paris. He was affable and polite. Nor did he necessarily alarm the administration when, after hearing nothing about his request, he peppered the White House with letters urging a reply. After all, Washington had no shortage of pushy eccentrics looking for a handout.

But things quickly grew worse. Guiteau spent his days sitting in Lafayette Park across from the White House and stalking members of the cabinet in the hopes of getting some word on his career choice. Secretary of State James Blaine became so sick of Guiteau's pestering that he finally blew up at him, hollering, "Never speak to me again on the Paris consulship as long as you live!" Guiteau could even be seen loitering in the White

→ Garfield spent eighty days on his deathbed while a team of experts (including Alexander Graham Bell) probed and prodded him with unsanitary medical instruments.

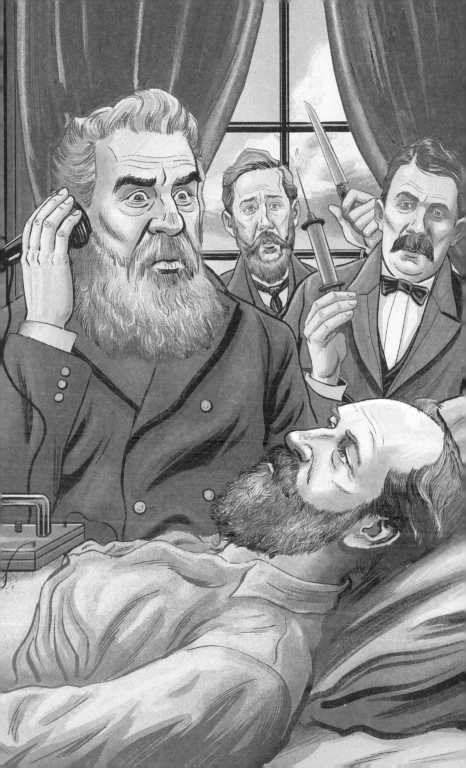

House itself, until the staff was given word that he was never to set foot inside the mansion again.

Finally, Guiteau allowed the last vestiges of his sanity to go right down the toilet. He purchased a British Bulldog pistol, was instructed by the salesman in how to use it, and—already aware of what he was about to do and what would happen to him as a result—visited the local prison to get a feel for his future digs. When the president was waiting for the train at the Baltimore and Potomac railroad station, Guiteau calmly walked up to him, drew his pistol, and fired twice. The first shot grazed Garfield's arm, but the second one lodged in his back and felled him.

IS THERE A [CLEAN] DOCTOR IN THE HOUSE?

During the eighty days it took him to die, Garfield's condition went from bad to worse to better, foiling predictions again and again. One thing seems certain: it wasn't Guiteau's bullet that killed him but all the subsequent probing with fingers and medical instruments, none of which had been sanitized. The harder his doctors tried to find the slug, the more damage they did to poor Garfield, who was awake through the whole ordeal (and suffering through the stultifying heat and humidity of summer). The bloody process took a tragicomic turn when Alexander Graham Bell was asked to help. He employed a sort of early metal detector in the hopes of locating the elusive piece of lead, but to no avail. The unhygienic investigations continued, and Garfield finally gave up the ghost. Doctors located the bullet during the autopsy.

As for Guiteau, he seemed quite pleased with himself. Interestingly, a jury found him sane, and he was hanged on June 30, 1882.

★ ★ ★ ★ ★

CHESTER A. ARTHUR

BORN October 5, 1829 **DIED** November 18, 1886	**NICKNAMES** "Elegant Arthur," "Our Chet," "Prince Arthur"

ASTROLOGICAL SIGN	PARTY	AGE UPON TAKING OFFICE
Libra	Republican	51

RAN AGAINST	VICE PRESIDENT
N/A	★ None ★

HEIGHT	SOUND BITE	TERM OF PRESIDENCY
6′ 2″ ↑	*"I may be president of the United States, but my private life is nobody's damned business."*	1881 – TO – 1885

harles Guiteau, the man who murdered James Garfield, wrote a letter from jail to the new president, Chester Arthur: "My inspiration is a Godsend to you.... It raised you from a political cypher to the president of the United States." For a lunatic, Guiteau had a decent grasp of politics; he understood that Arthur never would have made it to the White House if his boss hadn't been knocked off.

Chester Alan Arthur was the quintessential machine politician. A dapper, congenial, sweet-talking schmoozer, he had become the flunky of the flamboyant New York senator Roscoe Conkling, who was instrumental in appointing Arthur as customs collector in New York City during the Grant administration. Arthur returned the favor by using

the considerable money and influence of the New York customshouse to fill the coffers of the party and aid Conkling's agenda as head of the conservative Stalwart branch of the Republicans. He proved something of a genius at using the mostly illegal fundraising methods of the time, wielding patronage and bribes with ease and panache. Aside from that, he was essentially devoid of talent.

Enter Guiteau and his homicidal need for a posting in Paris. After assassinating Garfield, Guiteau repeatedly shouted, "I'm a Stalwart, and Arthur is now president!" This passionate show of support caused many to wonder if the Stalwarts had in fact hired Guiteau, and Arthur ducked out of sight during Garfield's deathwatch to avoid suspicion. When the press showed up at his home with news that Garfield had finally died, the new president was found slumped over a table sobbing.

His presidency was remarkable for its social events, fine dining, and little else (with the notable exception of ominous legislation that sought to limit Chinese immigration). The nattily dressed Arthur liked to eat well almost as much as he liked to buy new duds, and he reigned as the first gentleman of the land. To his credit, he turned his back on his old ways. The Pendleton Act sought to undo much of the spoils system he'd done so much to advance, and it grated on his old pals—who promptly dumped him at the next convention.

FAMILY TIES

Chester Arthur entered the White House a widower. His wife, Ellen Lewis Herndon Arthur, died in 1880, leaving Chester—who'd spent most of his marriage running around raising cash for the party—heartbroken. Though their time together was mostly tranquil, they did quarrel during the Civil War. Ellen, a native of Virginia, was sympathetic to the South. Arthur didn't let his devotion to the Northern cause eclipse his devotion

← Arthur was the first president to employ a full-time valet—and for good reason. He is rumored to have owned as many as eighty pairs of pants.

to his wife, however. He once used his influence as an officer in the New York militia to secure the release of her Confederate brother from a Union prisoner-of-war camp.

A TOUCH OF CLASS

Chester Arthur may have been short on talent, but he was long on taste. The guy had a bona fide love of clothes and was always dressed impeccably, earning him a reputation as a dandy. He was the first president to have a full-time valet—and he needed it. He is rumored to have owned as many as eighty pairs of pants. He could often be seen riding around in his lavishly appointed carriage, complete with gold lace curtains and the Arthur coat of arms displayed on the side. His extravagant sense of décor extended to the White House, whose dilapidated furnishings he determined to overhaul even before moving in. To raise money for the project (and to empty the old mansion of its piles of detritus), he held an auction. Some twenty-four wagonloads of presidential paraphernalia were sold to a crowd on the White House lawn, including an old pair of Lincoln's trousers and a hat that once belonged to John Quincy Adams. Much of it was priceless, and Arthur didn't really give a damn.

SLOOOOW DOWN, CHET

No one could ever accuse Chester Arthur of having worked too hard. After all, Gilded Age fops didn't have much use for long hours or dedication. As one administration official put it, "President Arthur never did today what he could put off until tomorrow." Arthur was always far too preoccupied with his nightly multicourse feed fests to bother with accomplishing anything. Former prez Rutherford Hayes was shocked at the Arthur White House: "Nothing like it before in the Executive Mansion—liquor, snobbery, and worse."

In the end, the secret to Arthur's lethargy was just that—a secret. He'd been diagnosed with Bright's disease, a fact he assiduously kept from the general public. Among the affliction's symptoms is an often profound lack of energy. The disease worsened and, with the help of a bout of malaria he contracted while fishing in Florida, finally caught up with him. He died only eight months after leaving the White House.

HOME SWEET HOME: THE WHITE HOUSE

"I pray heaven to bestow the best of blessings on this house and all that shall hereafter inhabit it," wrote John Adams to his wife, Abigail, from the "President's House" in Washington. He was the first to reside in the new mansion, a relatively vast structure that would eventually come to be known as the White House. And if he were to crawl out of his grave today and pay a visit, he would hardly recognize it.

For one thing, the building was gutted in 1814 by the British. Though the flames were quickly extinguished by rain, the heat had weakened much of the stonework, which had to be replaced. The result was a virtual rebuild, though one that closely followed the original design by James Hoban. Later extensive restorations during the administrations of Theodore Roosevelt and Harry Truman would result in a structure that was almost completely new. When you throw in such additions as the South Portico, a third floor, and extensions that include the West Wing, you have a building that only barely resembles the original.

Because of a stingy Congress, improvements to the White House often had to wait and were sometimes paid for out of the sitting president's own pocket. Running water wasn't installed until 1831, during Andrew Jackson's presidency, by which time such a convenience was already common in hotels and inns. Martin Van Buren added central heating in 1837, and the White House kitchen staff prepared meals with colonial-era pots over open flame until Millard Fillmore bought a real stove. (Fillmore made a personal trip to the patent office for instructions when his cook failed to understand the stove's operation.) Gas lighting replaced candle flame during James Polk's term, and by the time Zachary Taylor was in office, the gas bills were already astronomical—until it was discovered that private tenants along Pennsylvania Avenue were illegally tapping into the White House gas line.

★ ★

But if keeping up with the times was always a challenge at the White House, the old building's greatest problem came with four legs and a hairless tail. Rats infested the building throughout the nineteenth century. Andrew Johnson, a devout animal lover, took to leaving out flour and water for them, while his daughter, Martha, waged a losing battle with traps and poison. Rutherford Hayes claimed that rats nibbled on his toes while he struggled to sleep, and by Grover Cleveland's second term, the rodents were joined by armies of roaches and spiders. The tide finally turned during the presidency of Benjamin Harrison, who enlisted not only professional exterminators but also ferrets, which were allowed to roam throughout the building in search of their quarry. Hundreds of rats perished in the resulting carnage.

And what about the underground complex we've all heard about? If there really is a vast subterranean realm beneath the White House, it's a closely guarded government secret. It is known that Franklin Roosevelt built a bomb shelter during the Second World War. There is also a tunnel that extends from the Treasury Building into the White House basement below the East Wing. Though it was originally planned as part of the bomb shelter, its primary use throughout the twentieth century was for surreptitiously shuttling party guests into the White House. Many a staffer—and president—has had sexual partners escorted through the tunnel for a late-night rendezvous. At least the taxpayers' money hasn't gone completely to waste, right?

GROVER CLEVELAND

BORN March 18, 1837 **DIED** June 24, 1908	**NICKNAMES** "Uncle Jumbo," "Buffalo Hangman," "His Obstinacy"

ASTROLOGICAL SIGN	PARTY	AGE UPON TAKING OFFICE
Pisces 	Democratic 	47 / 55

RAN AGAINST	VICE PRESIDENT
James G. Blaine *(first term)* Benjamin Harrison *(second term)*	★ Thomas A. Hendricks ★ *(first term)* ★ Adlai E. Stevenson ★ *(second term)*

HEIGHT	SOUND BITE	TERMS OF PRESIDENCY:
5'11" ↑	*"Sensible and responsible women do not want to vote."*	1885 1893 – TO – – TO – 1889 1897

The only American president to serve two nonconsecutive terms, Grover Cleveland was one of the most honest men ever to have occupied the White House. But honesty doesn't feed the poor, of which the country had plenty during Cleveland's second stint, and this giant of the presidential pantheon (he weighed more than 250 pounds) hasn't been treated well by historians.

Though born in New Jersey, Grover Cleveland made his political fortune in New York State, serving as sheriff of Erie County and mayor of Buffalo before landing in the governor's mansion. Incredibly, he climbed his way up the ladder through hard work, fiscal responsibility, and telling the truth (no matter how much it hurt). By the presidential election of 1884, many Republican voters were so fed up with corrupt politics that they abandoned their own candidate and voted for Cleveland instead. At the end of a close election, he became the first Democratic president elected since 1856.

His was a conservative presidency, and Cleveland ran the country as if he were CEO of a failing corporation. From questionable pension payments for Union officers to drought relief for stricken Texans, anything that even remotely sniffed of a handout was vetoed. Indeed, his willingness to veto earned him the title "His Obstinacy," and by the time his second term was over, he'd killed three times as many bills as all of his predecessors combined. Cleveland was pedantic, stubborn, blunt, and, as always, honest—he seems to have taken particular delight in favoring the talented over the politically connected, appointing people of his own choosing, even when it burned bridges. Though he lost to Benjamin Harrison in 1888, he threw his hat back in the ring in 1892, by which time the Democrats had gained ground against a Republican Party that tried to do too much and accomplished little. Uncle Jumbo was back.

But the limited government that worked the first time around proved disastrous in 1893, when an economic panic quickly turned into widespread recession. While unemployment and hunger stalked the land, Cleveland wrestled with many in his own party who believed that the economic slowdown could be thwarted by adopting silver, rather than gold, as the currency standard. Cleveland stuck with gold, causing fissures among Democrats that would take years to heal. As for the poor and disenfranchised, he either ignored them or used force against them—as in the Pullman Strike of 1894, in which troops were ordered to break up striking railroad workers. Already averse to public scrutiny, his detestation of the press only made him look withdrawn, aloof, and insensitive. The severe recession lasted another four years, dooming Cleveland's second administration and his place in history.

But, hey—did we mention how honest he was?

BLOOD MONEY

If you were drafted during the Civil War, it was perfectly legal to hire someone else to take your place. And since Grover Cleveland preferred to avoid strenuous physical activity (except whatever effort was required to fill his ample stomach with sausage, corned beef and cabbage, and beer), he reached for his checkbook after being conscripted. He paid a thirty-two-year-old Polish immigrant to take his place for $150.

HANGING TOUGH

During his stint as sheriff of Erie County from 1871 to 1874, Cleveland threw the noose around the necks of two convicted criminals. He remains the only U.S. president to have hanged anyone (personally, anyway).

HELPIN' HALPIN

There is no finer example of Cleveland's outstanding honesty than the Maria Halpin story. Maria, a fellow Buffalonian, was a department store clerk with a weakness for drink and married men. She'd experienced plenty of both by the time she began a sexual relationship with Grover Cleveland, who was still a bachelor at the time. When told by Maria that she was pregnant, Cleveland—though doubtful that he was the father—decided to support the child anyway. It was an extraordinary move for a Victorian man eager to make it in politics. If the secret of his illegitimate son ever leaked, it could ruin him.

The leak sprang during the campaign of 1884. When his aides scrambled to compose a response to the charges, Cleveland's instructions were—and remain to this day—simply fabulous. "Tell them the truth," the candidate directed. The public learned that Cleveland had indeed

→   Cleveland became legal guardian of Frances Folsom when she was eleven years old—and then married her just ten years later.

fathered the child, and scandal broke out. But the voters got over it; more important, they came to respect this flawed but courageous man, and the incident helped Cleveland squeak past Blaine into the White House.

How's that for damage control?

WHO'S YOUR DADDY?

Grover Cleveland's friend and law partner, Oscar Folsom, had a daughter named Frances, born when Cleveland was twenty-seven years old. He bought Frances's first baby carriage and became quite attached to the little tyke, who referred to him affectionately as Uncle Cleve. Oscar died in a carriage accident when Frances was only eleven, and Uncle Cleve became her legal guardian.

Later, when Cleveland was president, Frances and her mother, Emma, would often visit him. Rumors started circulating—was the bachelor president wooing Emma Folsom? Wouldn't that be nice? Such a happy family the three of them would make.

As it happened, the rumors were only half right. The president was in fact hoping to marry twenty-one-year-old Frances. Thus, she and Grover became the only first lady and president to be married in the White House. Media coverage was so exhaustive that the newlyweds had to scramble for privacy at their secluded Maryland honeymoon spot. The experience gave the president a hatred of the press that became legendary.

MAKING CANDY FROM A BABY

Between Cleveland's two terms as president, he and Frances had a daughter, Ruth, who became immensely popular with the public—so popular, in fact, that Nestlé named a candy bar after her: Baby Ruth.

Ruth was the first of five Cleveland children. Another, Esther, was born during Cleveland's second term—the only president's child ever born in the White House.

TWO NAMES, ONE RIFLE

Grover Cleveland tended to balance long hours of work with food and beer. *Lots* of food and beer. He exercised rarely, though he did cultivate a love of hunting and fishing. His weapon of choice was a rifle that he called Death and Destruction.

THE HOLE TRUTH

Long after Grover Cleveland died, a doctor named William Keen revealed a secret he'd kept for twenty-four years: a dangerous operation had been performed on Cleveland while he was president to remove a cancerous tumor from his upper palate.

When, in 1893, Cleveland learned that the rough spot in his mouth was cancer and had to be removed, he insisted that the procedure be kept secret to avoid alarming the public. Extraordinary precautions were taken. A friend of the president's offered his private yacht for the operation. It sailed to Long Island Sound, where surgeons anesthetized Cleveland with laughing gas and then started cutting. Led by Dr. Joseph Bryant, the president's personal physician, they labored for an hour to remove the tumor. The operation was a success, and the doctors filled the resulting hole with a rubber prosthetic. Incredibly, the whole charade worked—Cleveland delivered a speech to Congress a month later without sounding as if his jaw had been torn apart. The press continued to follow up on strange rumors during the president's convalescence, but the truth didn't come to light until Keen spilled the beans to the *Saturday Evening Post* in 1917.

Pretty smooth for a president known for his honesty, eh?

★　★　★　★　★

BORN August 20, 1833 DIED March 13, 1901	NICKNAMES "Little Ben," "White House Iceberg"

ASTROLOGICAL SIGN	PARTY	AGE UPON TAKING OFFICE
Leo 	Republican 	**55**

RAN AGAINST	VICE PRESIDENT
Grover Cleveland	★ Levi P. Morton ★

HEIGHT	SOUND BITE	TERM OF PRESIDENCY
5' 6" 	*"We Americans have no commission from God to police the world."*	**1889** – TO – **1893**

B enjamin Harrison's administration is remembered primarily for being sandwiched between Grover Cleveland's two terms. It's fitting, too, because this guy's about as exciting as lunch meat.

Not that there wasn't cause to expect great things from Harrison. After all, he was the latest in a long line of distinguished Harrisons: his great-grandfather was a signer of the Declaration of Independence; his grandfather William Henry Harrison had been president (for a month); and his father, John Scott Harrison, had been a congressman. Benjamin was a rousing public speaker with a distinguished military career; as a brigadier general in the Civil War, he had impressed everyone—especially his own men—with his fighting spirit and leadership qualities. Such a record had allowed this native of Ohio to represent his adopted state of Indiana in the Senate.

His presidential administration, however, was pretty much a dud. He'd beaten Cleveland in a close race (he actually lost the popular vote, despite winning the electoral college) by supporting a high tariff, and he did it with the then largest campaign fund in history—plenty of prominent businessmen liked what he was saying. But aside from building up the navy and establishing the nation's first forest reserve, Harrison accomplished little by way of leadership.

The most conspicuous exception was when he turned the deaths of two U.S. sailors in a barroom brawl in Chile into an opportunity to flex American muscle. Until the Chileans apologized (their police were rumored to have used unnecessary force), the scuffle almost came to war. In the end, Harrison's most important contribution may have been appointing a young and ambitious Theodore Roosevelt to the civil service commission, thereby safeguarding the continuing overhaul of the patronage system.

The Republican-dominated Congress didn't make Harrison's administration any more successful. Known as the billion-dollar Congress, they wasted exorbitant sums of money, angered voters, and basically guaranteed that plenty of Democrats would win the congressional elections of 1890. This spelled bad news for Harrison's own reelection prospects, and his chances grew even worse when his beloved wife died in 1892. The tragedy took the wind out of his stumping.

After Cleveland's narrow victory, Harrison was relieved to go back to his law practice in Indianapolis, where he eventually married his late wife's niece—a move that alienated his children and drove him to cut them out of his will.

"HE'S MISTER WHITE CHRISTMAS, HE'S MISTER SNOW ... "

And you thought the Snow Miser was just a character in that silly holiday TV special. Perhaps—but, aside from the tights and a squad of singing elves, he bears a striking resemblance to Benjamin Harrison.

Sure, Harrison had a gift for public speaking. But in person, the staunchly Presbyterian president was a virtual corpse. *Chilly, frigid, frosty*—words like these were routinely used to describe the unpleasant experience of meeting privately with the man. "It's like talking to a hitching post" is how one stunned victim described his conversation. Senator Thomas Platt was the man who coined the moniker "White House Iceberg." As Platt explained, "Inside the Executive Mansion, in his reception of those who solicited official appointments, [Harrison] was as glacial as a Siberian stripped of his furs. During and after an interview, if one could secure it, one felt even in torrid weather like pulling on his winter flannels, galoshes, overcoat, mitts, and earflaps." Even Harrison's handshake was a flop, likened to "a wilted petunia." His supporters often kept voters at a distance after public speeches.

COME WHAT [CAPE] MAY

When Postmaster General John Wanamaker got a bunch of wealthy friends to buy Harrison a cottage in Cape May, New Jersey, the president was delighted. So was the press—after all, it looked as if Harrison was taking a plump bribe from real estate folks interested in developing Cape May. The whiff of scandal filled the air. Before the papers could get Harrison's opponents in government to act, the president flushed the whole matter down the toilet by sending Wanamaker a personal check for $10,000. See what a little publicity can do?

BY A WHISKER

Harrison may not be the most memorable chief executive in American history, but he did, in fact, embody the end of an era: he was the last president to have a beard.

← Just how frosty was Benjamin Harrison? Many referred to him as the White House Iceberg. The guy even cut his own children out of his will.

BORN January 29, 1843	NICKNAMES
DIED September 14, 1901	"Wobbly Willie," "Idol of Ohio," "Napoleon of Protection"

ASTROLOGICAL SIGN	PARTY	AGE UPON TAKING OFFICE
Aquarius	Republican	54

RAN AGAINST	VICE PRESIDENT
William Jennings Bryan *(both terms)*	★ Garret A. Hobart ★ *(first term)* ★ Theodore Roosevelt ★ *(second term)*

HEIGHT	SOUND BITE	TERM OF PRESIDENCY
5′7″ ↑	*"We need Hawaii just as much and a good deal more than we did California; it is Manifest Destiny."*	1897 – TO – 1901

"I have been through one war," William McKinley remarked during the first year of his administration, making reference to his service in the Civil War. "I have seen the dead piled up and I do not want to see another." For all the talk about peace, however, McKinley's administration would see quite a lot of violence.

William McKinley was a sweetheart. With the sponsorship of fellow Ohioan Rutherford Hayes, he had served in the House of Representatives and as governor of his home state. Through it all, he had impressed people with his ability to remember names, the way he turned people down while making them feel as if he'd done them a favor, the carnations he wore in his lapel (and that he was fond of handing out to disappointed office-seekers to mollify their hurt), his jovial sincerity, and—most of all—his endearing devotion to his epileptic wife. Even his enemies hated saying bad things about him.

But beneath the smiling politeness stirred a Machiavellian, a canny Washington insider who navigated the channels of power effortlessly. The nice guy image came in handy. As Secretary of War Elihu Root once said, "He had a way of handling men so that they thought his ideas were their own." Take the press, for example. Unlike his grouchy predecessor Grover Cleveland, McKinley welcomed coverage of his administration—indeed, he promoted it, building the first White House pressroom. By offering a constant flow of (carefully chosen) information, he soon had journalists eating out of his hand. Who was using whom?

Perhaps we shouldn't be surprised, then, that this avuncular, companionable bloke was also responsible for unleashing a violent grab for empire. Cuba offered the ideal excuse: it had been in revolt for years against its masters in Spain, threatening the millions of dollars that Americans had invested there. McKinley dispatched the battleship *Maine* to Havana harbor as a show of America's willingness to keep an eye on its interests. Not long after arriving, the ship blew sky high, taking more than two hundred Yankee sailors with it. Though the probable cause of the vessel's spectacular demise was a coal fire, America had its casus belli, and the whole nation seemed to quake with vengeance and wrath.

Except, at first, its president. McKinley insisted on having a commission investigate the *Maine* disaster, even after his own assistant secretary of the navy, Theodore Roosevelt, called him a "white-livered cur" for acting so cautiously. The commission finally concluded that the explosion was caused by a Spanish mine, and McKinley was swept up into the bloodsport.

The Spanish American War, such as it was, lasted some three months. Spain surprised no one by losing spectacularly—and eventually forking over Puerto Rico, the Philippines, and Guam to an insatiable United States. Cuba, though independent, became a virtual vassal state, and the president even persuaded Congress to annex Hawaii. The bloodshed was far from over, however. McKinley grew nicely into his new suit of armor, reacting with disturbing ruthlessness to a revolt in the Philippines. He also sent thousands of troops to China to help squelch the Boxer rebellion, in which Chinese xenophobes attempted to end centuries of crude European manipulation by slaughtering every foreigner they could get their hands on. Oh, the cares of empire!

Nothing pleases a voting public more than victory in war except a recovering economy. McKinley had both—the depression that began in 1893 was over, and everyone basked in the new, muscular America. In such heady days, it seems only an anarchist could find cause for concern—and one did. His name was Leon Czolgosz, and at the Pan-American Exposition in Buffalo, he shot McKinley just one day after the recently reelected president was welcomed by a giant sign that read, "Welcome McKinley, chief of our nation and empire." He died eight days later.

BANKING ON VICTORY

McKinley's opponent in both presidential elections was William Jennings Bryan, one of the greatest populists in American history. While McKinley conducted his campaign from his front porch in 1896, Bryan went whizzing around the country giving speeches before cheering crowds. But despite all his efforts, Bryan was bound to lose. His desire to use the silver standard in American currency earned him plenty of enemies in the nation's legions of businessmen, including Mark Hanna, a prominent Cincinnati financier. Hanna joined the McKinley team and contributed much of his own fortune toward his candidate's fight, bringing McKinley's campaign chest to more than $3 million. Bryan's friends weren't quite as rich—he had somewhere around $50,000 to spend on his campaign. When you factor in all the Republican businessmen who literally threatened their

→   Whenever First Lady Ida McKinley suffered an epileptic seizure—and she suffered them often—the devoted president would simply drape his handkerchief over her face.

employees with dismissal if they didn't vote for McKinley, the results of the 1896 election hardly seem surprising.

A NEW PRESIDENT FOR A NEW CENTURY

It wasn't just the naked use of force that distinguished McKinley as the first true twentieth-century president. He was also the last president to have served in the Civil War and the first to have his inaugural captured on film.

A MODEL MARRIAGE

First Lady Ida McKinley was an epileptic, though that word was carefully avoided by journalists when describing her. Her seizures could occur at any moment and often did—at state dinners, public gatherings, speeches, etc. The president was an inspiration to all in his respectful devotion to her. When the fits were particularly bad, he would merely drape his handkerchief over Ida's face. The darkness tended to soothe her, and when the seizures passed, the first couple would continue as if nothing had happened. McKinley was never too busy to interrupt whatever he was doing to go pay Ida a visit, and all of Washington was taken by the couple's obvious closeness.

McKinley's concern for Ida never left his harried mind, even when mortally wounded. Virtually the first words out of his mouth after being shot were to his secretary, George Cortelyou: "My wife—be careful, Cortelyou, how you tell her—oh, be careful!"

26 | THEODORE ROOSEVELT

BORN October 27, 1858 **DIED** January 6, 1919	**NICKNAMES** "TR," "Hero of San Juan Hill," "The Bull Moose"

ASTROLOGICAL SIGN	PARTY	AGE UPON TAKING OFFICE
Scorpio	Republican	**42**

RAN AGAINST	VICE PRESIDENT
N/A *(first term)* Alton B. Parker *(elected term)*	★ None ★ *(after McKinley assassination)* ★ Charles W. Fairbanks ★ *(elected term)*

HEIGHT	SOUND BITE	TERM OF PRESIDENCY
5′ 8″ ↑	*"No triumph of peace is quite so great as the supreme triumphs of war."*	**1901** – TO – **1909**

Speak softly and carry a big stick," said Theodore Roosevelt, "and you will go far." TR sure did go far. But he never spoke softly about anything in his life. He boomed and shrilled, gesticulated wildly, thrilled to action of all sorts. Not since Thomas Jefferson did a man of such varied talents lead the nation. An insatiable reader with a photographic memory, Roosevelt published more than forty books on everything from naval history to bird watching, wore a deputy sheriff's badge in the western Badlands, led troops in battle, and shot game in Africa. He was the last true Renaissance man to make it to the White House.

But TR was also a blatant militarist. Let's not dance around the facts: He sought out and reveled in the nerve-testing cauldron of battle. He believed there were important moral lessons to be learned from punching a bayonet through another man's belly. He racked up an impressive list of administrative posts, including New York City police commissioner, assistant secretary of the navy, governor of New York, and vice president and president of the United States. But his proudest moment would always be the day he charged up San Juan Hill during the Spanish-American War and killed a Spaniard with his bare hands.

By the time he became governor of New York, the Republican Party was wary of "that damned cowboy" and his alarming reformist views. Figuring he would do less damage as vice president, they elected him to the McKinley ticket—and assumed McKinley would live another four years. Oops.

As chief executive—the youngest, at his inauguration, in American history—TR would fight most of his battles against the big business "trusts," whose enormous wealth and power were killing competition and creating a gulf between rich and poor that most people thought had gone too far. By taking on J. P. Morgan's titanic Northern Securities Company, he did more than stop a conglomerate from fixing prices; he set a precedent for governmental regulation and remade the presidency into the most powerful and active branch of government. His efforts at cleaning up the food and drug companies did much to stop faulty advertising and the proliferation of bad meat. Though generally opposed to unions, he sided with labor during the coal miners' strike of 1902 and proved to be a conservationist dynamo by setting aside millions of acres of land for protection. He even won a Nobel Peace Prize for brokering an end to the Russo-Japanese War. But despite his popularity, he passed the torch in the 1908 election to his handpicked successor, William Taft, and went on safari in Africa. Then, in 1912, having fallen out with Taft, he ran against him on the Progressive, or "Bull Moose," ticket—and succeeded only in making it easier for both of them to lose to Democrat Woodrow Wilson.

← While boxing in the White House with heavyweight champion John Sullivan, Roosevelt received a blow to the face that left him blind in his left eye.

With his rather odd mixture of conservative and liberal qualities, the incomparable, charismatic TR has become the darling of both the left and the right. A lover of animals who took pleasure in blowing them away, a believer in the separation of the races who broke bread with Booker T. Washington in the White House, a highly educated aristocrat who wanted nothing more than to receive approval from cowpokes and ruffians, a war worshipper renowned for making peace, a believer in rugged individualism who wanted to use the government to help those in need—this guy's record is a little hard to follow. But you'd be hard pressed to find a more colorful character.

BODY POLITIC

As a boy in New York City, Theodore Roosevelt was a sickly, asthmatic weakling. Urged by his father to do something about it, he determined to remake his own body. The family's wealth was harnessed in the effort, turning part of their brownstone into a gym, and Theodore began spending plenty of time lifting weights. He took up all manner of strenuous physical activity, especially boxing. As a student at Harvard, he came close to winning the lightweight championship. His heart, however, remained weak—although that didn't stop him from climbing the Matterhorn in Europe after graduation.

TR's preoccupation with "the strenuous life," as he liked to call it, would never abate, and it came to define his rugged, no-holds-barred image. After moving into the White House, he replaced the old greenhouses with a tennis court, on which he was fond of playing as many as ninety games in a day. He continued to box with anyone crazy enough to take him on, and he even studied martial arts. Visiting friends and dignitaries were often obliged to jog with him around the White House grounds or embark upon his infamous "point-to-point" sojourns—a distant point in the wilderness would be chosen, toward which the day-trippers would hike at a breathless pace, taking on every obstacle in between. Those too frail (or sensible) to keep up were often derided as soft by the president, who could not abide laggards.

GO WEST, YOUNG MAN

Next time you find yourself single on Valentine's Day and mired in your own self-pity, remember that your sadness cannot possibly be greater than Theodore Roosevelt's. For on that day in 1884, his mother and his wife, Alice, both died. Overwhelmed with grief, he entrusted his only child at the time, also named Alice, to her aunt and took off to the Badlands to become a cowboy. Impressively, the Harvard-educated Eastern aristocrat held his own among the indelicate crowd he encountered there, despite his spectacles and large vocabulary. Some of the men he befriended during those years would fill the ranks of the Rough Riders recruited by Roosevelt to fight in the Spanish-American War.

TR would later marry Edith Kermit Carow, whom he had known from his childhood in New York City. They would have five children together. He never again mentioned his first wife, Alice, even in his autobiography.

PASS THE EGGS, PLEASE

Roosevelt may have been a tireless, self-made athlete, but he loved to overeat. His muscular frame couldn't hide a stomach born of massive meals. A typical breakfast, for example, included giant mugs full of coffee and twelve eggs. Yes, twelve. The result was the arteriosclerosis that probably killed him.

ROUGH-HOUSING

War was a preoccupation of TR's, and he wanted desperately to get into one. Any one, he wasn't picky. He would've preferred a fight against someone like Germany or another great power. But when Spain became a possibility, he sank his teeth into the idea and never let go. As assistant secretary of the navy, TR was in his element. Because his boss, Secretary of the Navy John Long, was constantly sick or incapacitated, Roosevelt had the run of things and raised holy hell after the *Maine* exploded in Havana harbor. But once he got his way and Congress declared war, TR resigned. His chance at blood had come, and he wasn't going to fritter it away in Washington.

He'd never spent a day in uniform in his life, but that didn't stop him from raising a regiment of volunteer soldiers. Quickly dubbed the Rough Riders by the press, the First Volunteer Cavalry was Roosevelt's baby, and it reflected his own bizarre background: Western buckaroos rubbed shoulders with Ivy League athletes, and not one of them had any military experience whatsoever. TR had the sense to get career soldier Colonel Leonard Wood to train the troops and became a lieutenant-colonel himself. Interestingly, their famous moment in Cuba—the charge up Kettle Hill and San Juan Hill—was done without their horses, which had been left behind in Florida during the chaos of boarding troop transports. TR had a horse, but he dismounted to be with his boys and loved every blood-spattered minute of it. "The charge up the hill was great fun!" wrote an ebullient Roosevelt to a friend. "I killed a Spaniard with my bare hands like a jackrabbit." Hey, neat!

Along with a brief skirmish just days before, this one scrape—against a foe outnumbered fifteen to one, mind you—remains the extent of Theodore Roosevelt's military experience. By the time the media got hold of it, however, you'd think he had seen more action than Ulysses Grant, George Washington, and Julius Caesar combined. Roosevelt, terribly pleased, did nothing to deflate the enormity of it all. While stumping for the governorship of New York, he toured with several of his fellow Rough Riders and announced every speech with a bugle call.

BURSTING HIS BELLICOSE BUBBLE

Roosevelt roundly criticized Woodrow Wilson for not trying to rush America into World War I. He even offered to lead a volunteer unit into Europe, but Wilson—to Roosevelt's undying rage—would have none of it. "The problem with Mr. Wilson," wrote the spurned warrior to French premier Georges Clemenceau, "is that he is merely a rhetorician, vindictive and yet not physically brave." After years of hollering for military preparedness and intervention, TR had much of the war whoop taken out of him in 1918, when his youngest son, Quentin, died in a fighter plane over the Western Front. The whole business didn't seem quite so glorious anymore.

IT'S OFFICIAL

Though the Executive Mansion had for years been commonly referred to as the White House, it was TR who first used the phrase on presidential stationery. The building has been known officially as such ever since.

ACTION FIGURE (BATTERIES INCLUDED)

Theodore Roosevelt wasn't one to sit home and play cribbage. He was the first president to ride in an automobile, the first to fly in an airplane, the first to go diving in a submarine, and the first to travel outside of the United States while in office (to Panama, in 1906). But living like the inspiration for *Jonny Quest* comes at a price, and TR had more than his fair share of accidents. Consider:

- During a collision between his vessel and another in the Gulf of Mexico, Roosevelt was hurled through a glass window.

- While boxing in the White House with heavyweight champion John Sullivan, Roosevelt received a blow to his face that left him blind in his left eye (an injury that he kept secret for years).

- Roosevelt twice suffered a broken arm: one from a spill during a fox hunt and the other from a bout of "stick-fighting" with his old comrade in arms, Colonel Leonard Wood.

TR's worst injury resulted from a collision near Pittsfield, Massachusetts, between his carriage and a trolley. Everyone in the carriage went flying, including the president, his secretary, the governor of Massachusetts, and a Secret Service agent, who was killed. Roosevelt, who landed on his face, received a large bruise on his leg—which proceeded to swell painfully until doctors cut all the way down to the bone in an effort to remove the dying tissue. The president was confined to a wheelchair for weeks.

BEAR HUG

In 1902, while on a hunting trip in Mississippi, TR found—and took mercy on—a bear cub. The press lapped it up like honey, giving a toy designer the idea for a stuffed bear. Thus the "Teddy Bear" was born. The kicker? TR hated being called Teddy.

PANAMA HACK

Always a fan of flexing American muscle, TR did his part to strengthen the military and show it off. He even sent the navy's new fleet of battleships on a trip around the world to impress and intimidate anyone who might have forgotten who wore the pants in the Western Hemisphere. Intent on providing a means for American warships to steam quickly between oceans, he decided to get serious about creating a canal through Central America. Panama, a province of Colombia, was the ideal spot—but the Colombian government rejected America's offer of money in exchange for digging rights. So TR did what any self-respecting imperialist would do: he promised Panama that, should they decide to, oh, say, *revolt* against their government and become independent, why, America would just love to do business with them instead of Colombia. Not surprisingly, a Panamanian revolution ensued—TR even aided his new business partners with a navy cruiser.

Roosevelt had nagging doubts about the legality of it all (gee, can't imagine why) but defended himself adamantly when those in government and the press cried foul. Secretary of War Elihu Root didn't make him feel any better when he told him, "You have shown that you were accused of seduction and you have conclusively proved that you were guilty of rape."

THE OTHER SIDE OF THE COIN

Even though Roosevelt became one of the most popular presidents of his age, not all of his initiatives met with approval. In fact, a couple nearly got him laughed out of office. He believed that "In God We Trust" should be removed from American currency—it was blasphemous, he insisted, to have such a conviction stamped on the coins with which people bought their booze or brassieres.

He also fought to have the spelling of American English overhauled to make it more phonetic. A group of academics calling themselves the Simplified Spelling Board provided new guidelines that the president instructed the government printing office to adopt, inciting a veritable hurricane of ridicule. As the *Louisville Courier-Journal* wrote, "Nuthing escapes Mr. Rucevelt. No subject is tu hi fr him to takl, nor tu lo for him tu notis." Roosevelt came around (though never repented), and the matter was put mercifully to rest.

BULL ROAR

Having thrown his hat back into the ring on the Progressive ticket in 1912, TR was making a stop in Milwaukee to give a speech when John Schrank, a local saloon-keeper suspicious of TR's quest for a third term, shot him. The bullet went through Roosevelt's eyeglasses case before hitting flesh, where it lodged in some muscle tissue. It was clearly not fatal, but a gunshot wound is a gunshot wound, and his aides were preparing to get him to the hospital. The stricken candidate, however, got up on the podium and gave his hour-long speech anyway. "I don't know whether you fully understand that I have been shot," he told the stunned audience, "but it takes more than that to kill a Bull Moose."

What some folks will do for votes!

| BORN September 15, 1857 | NICKNAME |
| DIED March 8, 1930 | "Big Bill" |

ASTROLOGICAL SIGN	PARTY	AGE UPON TAKING OFFICE
Virgo	Republican	51

| RAN AGAINST | VICE PRESIDENT |
| William Jennings Bryan | ★ James S. Sherman ★ |

HEIGHT	SOUND BITE	TERM OF PRESIDENCY
6′ 2″	*"What's the use of being president if you can't have a train with a diner on it?"*	1909 – TO – 1913

O f all the people Theodore Roosevelt could've picked as his preferred successor, he chose a guy with whom he shared virtually nothing in common. William Howard Taft was lethargic, unsure of himself, retiring, unimaginative, and grossly overweight—a far cry from the tireless, overconfident powerhouse who preceded him. The mistake would become all too obvious: by the time Taft's term as president was drawing to a close, Roosevelt—and virtually every other American—couldn't wait to get rid of him.

In fact, Taft had racked up an impressive record of public service by the time he'd become TR's beloved pal and protégé. He had been an assistant county prosecutor, collector of internal revenue, and state superior court judge in his home state of Ohio, as well as solicitor general of the United States and a federal judge. McKinley made him governor of the Philippines, in which capacity he helped the newly acquired islands make the transformation from martial to civil law. But it was the appointment as secretary of war in Roosevelt's administration that changed his life. He would become bosom buddies with the most charismatic man in the nation and allow himself to be convinced that he could carry TR's torch.

Taft never truly wanted to be president. But his wife, Nellie, had married him for his presidential potential; she'd dreamed of being first lady ever since she spent a few months in the White House during the Hayes administration. And who was he to disappoint Nellie? Or Theodore Roosevelt? After all, Taft coveted affirmation, and he found it in TR (who, for that matter, basked in Taft's obsequiousness), which goes a long way toward explaining the odd couple's relationship.

Roosevelt wasn't the only one who liked Big Bill. In the election of 1908, seemingly everyone was taken by the affable Taft: Roosevelt supporters, because he was the chosen one; imperialists, because of Taft's extensive travels and stint in the Philippines; and conservatives, who thought the legalistic Taft would put an end to TR's law-stretching progressivism. But there would soon be more than enough disappointment to go around, for the presidency fit Taft about as well as a pair of Speedos.

He promised to pursue the Progressive-backed lower tariff but ended up signing into law one that actually *raised* rates on numerous items (and then called it a victory). His lackluster foreign policy failed to make a dent in the European control over Chinese markets and created animosity in Latin America through sloppy interventionism, especially in Nicaragua. And, though a self-proclaimed conservationist, his strict judicial approach prohibited the sort of dramatic accomplishments that Roosevelt had been able to make through sheer force of will.

Despite taking a much harder stance on big business than his "trust-buster" predecessor, Taft couldn't escape the derision of Roosevelt and the Progressives. To them, he'd thrown away all the hard work of the previous administration. Nevertheless, the Republicans nominated him for another term, which infuriated Roosevelt, who had reentered politics to save the country from his erstwhile friend. He and his supporters broke away into the Bull Moose Party, creating a three-way race that sent Woodrow Wilson to Washington. Taft received an abysmal 23 percent of the popular vote in 1912—the lowest of any presidential incumbent in American history.

But if the nation was happy to see him go, Taft was born anew by his defeat. "Politics makes me sick," he'd once said, and his judicial dreams could now be realized. In 1921, he was appointed to the Supreme Court. For the record, he made a much better judge than he did a president.

WHAT'S FOR DINNER?

While governor of the Philippines, Taft once wired Washington, "Took long horseback ride today; feeling fine." Secretary of War Elihu Root shot back, "How's the horse?" At a whopping 325 pounds, William Howard Taft was the largest president in American history. During a visit to the czar of Russia, Taft's pants split up the seam while getting out of his carriage; he had to back his way out of the czar's presence to avoid exposing his backside. This was a man whose girth prevented him from tying his own shoes—his valet had to do it. The president installed banisters in executive buildings to help support his weight while ascending stairs. He even had trouble getting out of the bathtub. After getting stuck a few times, he had a new one installed in the White House. It was seven feet long, weighed about a ton, and accommodated four average-sized men.

DOZING OFF

Perhaps because of his weight, William Taft had the alarming habit of dozing off at the drop of a hat. Nothing was so important that it couldn't be slept through—including cabinet meetings, funerals (he was in the front

→ At 325 pounds, Taft often found himself stuck in the White House bathtub. His advisers sometimes had to help pull him out.

row of one when a catnap overtook him), and campaign engagements. He once slept through a campaign motorcade in New York City—his open car cruised the streets, with the great man snoring for all the city to see. His military aide, Archie Butt, made it his responsibility to clear his throat whenever he saw his boss nodding off, but he didn't always catch him in time.

HITTING THE LINKS

William Taft was the first to embark upon that presidential pastime we all take for granted today: golf. Though he had never played before being elected, he soon became an avid (if mediocre) player, and the burdens of the White House always seemed much smaller from the vantage point of the links. In fact, his habit of ducking out for a game only further worried those who thought Taft took his responsibilities too lightly. During the ceremonial signing of one of his administration's most important achievements, the General Arbitration Treaty with Great Britain (which provided for the peaceful settlement of whatever disagreement might arise between the powers), the president was conspicuously absent; he'd noticed a break in the clouds and had snuck out for a game of golf. Military aide Archie Butt was left to feed the British ambassador a line about Taft's having been called to the White House for a matter of grave importance.

DRIVING IN STYLE

William Taft was the first president to make automobiles his primary means of getting around. Thanks to a $12,000 appropriation from Congress, he bought four of them—including a giant, steam-driven monstrosity manufactured by the White Sewing Machine Company. Called the White Steamer, it could seat seven people, but Taft liked to have the back seat all to himself, where he could doze during drives with his chauffeur.

★ ★ ★ ★ ★

BORN **December 28, 1856** DIED **February 3, 1924**	NICKNAMES "The Schoolmaster," "Big One of the Peace Conference"

ASTROLOGICAL SIGN Capricorn 	PARTY Democratic 	AGE UPON TAKING OFFICE **56**

RAN AGAINST William Taft, Theodore Roosevelt *(first term)* Charles Hughes *(second term)*	VICE PRESIDENT ★ Thomas R. Marshall ★

HEIGHT 5'11" 	SOUND BITE *"The use of a university is to make young gentlemen as unlike their fathers as possible."*	TERM OF PRESIDENCY **1913** – TO – **1921**

Woodrow Wilson was the best-educated president in American history. But the most important lesson, in the end, was his to learn. After years of brilliantly lecturing the world on how to govern itself, he was forced to realize that the most important students in his classroom weren't listening.

Though born in Virginia and raised in Georgia, it was in New Jersey that Thomas Woodrow Wilson first made his mark. Being named president of Princeton University was the capstone of a teaching career that had spanned Bryn Mawr and Wesleyan colleges, and he proved an able

and dedicated administrator. It wasn't long before he was governor of New Jersey and attracting the attention of a Democratic Party intent on ending the Republican domination of the White House. Thanks to the three-way race with Roosevelt and Taft in 1912, that's exactly what happened.

Wilson had a Ph.D. from Johns Hopkins, authored several impressive books on American history and politics, and boasted a lot of experience as a progressive reformer. But his most important asset as president was the Democratic majority in Congress, which helped him pass one of the most impressive legislative programs in history. It included a lower tariff, antitrust legislation, the Federal Trade Commission Act, and the Federal Reserve Act, which stabilized the country's finances through the creation of twelve Federal Reserve Banks and a board to oversee them. Another wave of reform in 1916 took on child labor and other progressive agendas.

But while the schoolmaster's curriculum at home was making impressive strides, it was running into serious trouble abroad. Wilson was so determined to keep his country out of World War I that he didn't even let such disasters as the sinking of the *Lusitania* by a German U-boat (which claimed more than 120 American lives) make a dent in America's neutrality. But additional unrestricted German submarine warfare, along with the interception of a telegram in which Germany attempted to instigate a Mexican invasion of Texas, proved too much to bear. Wilson reluctantly asked Congress for a declaration of war in 1917. For years he had been imploring the European powers to stop killing one another—now it seemed the only way he was going to create an idyllic world order was by resorting to the one thing he wanted most to destroy: war.

And what a war it turned out to be. Wilson the archliberal found himself presiding over a government that exhorted its masses to battle with hideous, sanguinary propaganda. Those who spoke out against the war—or, for that matter, against the proliferation of violence against German Americans—were shamelessly and hurriedly jailed. Despite all

← Wilson was a big fan of D. W. Griffith's *Birth of a Nation*, a film that glorified the actions of the Ku Klux Klan.

the ugliness, Wilson, ever the optimistic Presbyterian, never lost sight of the prize: a peaceful future. So that there'd be no excuse for failure, he even made it easy for the world by creating his Fourteen Points, which envisioned the upcoming peace settlement as an opportunity to create a League of Nations to settle disputes by arbitration.

Unfortunately, many of the professor's students weren't taking notes—indeed, some of them were skipping class altogether. The president may have been welcomed as a virtual messiah in Paris, but European leaders had revenge on their minds and couldn't wait to kick a defeated Germany where the sun doesn't shine. Even worse, Wilson's own backyard was doing some kicking of its own, walloping his posterior with a Republican takeover of the Senate that started picking over his Fourteen Points like vegans at a Texas barbecue. Wilson ended up compromising with the Europeans, but when senators started making some sobering edits to the final treaty before ratifying it, Wilson dug in his heels, took the debate to the American people by embarking upon an ambitious national tour . . . and had a stroke. While Wilson languished at death's door, his opponents finally got their way, and the League of Nations came into being without the nation whose president had cooked up the idea in the first place (and who won a Nobel prize for it, no less). Now *that's* humiliation.

Wilson lived until 1924, long enough to see a Republican elected to replace him in a resounding repudiation of all things Wilsonian. He remains the only president buried in Washington, D.C. (within the National Cathedral). What grade would the schoolmaster have given himself in the end? Despite some profound achievements, history offers something like a B-. Betcha he would've asked for an extension.

UNCONSTITUTIONAL

Wilson suffered from a myriad of ailments his entire life. As a boy, he was dyslexic and could not read until he was nine. As a young man, he suffered from constant bouts of nausea, constipation, and heartburn. He even used a stomach pump to combat the build-up of acid in his stomach with infusions of water. Most attribute the cause of his frailty to excessive tension which led to problems with his stomach and, eventually, his heart. Little wonder that the pressures of stumping on behalf of the League of Nations finally caused the stroke that paralyzed his left side and prevented him from concluding his presidency with a bang.

BERMUDA LOVE TRIANGLE

Wilson's handshake was once compared to "a ten-cent pickled mackerel in brown paper." There's no doubt that he was austere, aloof, sanctimonious, and generally ill at ease in intimate social circumstances. But Wilson, surprisingly, had a romantic side that burned like a furnace. The letters he wrote to his first wife simmer with sexual desire, and thousands of them survive. It was a truly touching correspondence, and it stands in stark contrast to the strictly reserved image we have of Wilson as the repressed son of a Presbyterian minister.

But the marriage was not without its share of missteps. In 1907, Wilson traveled to Bermuda on his doctor's orders to relieve some of the stress that was burning a hole in his stomach. There he met one Mary Allen Hulbert Peck, a worldly divorcée whose charm burned a hole in Wilson's heart. Though it is not known whether the two consummated their obvious closeness, Wilson made several trips to Bermuda, always with the intent of seeing Mrs. Peck. While the relationship threatened both Wilson's marriage and his presidential campaign, it ultimately failed to mess up either. (Peck refused to sell her letters from Wilson to the Republicans, and Wilson's wife, Ellen, forgave him.)

TITILLATING TYPO

When Wilson's first wife, Ellen, died of Bright's disease in 1914, the loss nearly resulted in the first presidential suicide. He was utterly heartbroken and descended into depression. But Wilson soon met Edith Bolling Galt, and they were married in December 1915. Reporting on one of their first dates to the theater, the *Washington Post* made an infamous typo when it wrote that, rather than entertaining his lady friend, "the President spent most of his time *entering* Mrs. Galt." Edith became his closest confidante and adviser—she even encoded and decoded his messages to the diplomatic corps abroad and, after his stroke, carefully screened his visitors, leading many to conclude that she was acting president.

PEACE, LOVE, HARMONY, YADDA, YADDA, YADDA

Wilson was a visionary when it came to international peace and fighting for common workers against big business. But his plans for bettering the lot of humanity didn't quite extend to African Americans. A white supremacist, Wilson allowed segregation to creep into the Treasury Department and the U.S. Post Office. He was a big fan of D. W. Griffith's *Birth of a Nation*, a film that portrayed blacks as virtual animals and glorified the actions of the Ku Klux Klan. "It's like writing history with lightning," Wilson said about the racist epic, "and my only regret is that it is all so terribly true."

He didn't like women voters, either. He was slow to come around to the suffrage movement, whose picketers once converged on the White House and turned down the president's invitation to come in for tea. First Lady Edith was no fan of suffragettes, either; she called them "disgusting creatures." Despite Wilson's feelings, the 19th Amendment was ratified in 1920, giving women the right to vote.

★ ★ ★ ★ ★

29 | WARREN G. HARDING

BORN November 2, 1865 DIED August 2, 1923	NICKNAME "Wobbly Warren"

ASTROLOGICAL SIGN	PARTY	AGE UPON TAKING OFFICE
Scorpio	Republican	55

RAN AGAINST	VICE PRESIDENT
James M. Cox	★ Calvin Coolidge ★

HEIGHT	SOUND BITE	TERM OF PRESIDENCY
6′	*"I am a man of limited talents from a small town; I don't seem to grasp that I am president."*	1921 – TO – 1923

Warren Gamaliel Harding won the 1920 election by an enormous landslide, served an uneventful two years as president, and then died a beloved national figure. Not bad for a guy who didn't know what the hell he was doing.

Harding was editor of the Marion, Ohio, *Star*, a small-town newspaper, and he loved every minute of it. He had to be persuaded to run for the Senate, where he served from 1915 to 1919, and liked it only because the workload was light and he felt as if he'd become a member of a fashionable gentlemen's club. The presidency would never even have occurred to him were it not for his domineering wife, Florence Kling De Wolfe, who was dead set on getting her husband into the White House. (Harding referred to her as the Duchess.) She had run the business end of the *Star* and ran the business end of his campaign with the same skill and hard-driving devotion. The 1920 election was the first in which women could vote, and, with their help, Harding won an unprecedented 60 percent of the popular vote.

His striking good looks, impressive build, and easygoing nature endeared him to virtually everyone he met. But he was utterly befuddled by the enormous responsibilities of his office and always felt like a fish out of water. His time as president witnessed a historic naval limitation treaty signed by the United States, Great Britain, Italy, France, and Japan; a protectionist tariff; and onerous immigration legislation that began limiting the influx of people from the "less desirable" regions of southern and eastern Europe. Congress led the way through nearly all of it, however—Harding was more than pleased to let Congress govern while he golfed, played poker, and had sex in White House closets with his mistress.

Harding may not have had many enemies, but he did have plenty of friends—and they ended up being just as harmful. Though his cabinet featured some talent, he stocked much of the executive branch with buddies from his Ohio days. Many of them would take advantage of him, most notably in the Teapot Dome scandal, in which government oil reserves in Wyoming were leased to unscrupulous, high-paying business interests. By the time the investigations were over, Secretary of the Interior Albert Fall would become the first cabinet officer in American history to go to jail, and two of Harding's pals would commit suicide.

But none of this came to light until well after Harding's term was cut short. Just two years into his presidency, he suffered a heart attack in a San Francisco hotel and died. Largely ignorant of the scale of the late president's incompetence, the nation mourned the passing of its agreeable, debonair leader.

→   Poker was Harding's obsession. During one heated game, he bet an entire box of priceless White House china and lost it.

CLOSETED AFFAIRS

As Harding's wife, "the Duchess," once said, "I know what's best for the president. I put him in the White House." But her husband had his own ideas about what was best for him, and the Duchess wasn't one of them.

And so he had affairs, two of which are infamous. The first was with Carrie Fulton Phillips, the wife of an old friend. It began in 1905 and ended only when Harding won the Republican nomination, forcing him to clean his closet. Carrie and her husband were sent on an all-expenses-paid tour of the world, care of the Republican Party.

The other, begun in 1917, was with Nan Britton, thirty years Harding's junior. While Harding was president, Nan was routinely ushered through the West Wing of the White House for their liaisons by Secret Service agents who were instructed to keep it all a secret from the first lady. Harding and Britton were not above resorting to closets for their lovemaking, especially when the Duchess was known to be nearby. Britton eventually bore an illegitimate child by Harding, Elizabeth Ann Christian, in 1919. He would never set eyes on her.

IT'S IN THE CARDS

Poker was a lifelong obsession for Harding. Back in his Ohio days, he won a controlling interest in the Marion *Star* by winning at cards. Once in the White House, his "poker cabinet" gathered regularly to play and—Prohibition notwithstanding—drink whiskey. (He'd conveniently forgotten that before becoming president, he supported the 18th Amendment, which banned the sale of alcohol.) As he used to say, "Forget that I'm president of the United States. I'm Warren Harding, playing poker with friends, and I'm going to beat hell out of them." He didn't always, though. He once bet an entire box of priceless White House china and lost.

GAY OL' TIME

President Harding never let his pressing responsibilities prevent him from visiting the Gayety Burlesque. The theater had a private box just for him in which he could watch the girls unnoticed.

CONFIDENCE MAN

Warren Harding never had much faith in himself. Though he loved working in the newspaper business, the pressures of the job sometimes overwhelmed him, and he once suffered a nervous breakdown. Being president of the United States couldn't have been any easier.

Fortunately for the country, Harding didn't suffer another breakdown after becoming president. But he whined incessantly about his new job. "May God help me, for I need it," he said to the Duchess upon learning of his victory. His anxiety only grew with time; he once flat-out admitted, "I am not fit for the office and should never have been here." To his mistress Nan Britton, he once wrote, "I'm in jail and I can't get out." He was just as blunt with Senator Frank Brandegee: "Frank, it is hell! No other word can describe it." But nothing offers a window into Harding's confused, horrified mind quite like the time he fell apart in front of a White House secretary over a tax issue: "I don't know what to do or where to turn in this taxation matter. Somewhere there must be a book that tells me all about it, where I could go to straighten it out in my mind. But I don't know where the book is, and maybe I couldn't read it if I found it. . . . My God but this is a hell of a place for a man like me to be!"

30 | CALVIN COOLIDGE

BORN July 4, 1872	NICKNAME
DIED January 5, 1933	"Silent Cal"

ASTROLOGICAL SIGN	PARTY	AGE UPON TAKING OFFICE
Cancer	Republican	51

RAN AGAINST	VICE PRESIDENT
	★ None ★
	(after Harding's death)
John Davis	★ Charles G. Dawes ★
	(elected term)

HEIGHT	SOUND BITE	TERM OF PRESIDENCY
5′ 10″ ↑	*"When a great many people are unable to find work, unemployment results."*	1923 – TO – 1929

I n September 1919, when Calvin Coolidge was governor of Massachusetts, the Boston police force went on strike. Coolidge responded forcefully by breaking up the union and issuing the famous proclamation, "There is no right to strike against the public safety by anybody, anywhere, any time." It was a bold statement that earned him national attention and made him the Republican Party's choice for vice president on the Harding ticket. But once Harding's death launched Coolidge into the presidency, he would become famous for saying—and, for that matter, doing—as little as possible.

In addition to serving as governor, Coolidge had been a city council-man, state representative, mayor, state senator, and lieutenant governor. The Boston police strike notwithstanding, his political convictions reflected a belief in limited government that fit well in the unambitious Harding administration. Coolidge was vacationing at his father's farm in Plymouth, Vermont, when word of Harding's death arrived by messenger. (The New England homestead had no electricity or phone.) At 2:47 A.M., on August 2, 1923, Coolidge changed out of his bedclothes and into a black suit to be sworn in as president of the United States by his own father, a notary public. He then changed out of his suit, crawled into bed, and descended into the state that would consume much of his presidency: sleep.

"I think the American public wants a solemn ass as president and I think I'll go along with them," said the new chief executive. Solemn he was—as well as taciturn, stoic, and shamelessly sluggish. Aside from hunting down the malcontents who had steeped Harding's administration in corruption and scandal, his chief exertion was vetoing things—especially bills geared toward relieving the hardship of economically stricken Americans. He further widened the gap between rich and poor by giving the country's wealthiest a giant tax cut in the hopes of increasing productivity. And he remained conspicuously silent on social issues at a time when the Ku Klux Klan, whose legions had swelled to more than five million members, marched on Washington in a show of racist solidarity. In an age when government was expected to avoid intervening in the affairs of business and cultural matters, President Coolidge did his part—by dozing away the afternoons and spending his time smoking cigars in the rocking chair he put on the White House porch.

His term wasn't without tragedy. On July 7, 1924, his sixteen-year-old son, Calvin Jr., died after contracting blood poisoning from a blister he'd suffered while playing tennis on the White House courts. The president, already maudlin, became an emotional void. Though he was reelected that year, the office increasingly held no joy for him. On August 2, 1927, while vacationing in South Dakota, he summoned reporters to an impromptu press conference and handed them all a slip of paper on which was printed, "I do not choose to run for president in 1928." He answered no questions. It was the terse conclusion to a terse presidency. Coolidge

lived long enough to witness the Great Depression that most historians believe his inactivity helped to bring about; he passed the time writing newspaper articles that promoted his tragically outdated maxims on government frugality. Dorothy Parker captured the frosty essence of the man when, upon hearing that doctors had declared him dead, she asked, "How can they tell?"

MOUTH OFF

No president has ever tried so hard to say so little as Calvin Coolidge. Silence was a religion to him. "Nine-tenths of a president's callers at the White House want something they ought not to have," he said to successor Herbert Hoover. "If you keep dead still they will run down in three or four minutes. If you even cough or smile they will start up all over again." When First Lady Grace Coolidge was met by a woman who was going to be seated next to the president at an upcoming state dinner, Mrs. Coolidge replied, "I'm sorry for you. You'll have to do all the talking yourself." Another woman approached the president at an engagement and told him that she'd made a bet that she could get more than two words out of him that night. "You lose" was his reply. Even his press conferences were a joke. Here's one from the 1924 campaign:

"Have you any statement from the campaign?"

Coolidge: "No."

"Can you tell us something about the world situation?"

Coolidge: "No."

"Any information about Prohibition?"

Coolidge: "No."

The best part? As the disappointed reporters made for the door, Coolidge reminded them all not to quote him.

← Coolidge slept at least ten hours every day. He was in bed by ten, often woke at eight, and always took an afternoon nap.

EARLY TO BED, LATE TO RISE

As H. L. Mencken once wrote, "Nero fiddled while Rome burned, but Coolidge only snores." Calvin Coolidge's favorite pastime was sleeping. He was in bed every night by ten and usually rose between six and eight in the morning. His daily afternoon naps ran between two and four hours, and he never missed one. It all made for a total of at least ten hours of sleep a day. The president's drowsy demeanor was no secret—at a performance of the Marx Brothers' show *Animal Crackers*, Groucho Marx discovered Coolidge in the audience and cried out to him, "Isn't it past your bedtime, Calvin?"

EASY RIDER

Coolidge wasn't exactly big on physical activity. His main form of exercise was riding an electric horse that he kept in the White House. Bucking and jouncing away the pounds became a daily routine for the president, and his Secret Service detail usually joined in the fun.

OUT WITH A BANG

The weather was wet and foul on Coolidge's last day as president, and he decided to wear rubber galoshes to his successor's inauguration. One of them, however, turned up missing. It took the efforts of eight Secret Service men to find it, very nearly delaying the transfer of power to Herbert Hoover.

★ ★ ★ ★ ★

FAMOUS FIRST LADIES

First ladies of the first order (and a few who were just weird):

DOLLEY PAYNE TODD MADISON: Originally born of Quaker stock, this buxom, flirtatious socialite set the standard for White House hostesses. (She was the first to serve ice cream at presidential receptions.) Her sense of style was legendary (she even wore turbans), as was her frank and unpretentious demeanor. She was fond of Parisian finery, which cost her husband dearly, and of snuff, which stained her fingers. Unfortunately, she coddled her son from a previous marriage, John Payne Todd, whose debts nearly ruined her. Though she spent her final years in virtual bankruptcy, it was customary for all newly elected presidents to call on her and receive her blessing until her death in 1849.

ELIZABETH KORTRIGHT MONROE: James Monroe's wife broke with Dolley Madison's popular custom of dutifully calling on Washington socialites, insisting instead that they call on her, proceeding to alienate many who thought her unsociable and aloof. She seems to have suffered from some sort of debilitating sickness (perhaps epilepsy), which would account for much of her aversion to public appearances.

JULIA GARDINER TYLER: This second wife of the tenth president was by all accounts a high-spirited beauty. Born and raised in East Hampton, Long Island, she was thirty years her husband's junior and would go on to bear seven of his fifteen children. She was fond of being addressed as "Mrs. Presidentress" and held receptions at the White House in which she was seated on a dais surrounded by female friends and relatives, wearing a wreath of flowers upon her head. Among her more noteworthy accomplishments was getting her fusty husband to loosen up and start dancing.

JANE MEANS APPLETON PIERCE: The wife of Franklin Pierce never liked politics or Washington and despised the notion of her husband becoming president. Shortly after Pierce's victory in the election, their son Bennie was killed in a train accident—the third Pierce son to die prematurely. Jane sank into a mire of melancholy and despair. The new first lady spent her first year in the White House staring blankly at the wall of her room, which she almost never left. She never stopped dressing in mourning black and demanded that black bunting be strewn throughout the Executive Mansion, which soon resembled a tomb. Her nights were spent writing letters to Bennie, and she took to inviting mediums into the White House in a desperate attempt to reach the spirits of her dead sons.

MARY TODD LINCOLN: When President Abraham Lincoln was reviewing Union troops at City Point, Virginia, beside him rode Mrs. Ord, the attractive wife of the unit commander. It was a trivial matter, but it was enough to send Mary Todd Lincoln into a screaming rage (and in front of the troops, no less). It was merely the most sensational of Mary's frequent jealous fits. Her other qualities were just as endearing. After she lost her son Edward in infancy and another son, Willie, while in the White House, Mary Todd's screws only got looser, and her bouts of screaming grief became legendary. Her love of spending the government's money on White House décor and an extravagant wardrobe (she once went $6,700 over budget, a sum Lincoln insisted on paying out of his own pocket to avoid scandal) was also well known. Though Lincoln was sympathetic to spiritualist beliefs, he drew the line at some of the fakes who sought to exploit his wife's grief by holding seances in the White House. One of them, Lord Colchester, was found to have faked the rappings of Willie's spirit by tapping with a rod that was attached to his arm. After Lincoln was shot, Mary went predictably berserk, ensconcing herself upstairs in the White House for weeks, making it difficult and awkward for new president Andrew Johnson to move in.

JULIA BOGGS DENT GRANT: Ulysses S. Grant's wife was a graceful, intelligent, and devoted White House hostess who loved her years as first lady.

She was also severely cross-eyed, the unfortunate result of being accidentally whacked by an oar as a child. Her condition rendered her incapable of seeing any distance without tilting her head, and she usually required the support of someone's arm when crossing a crowded room.

LUCY WARE WEBB HAYES: The wife of Rutherford B. Hayes was a graduate of Wesleyan Women's College and the first first lady to have a college education. Known as "Lemonade Lucy," she was a temperance powerhouse. The Women's Christian Temperance Union was so impressed by her that they commissioned a portrait, which hangs in the White House to this day.

IDA SAXTON MCKINLEY: Doctors usually kept the epileptic wife of William McKinley medicated, making her look something like a smiling mannequin. She was terribly in love with—and totally dependent on—her husband, whose assassination made her want to join him in the beyond. Fate wouldn't have it—she lived another six years, during which, it is rumored, her seizures all but vanished.

HELEN "NELLIE" HERRON TAFT: William Howard Taft's wife was more excited to get to the White House than her husband had been and viewed it as the fulfillment of a lifelong dream. Not even a stroke, which she suffered only a month into Taft's term, could ruin her experience as first lady. She was the first woman to be allowed a seat within the bar of the Supreme Court, the first first lady to have her memoirs published, and the first to be buried in Arlington National Cemetery. But her greatest legacy remains the thousands of cherry trees that grace Washington, D.C. —they were her idea.

LOU HENRY HOOVER: Herbert Hoover's wife was an impressive public figure on her own terms before she became first lady. In addition to being an inveterate outdoorswoman, she had a degree in geology, spoke fluent Chinese, studied ancient Egyptian culture, and had translated an obscure Latin text. She was an avid spokeswoman for charity during the Great Depression and even found time to be a sponsor of the Girl Scouts.

ELEANOR ROOSEVELT: Partly because of FDR's inability to get around easily, his wife, Eleanor, became a spokeswoman for the administration. Through numerous public appearances, she overcame her innate shyness to evolve into one of the twentieth century's most effective progressive activists. It is speculated by many that she shared a romantic relationship with Associated Press writer Lorena Hickok—in any event, her relationship with Franklin was sexless after the birth of their sixth child. She was the first first lady to hold her own press conferences and wrote regular newspaper columns about her active political life. She even carried a gun for protection, though it is reported that she was a terrible shot.

MAMIE GENEVA DOUD EISENHOWER: Among the maladies that afflicted Dwight Eisenhower's wife were asthma, heart flutters, and claustrophobia. She also had an inner-ear condition that threw off her balance and made many think she was an alcoholic. But perhaps her worst sickness was a weakness for the color pink—everything in the presidential bedroom was adorned in the rosy hue, from the wastebasket to the nightgown she wore to bed.

JACQUELINE LEE BOUVIER KENNEDY: Probably the most glamorous first lady of all time, John Kennedy's wife was born of stock as wealthy and privileged as her husband's. She was keenly intelligent, well bred, beautiful, and frighteningly tolerant of her husband's countless extramarital affairs. Jackie restored the country's respect in its Executive Mansion by giving a nationally televised tour of the White House in 1962. It had been refurbished by the first lady with numerous antiques at a staggering cost. In fact, spending money was Jackie's strong suit—she blew more than $121,000 on her wardrobe in 1962 alone.

ELIZABETH BLOOMER WARREN FORD: Gerald Ford's wife openly spoke about the radical mastectomy she underwent to remove a lump in her breast during her term as first lady, courageously promoting awareness of breast cancer and the need for its prevention. She was a huge supporter of the Equal Rights Amendment and the women's liberation movement, and she liked to chat on CB radios. (Her handle was "First Mama.") Her other loves included alcohol and painkillers, to which she became addicted long before entering the White House. She finally came to terms with her demons by entering a clinic after her husband's presidential term. She went on to found the Betty Ford Center to help other addicts overcome their dependencies.

ROSALYNN SMITH CARTER: When Jimmy Carter's wife visited Latin America, she went as an official representative of the Carter administration—the first time a first lady set out alone on an official diplomatic mission. She went on to become one of the most most-traveled first ladies, visiting sixteen foreign countries in her first year alone.

NANCY REAGAN: When she was first lady, Nancy Reagan's pet project was getting America's kids to avoid drugs. "Just Say No" was the slogan she had plastered all over the media. But she really made history by saying yes to an offer from the writers of *Diff'rent Strokes* to make an appearance on their television sitcom, a show that—for reasons that continue to mystify—was wildly popular at the time. To everyone involved, it seemed a match made in heaven: *Diff'rent Strokes* (starring the diminutive Gary Coleman) was doing an antidrug episode, and the first lady was the nation's antidrug spokesperson who'd once been an actor herself. She went to California to do her part, so to speak, and the episode aired on March 19, 1983. Ironically, only those viewers who were on drugs appreciated her performance.

BARBARA PIERCE BUSH: George Bush's wife became more popular than her husband for her delightfully frank, self-deprecating humor. "One of the myths is that I don't dress well," she once said in reference to her frumpy appearance. "I dress very well—I just don't look so good." Astute readers may have noticed a familiar ring to her maiden name—it's courtesy of President Franklin Pierce, from whom she was descended.

BORN August 10, 1874	NICKNAME
DIED October 20, 1964	"The Great Engineer"

ASTROLOGICAL SIGN	PARTY	AGE UPON TAKING OFFICE
Leo	Republican	54

RAN AGAINST	VICE PRESIDENT
Al Smith	★ Charles Curtis ★

HEIGHT	SOUND BITE	TERM OF PRESIDENCY
5′11″	*"I outlived the bastards."* (referring to the many people who blamed him for the Great Depression)	1929 – TO – 1933

We in America today are nearer to the final triumph over poverty than ever before in the history of any land," said Herbert Hoover in his acceptance speech at the Republican national convention in 1928. "The poorhouse is vanishing from among us." Just seven months after assuming the presidency, Hoover was forced to eat his words as the Great Depression started turning America into a nation of poorhouses.

In fact, the country had every cause to be optimistic about a Hoover administration. Calvin Coolidge called him the "wundah boy," and for good reason. Orphaned at the age of nine, Hoover became a rags-to-riches poster child. He graduated from Stanford University with a degree in engineering and quickly set about building an international mining empire, becoming a millionaire by the age of forty. His business sense was matched by an equally impressive call to public service. In 1914, he organized relief for Belgian war refugees; President Wilson named him food administrator after America's entry into World War I; and Hoover played a central role at the Versailles peace conference as Wilson's economic adviser. Such credentials got him the post of commerce secretary during the Harding and Coolidge administrations, where he proved adept at fostering business and industry without creating a bloated bureaucracy.

Little wonder, then, that he won the 1928 election. His Democratic opponent was Al Smith, America's first Roman Catholic candidate, and Hoover won by a comfortable margin. The nation looked at its new president with a sense of awe: he was an administrative genius, a genuine humanitarian, a scholar who published works on politics and engineering, and a brilliant businessman. He could do no wrong.

Until the stock market crash of October 29, 1929. Unlike every president before him who faced a stricken economy, Hoover confronted the calamity head-on. He worked long hours and even weekends to get a grasp of the situation, initiating tax cuts and public works programs and issuing proclamations to the press that recovery was just around the corner. But nothing he did worked, and soon his name became the embodiment of misery and hardship. "Hoovervilles"—shantytowns that sheltered the unemployed—carpeted the nation, and citizens took to using the word "Hoover" as a curse. Despite his tireless efforts, he always opposed direct government relief for the poor, and his fear of big government prevented him from spending the enormous amounts of money that were needed. The Great Depression continued unabated by 1932, unemployment had reached 25 percent.

The president took to feeling sorry for himself. His hair went white, he lost more than thirty-five pounds, and his mood (understandably) turned melancholy. He didn't have a snowball's chance in hell of beating Franklin Roosevelt in 1932, and he knew it. The election results proved him right. As the two rode side by side in the car that took FDR to his inauguration, Hoover barely said a word, remaining steeped in a cloud of gloom while his successor stammered out a series of awkward attempts at conversation. For Hoover, passing the cheering crowds—whose adulation, he knew, wasn't meant for him—was like running the gauntlet.

Herbert Hoover went on to write books and advise presidents, but he never could shake the stigma of being attached to the Great Depression. He lived to the ripe old age of ninety—more than enough time to see his reputation slammed by a whole slew of historians.

BY APPOINTMENT ONLY

Hoover had never campaigned for any government post before the presidency. All of the jobs that made him a famous public figure were appointed by higher-ups. Before 1928, the last office to which he'd been elected was class treasurer at Stanford University.

SECRET SERVICE

The Hoovers had a bizarre relationship with the White House servants. First Lady Lou Hoover communicated with the staff through a sign language she developed for the sake of efficiency. (Touching her hair meant dinner was to be announced to guests, for example.) The president also avoided verbal communication and preferred not to see the servants at all. The mansion's bell system was used to keep a distance between Hoover and the people who served him: three rings announced his approach, requiring staff to hide in the nearest closet until he was out of sight. The same went for the groundskeepers, who found themselves jumping behind shrubs when the president was rumored to be nearby. Those staff members with an insufficient cloaking device faced the possibility of dismissal.

→ White House servants and groundskeepers received strict orders to hide whenever President Hoover passed by. Those who failed to do so risked dismissal.

DEPRESSION? WHAT DEPRESSION?

Though Herbert Hoover routinely gave to charities while president, he always did so anonymously, and his public image remained stiff and officious. (The guy even wore a tie while fishing, for crying out loud.) The Hoovers' lavish lifestyle only made things worse. While the rest of the nation wallowed in hunger, those in the White House carried on like aristocracy. Both lunch and dinner usually required formal attire, and virtually every meal was a seven-course feast. Hoover may have thought he was maintaining an air of confidence, but it only backfired; after all, few soup kitchens at the time offered seven courses.

32 | FRANKLIN DELANO ROOSEVELT

BORN January 30, 1882
DIED April 12, 1945

NICKNAMES
"FDR," "The New Dealer,"
"That Man in the White House"

ASTROLOGICAL SIGN	PARTY	AGE UPON TAKING OFFICE
Aquarius	Democratic	51

RAN AGAINST

Herbert Hoover *(first term)*
Alfred M. Landon *(second term)*
Wendell Wilkie *(third term)*
Thomas E. Dewey *(fourth term)*

VICE PRESIDENT

★ John N. Garner ★
(first and second terms)

★ Henry A. Wallace ★
(third term)

★ Harry Truman ★
(fourth term)

HEIGHT
6′1″

SOUND BITE

"Be sincere;
be brief;
be seated."

(on the art of public speaking)

TERM OF PRESIDENCY
1933
– TO –
1945

To those Americans who came of age during the Roosevelt years, it seemed as if FDR had been president forever. He remains the only chief executive to serve more than two terms. (The 22nd Amendment, passed in 1951, put the limit at two terms for president.) While discussing the arrangements for his third inauguration, Chief Justice Charles Evans Hughes joked to Roosevelt, "Don't you think this is getting just a little monotonous for both of us?"

For a man who did so much for the common people, Franklin Delano Roosevelt was anything but common. He was born to New York aristocracy and bred for a life of yachting and cocktail parties. But, unlike so many of his class, FDR embraced the call to public service with an emphasis on bettering the lot of his fellow Americans. After serving in the New York state senate and as Woodrow Wilson's assistant secretary of the navy, he ran as the Democratic vice presidential candidate in 1920 with James Cox. Though they lost to Warren Harding, FDR had arrived as an impressive figure in the Democratic Party.

In 1921, he was stricken with polio, from which he was to lose full use of his legs for the rest of his life. It didn't stop him, however. After a lengthy recovery, he got right back into politics, stunning everyone with his determination to carry on despite daunting physical challenges. As governor of New York from 1929 to 1933, he initiated programs to help ease the misery brought about by the Depression, setting himself up for the White House. He had charm, style, good looks, and a disarming sense of humor. Most conspicuous of all was his infectious optimism, a quality he would rely on time and again while leading the country out of its economic woes.

His strategy for tackling the Depression was simple: Try something, anything, and if it didn't work, try something else. FDR first spoke of the "New Deal" during his acceptance speech at the Democratic national convention in 1932, and it became the catchphrase for his ambitious campaign to reinvigorate the economy. Among the numerous projects he pushed through were the Civilian Conservation Corps, a public works department that employed the poor; the Federal Emergency Relief Administration, which offered direct government assistance to the impoverished; and the National Industrial Recovery Act, which helped states fund construction projects. Compared with the terse defeatism of Herbert Hoover, FDR was a beacon of hope and action, and his ceaseless efforts—combined with his twice-yearly "fireside chats," in which he spoke directly to the nation over

← Between Franklin, Eleanor, Lucy, Missy, and Lorena, the Roosevelt White House saw more adultery than a 1970s key party.

the radio—were a boon to a populace weary of government lethargy.

Yet the New Deal's results were spotty at best. Moreover, it ran into opposition at every turn—the Supreme Court ruled that some of it was downright unconstitutional, an abuse of executive power. In the end, total relief from the Great Depression would come not through government programs but from the unlikeliest of sources: the Japanese.

When the United States Pacific fleet got bombed at Pearl Harbor on December 7, 1941, it vaulted Americans into a fight that FDR had been trying to join for years. Nazi Germany, his chief concern, made things easier by declaring war on America three days after Congress declared war on Japan. The conflict was now truly global. As commander in chief, FDR presided over an industrial power that quickly went from moribund to massive, an industrial juggernaut the likes of which the world had never imagined. Though he forged a close and friendly bond with British prime minister Winston Churchill, his other ally, Joseph Stalin, proved much harder to handle. At the Allied conferences near the conclusion of the war, Roosevelt, though convinced that he could deal with the Soviet premier, was duped into giving the Russians firm control over Eastern Europe, sowing the seeds of the Cold War. Many historians have also given FDR a lot of guff about the plight of the Jews; he was entirely in the know about the Holocaust yet steadfastly insisted on winning a military victory rather than intervening in the genocide. Nevertheless, he saw his country through history's most disastrous conflagration, and he did it masterfully.

FDR's vice president after the election of 1944 was a little-known machine politician named Harry Truman, with whom the president shared virtually no information—including that America was developing an atomic bomb. Ironically, it was Truman to whom the decision to use it would fall. On April 12, 1945, FDR was in his home-away-from-home at Warm Springs, Georgia, sitting for a portrait when he suddenly announced that he had "a terrific headache." Just hours later, he was dead from a cerebral hemorrhage. For a people who had gotten used to the image of FDR leading them through their worst nightmares, it was like losing a parent.

FAMILY MAN

In 1905, Franklin Delano Roosevelt married Eleanor Roosevelt. They were fifth cousins once removed. Eleanor's uncle Theodore Roosevelt remarked, "It's a good thing to keep the name in the family." Hmmm.

But Uncle Teddy wasn't the only famous person in the family tree. FDR could count George Washington, John Adams, James Madison, Martin Van Buren, Zachary Taylor, Ulysses S. Grant, and William Howard Taft as his distant relatives. He was even related to Winston Churchill, who was a seventh cousin once removed.

BRACING FOR THE WORST

Franklin Roosevelt's vast accomplishments as president are all the more impressive when one considers the physical hurdles he had to overcome. He was the only paraplegic to occupy the White House—and he did it through more than three terms.

He had plenty of help. Through a gentleman's agreement that seems impossible today, the media obeyed the administration's wish to avoid photographing the president in his wheelchair. But the subterfuge went much further and was so effective that, incredibly, many Americans never knew the full extent of Roosevelt's condition. He wore steel braces that were heavy and often dug into his flesh. They were as much a burden as an aid and could be relied upon to support him for only brief periods. As a result, Secret Service agents were often called upon to handle FDR as if he were a great sack of grain: they lifted him out of his car, carried him across barriers, and always remained on the lookout for eager photographers—whose cameras were quickly knocked to the ground. At House Speaker William Bankhead's funeral in 1940, the street outside was raised to the same level as the church floor so that Roosevelt could seem to walk in under his own power. The president didn't always need help, though—especially when he was driving one of the cars he had specially fitted with hand controls to let him speed about with impunity.

TOUGH TARGET

In February 1933, FDR was finishing a speech in a Miami park when a man stood up on a bench and fired five shots at him. The assassin's name was Joseph Zangara, and apparently his aim was terrible. The bullets struck five people unfortunate enough to be standing next to Roosevelt, including Chicago mayor Anton Cermack, who later died.

TAKING NO CHANCES

FDR was extremely superstitious. He never lit three cigarettes off a single match, refused to sit at a table set for thirteen, and wouldn't begin a trip on a Friday. Strangely enough, the funeral train that took his body back home from Georgia began its journey on Friday the thirteenth.

LUCY AND MISSY

In 1918, Eleanor Roosevelt discovered a collection of love letters between her husband and her own social secretary, Lucy Mercer. Eleanor confronted Franklin, vowing to sue for divorce unless he stopped seeing Lucy. FDR's mother, Sara Roosevelt, helped make the decision easier by threatening to cut off his share of the family finances unless he complied. And so he did. The result was a marriage that thereafter remained almost completely devoid of physical contact.

FDR eventually replaced Mercer with another mistress. Missy LeHand became one of his secretaries while he was governor of New York, and she would stay with him right into the White House. Stories abound of people walking into the president's office to discover Missy sitting on Roosevelt's lap. Eleanor seemed far less bothered by LeHand than she'd been by Mercer—perhaps because she was said to have her own mistress by this time. Reporter Lorena Hickok lived in a room in the White House right across from the first lady's, and it seems certain to many that the two shared more than just a deep friendship.

When Missy LeHand died in 1944, FDR mourned her passing . . . and then started up with Lucy Mercer again. Because Eleanor's ban on Mercer was still in effect, the relationship remained a secret (with the help of the Secret Service, of course, who regularly arranged for illicit meetings between their boss and his old flame). Mercer was with FDR when he died in 1945. By the time Eleanor arrived, all evidence of Mercer's presence had been removed from the home.

★ ★ ★ ★ ★

33 | HARRY S TRUMAN

BORN May 8, 1884	NICKNAMES
DIED December 26, 1972	"The Haberdasher," "Give 'Em Hell Harry"

ASTROLOGICAL SIGN	PARTY	AGE UPON TAKING OFFICE
Taurus	Democratic	60

RAN AGAINST	VICE PRESIDENT
Thomas E. Dewey	★ None ★ (after FDR's death)
	★ Alben W. Barkley ★ (elected term)

HEIGHT	SOUND BITE	TERM OF PRESIDENCY
5′ 7″ ↑	*"I fired MacArthur because he wouldn't respect the authority of the president. I didn't fire him because he was a dumb son of a bitch, although he was, but that's not against the law for generals. If it was, half to three-quarters of them would be in jail."*	1945 – TO – 1953

Harry S Truman began his presidency with a glass of bourbon in his hand. He was having a cocktail with Speaker of the House Sam Rayburn in the Capitol Building lounge when word came that President Roosevelt was dead. "Jesus Christ and General Jackson!" exclaimed Truman. His words were a little graver the next morning when he assembled a group of reporters: "Boys, if you ever pray, pray for me now."

If Truman was pessimistic about his own abilities, he was in good company; virtually nobody expected great things from this little-known politician from Missouri. "Now, Harry," said Speaker Rayburn to the new president, "a lot of people are going to tell you you are the smartest man in the country, but Harry, you and I know you ain't." He remains the only twentieth-century president without a college degree. When Truman walked into the room at FDR's funeral, nobody stood up. After twelve years of Roosevelt's commanding presence, no one could bear to think of this bespectacled haberdasher as the chief executive.

In his younger days, Truman had been a mailroom clerk, a bookkeeper, and a farmer. At the age of thirty-three, he volunteered for the army and became a captain of artillery during World War I. Then he came home, opened a men's clothing store in Kansas City, watched it go bust, and decided to give politics a try. The local Democratic machine was as corrupt as they come, and it overlooked Truman's honesty to make him a judge of Jackson County, Missouri. He went on to the U.S. Senate, where his investigation of defense contracts saved the government billions of dollars. Though Truman loved being a senator, Franklin Roosevelt had bigger plans for him. FDR eventually convinced the irascible Missourian to become his vice presidential candidate in 1944.

Truman was woefully unprepared to fill his predecessor's gigantic shoes when FDR died in April 1945. Nevertheless, the new president was soon rubbing shoulders with Churchill and Stalin at the Potsdam conference and authorizing the use of atomic bombs against Japan. Winning the war was the easy part—picking up the pieces would prove far more difficult.

Due in large part to postwar economic hardships, Truman's popularity had waned so severely by 1948 that almost nobody thought he could win reelection. After a vigorous "whistle-stop" campaign fought in large part from the back of a railcar that toured the country, Truman pulled off the impossible and beat Thomas Dewey. Nobody was more shocked than the *Chicago Daily Tribune*, which had gone ahead and printed "DEWEY DEFEATS TRUMAN" on the front page of its postelection edition.

Delight over the surprise victory had barely subsided before another struggle overwhelmed the administration: the Cold War. Before reelection, Truman responded forcefully to Soviet bullying with the "Truman Doctrine," a plan that emphasized containment—communism would be bottled up where it was and prevented from spreading. The "Marshall Plan," named for Secretary of State George Marshall, succeeded in helping war-torn nations with heaps of financial aid. And in 1948, Truman succeeded in airlifting supplies to West Berlin when that city was blockaded by Stalin's troops.

But his second term witnessed a slew of nasty surprises. China soon fell to communist rule, and the Soviet Union detonated its first atomic bomb. Communist North Korea invaded its southern neighbor, starting a war that would draw in not only the United States and the United nations but China as well. And as if all that weren't bad enough, the general sent to win the Korean War, the immensely popular Douglas MacArthur, started openly criticizing the president. Truman did the only thing he could: he sacked the general, a move for which he was widely and viciously criticized.

As the Korean War dragged on, Senator Joseph McCarthy's witch hunts had everyone at home believing that a communist spy lurked in every pantry. Poor Harry was seen as light on communism, an old New Dealer whose civil rights agenda, noble as it was, didn't address important security issues. Truman's decision not to run for a second elected term was an easy one; as 1952 approached, his approval ratings were the worst of any president in American history. Posterity, however, has been much kinder to him. Long after he was shouted out of the White House, Truman has come to represent earthy, straightforward, tough-talking simplicity—a quality that's hard to come by in a politician these days.

→   "Give 'Em Hell" Harry set new heights in presidential profanity—at least until Richard Nixon came along.

"S" IS FOR "STUCK IN THE MIDDLE"

There is no period after the "S" in Harry S Truman's name. That's because it doesn't actually stand for anything. When he was born, a disagreement arose over whether to make his middle name Shippe, after his paternal grandfather, or Solomon, after his maternal grandfather. The issue was never resolved, and "S" was put on the birth certificate as a compromise.

SWEARING IN

Harry Truman had a fondness for harsh language, and he rarely hesitated to use it. When first told that FDR wanted to make him his running mate, Truman said, "Tell him to go to hell." During a speech in Washington, he took umbrage with all those who made cabinet recommendations, proclaiming that "no S.O.B. is going to dictate to me who I'm going to have!" He didn't calm down after leaving the White House, either. While stumping on behalf of John Kennedy in 1960, Truman told a Texas crowd that anyone who voted for Nixon should "go to hell."

DADDY'S LITTLE GIRL

Truman's temper was notorious. Once, when an ambassador canceled a dinner engagement with him at the last minute, Truman blew a gasket and demanded that the diplomat be sacked immediately. Undersecretary of State Dean Acheson joined forces with First Lady Bess Truman to talk Truman down. It was standard practice at the White House—Mrs. Truman and many of the president's cabinet went out of their way to intercept Truman's mail in case he sent out a dangerously wrathful reply that might get him in trouble.

Sometimes they failed. The most notorious instance involved *Washington Post* music critic Paul Hume, who gave a scathing review of a singing recital given by the president's daughter, Margaret. Truman read the review and flipped out. "You sound like a frustrated old man who never made a success, an eight-ulcer man on a four-ulcer job and all four ulcers working," penned a fuming Truman in his 150-word letter to Hume. "Some day I hope to meet you. When that happens you'll need a new nose, a lot of beefsteak for black eyes, and perhaps a supporter below!" Despite his rage, Truman maintained the presence of mind to realize that the letter would never get through his advisers if he sent it through the normal channels. So he stamped the letter himself, went for a walk, and posted it personally to ensure that it would be delivered. It soon appeared on the front page of the *Washington News*, causing a scandal. Sadly, it did little for Margaret's singing career.

IT'S A BIRD! IT'S A PLANE!
IT'S . . . THE PRESIDENT?

Truman had a presidential DC-4 airplane called the Sacred Cow, whose pilot he once talked into buzzing the White House while Bess and Margaret were on the roof. Unfortunately, none of the Secret Service agents knew the president was on the plane. As the swooping machine roared over the White House, terrifying the first family and staff, the mansion's security—convinced that some assassin had commandeered the plane—flew into action. By the time the truth was discovered, even Air Force security units had been scrambled. Thankfully, nobody was hurt (but the president was mightily embarrassed).

CURIOSITY (ALMOST) KILLED THE CAT

While the White House underwent an extensive renovation in 1950, the Trumans stayed at Blair House, a government-owned building across the street. There, on November 1, the president was the target of an assassination attempt that very nearly succeeded.

Not that the would-be assassins knew what the hell they were doing. Oscar Collazo and Griselio Torresola were determined to strike a blow for the Puerto Rican independence movement by assassinating the president of the United States. After having Blair House identified by their taxi driver, they attempted to get in—through the heavily guarded front door.

Once the shooting started, Truman, who had been taking a nap upstairs, got out of bed and stuck his head out the window to see what was going on. Had the assassins only looked up, they might have gotten a shot at their target. But despite Truman's cooperation, it wasn't to be. Torresola was dead and Collazo wounded. They'd taken a White House police officer with them.

DAUGHTER OF THE CONFEDERACY

Some of Harry Truman's ancestors on his mother's side had been Confederates who did time in a Union internment camp during the Civil War. His mother, Martha Ellen Young Truman, forever held a grudge against the federal cause. After her son became president, she visited the White House and was invited to sleep in the Lincoln bedroom. She said she'd rather sleep on the floor.

★ ★ ★ ★ ★

34 | DWIGHT DAVID EISENHOWER

BORN October 14, 1890	NICKNAME
DIED March 28, 1969	"Ike"

ASTROLOGICAL SIGN	PARTY	AGE UPON TAKING OFFICE
Libra	Republican	
		62

RAN AGAINST	VICE PRESIDENT
Adlai E. Stevenson	★ Richard M. Nixon ★

HEIGHT	SOUND BITE	TERM OF PRESIDENCY
5′10″ ↑	*"I just won't get into a pissing contest with that skunk."* (referring to Senator Joe McCarthy)	1953 – TO – 1961

fter World War II, when supporters began suggesting that Dwight Eisenhower run for public office, he acted as if they were out of their minds. "I cannot conceive of any circumstance that could drag out of me permission to consider me for any political post from dogcatcher to Grand High Supreme King of the Universe." But Dwight wasn't fooling anybody. It was only a matter of time before the most important general in the greatest military conflict in history gave in to the pressure to become commander in chief.

Eisenhower grew up in a Kansas family as large as it was poor. After his father's general store went belly up, he and his five brothers were lucky to have shoes on their feet. Dwight decided on a military career and went

to West Point. Athletics always meant more to him than his studies, and he graduated in the middle of his class. After a knee injury demolished his dreams of being a football player, he resigned himself to a career in the army. (Thank goodness for the civilized world.) His mediocre academic performance belied an extraordinary intelligence, however. He proved so good at training troops during World War I that his superiors kept him back home, ruining his hopes for martial glory. He then went on to serve with General MacArthur in Washington, D.C., and the Philippines, where his uncanny organizational skills won him renown in the officer corps. After the Japanese attack on Pearl Harbor, Eisenhower's star had risen high enough to catch the attention of the nation's top soldier, General George Marshall.

As commander of all Allied forces in Europe during World War II, Ike earned a reputation as a gifted conciliator. His American and British underlings were often as eager to pummel each other as they were to pummel the Germans, and Ike struggled to make them operate effectively against the Third Reich. It was the sort of brilliant leadership ability that many thought had "White House" written all over it.

Many, that is, except Eisenhower. Determined not to be a "glory-hopper," he did everything but run for office: He served as army chief of staff and president of Columbia University and even wrote a best-selling memoir of World War II. The pressure to run grew too great, however, and he finally ran as a Republican in 1952 against Adlai Stevenson. He won in a landslide.

The last Republican to occupy the Oval Office had been Herbert Hoover, and Ike bent over backward to distance himself from the old guard. His domestic agenda bore a striking resemblance to those of his Democratic predecessors. He expanded Social Security and spent lavishly on public works projects such as the interstate highway system. Though mostly silent on issues of race, he intervened forcefully to support desegregation of

← Eisenhower spent as many as 150 days a year on the golf course and even installed a putting green on the White House lawn (it was plagued by squirrels).

schools in Little Rock, Arkansas. He was also just as disgusted as Harry Truman had been by Senator Joe McCarthy's rabid anticommunist rabble-rousing.

Not that communism didn't keep him up at night. To the contrary: he continued Truman's containment policy and bullied the North Koreans into an armistice. With communist rumblings in Southeast Asia and violent Soviet repression in Eastern Europe, it looked to many as if the U.S.S.R. was upping the ante. The launching of Russia's *Sputnik* satellite in 1957 only made things worse, and Ike began the stockpiling of nuclear weapons that would define the Cold War.

For a guy who made such a huff about not running for president, Eisenhower seemed made for the job. An economic boom during his first term helped him crush Adlai Stevenson again in 1956, and Ike maintained a high approval rating. But Eisenhower had planted a terrible seed whose blossom would loom large over his successors: part of his containment policy involved sending a small group of military advisors to a little-known corner of the world called Vietnam.

WHERE DID WE GO WRONG WITH THAT BOY?

Eisenhower's parents were members of a fundamentalist religious sect known as the River Brethren. They were strict pacifists. The couple who raised one of the most effective soldiers in history could not abide the taking of another life. The only time the Eisenhower brothers saw their mother cry was the day she left Ike at the train station to go to West Point.

IN THE FLESH

Ike's lackluster academic performance at West Point may not have been the only reason he graduated 61st in a class of 164. He was also a notorious prankster. On one occasion, he was summoned by his commanding officer to appear in full dress coat. Ike promptly showed up dressed in his coat—and nothing else.

PUTTERING AROUND

Eisenhower was an inveterate card player. He and his wife, Mamie, were obsessed with bridge and canasta and even had friends flown in to the White House on occasion to make sure they had enough players. But golf was Ike's first passion. Incredibly, he spent as much as 150 days of the year on the links during his administration and even had a putting green constructed on the White House lawn. (It was constantly plagued by squirrels.) He loved to win and usually behaved poorly when he lost. After one particularly bad shot, he threw his iron at fellow golfer Dr. Howard Snyder, hitting him in the shin and nearly fracturing the man's leg.

REVVING HIS ENGINE

While he was stationed in England during World War II, Eisenhower's personal driver was an attractive woman named Kay Summersby. Ike was impressed enough with Kay's driving (ahem) to request that she be his full-time—er, *driver* for the rest of the war. It is widely believed that the two shared a physical relationship, though according to Summersby, Ike's stick didn't shift too well. In *Past Forgetting: My Love Affair with Dwight D. Eisenhower*, a ghost-written tell-all, she claims he was virtually impotent.

CLOSE CALLS

No spring chicken when he began his presidency, Eisenhower suffered a few serious physical setbacks during his two terms in office. In 1955, while golfing in Denver, he was called from the links four times in one day to take phone calls from Washington. Ike despised having his golf game interrupted, and he became furious. His anger took its toll—that night, he suffered a massive heart attack. Dr. Snyder, Ike's personal physician, was so worried about the president's condition that he broke down in tears. When the press learned of the information, all hell broke loose—the following Monday, the stock market lost $14 billion. Ike eventually recovered, but it was merely the first of many heart attacks he would suffer before his death in 1969.

In 1956, while campaigning for his second term, Eisenhower was diagnosed with ileitis, an intestinal affliction. He had to undergo surgery—twice. But his scariest brush with death by far occurred in 1957. While sitting at his desk, he was overcome with dizziness and retired to his bed. He later rose, went downstairs, and—when asked by his wife, Mamie, what he was doing out of bed—stuttered out a bunch of incoherent words. He had suffered what doctors call a cerebral occlusion, which disrupts the part of the brain dedicated to speech. The president took to pounding his fists in frustration at not being able to enunciate his own thoughts. With several weeks of rest (during a critical period of the Cold War), he eventually recovered.

THE PRICE OF GLORY

After years as one of the most important men on the face of the planet, Eisenhower had grown accustomed to having the little people attend to details. While he was president, he even had someone dress him. Among valet John Moaney's responsibilities were putting Eisenhower's watch on while the president held out his wrist and pulling up his boss's boxer shorts. Such a lifestyle came back to haunt Ike once he left the White House. After leaving public office, he was almost completely ignorant of how to pay for things at a department store, adjust a TV set, get past a tollbooth on the highway, or dial a phone (yes, dial a phone).

IKE ALIKE

How did "Dwight" translate into "Ike"? Actually, it didn't. Ike was an Eisenhower family nickname—all six of the Eisenhower boys were nicknamed Ike at one time or another.

★ ★ ★ ★ ★

35 | JOHN FITZGERALD KENNEDY

BORN **May 29, 1917**
DIED **November 22, 1963**

NICKNAMES
"Jack," "JFK"

ASTROLOGICAL SIGN
Gemini

PARTY
Democratic

AGE UPON
TAKING OFFICE
43

RAN AGAINST
Richard Nixon

VICE PRESIDENT
★ Lyndon B. Johnson ★

HEIGHT
6′1″

SOUND BITE
*"Forgive your enemies,
but never forget their names."*

TERM OF
PRESIDENCY
1961
– TO –
1963

How do you become one of the most beloved icons of all time after serving only three somewhat unproductive years as president? You begin by having a father who's incredibly ambitious, utterly unscrupulous, and filthy rich. It also helps to have charm, humor, and movie-star good looks. And it doesn't hurt to get cut down by a sniper before your domestic legislation has a chance to get cut down by Congress. John F. Kennedy had it all—and no amount of truth, no matter how ugly, can remove the shining aura from his memory.

"Jack" Kennedy grew up in a Catholic Massachusetts household in which being frail and sickly—which he was—couldn't be tolerated. His father, Joseph Kennedy Sr., had amassed a ghastly fortune from Wall Street speculation, investment in Hollywood films, and bootlegging during Prohibition. He ran his household like a boot camp for future achievers. In the clan's ubiquitous touch football games, winning was everything, and losers learned to hang their heads in shame. Joe's wife, Rose, contributed to the healthy family atmosphere by keeping her mouth shut and withholding affection from their nine children. When Joe was appointed ambassador to Great Britain by President Franklin Roosevelt, he made an ass of himself by insisting that the British were going to lose the war with Hitler's Germany. FDR fired him, and by backing the wrong horse, Joe Kennedy ruined his dream of becoming president.

He then projected all his grandiose hopes on his sons. Joe Jr. was the eldest; unfortunately, his bomber got blown out of the sky over Europe, so Joe Sr. focused his energies on son number two: Jack. After graduating from Harvard, Jack joined the navy and saved the lives of his crewmen after the PT boat he commanded was rammed by a Japanese destroyer. By playing up his "war hero" status and playing down his chronic health problems and womanizing, JFK—with a lot of help from Dad—got elected to the House of Representatives and then the Senate. As the 1960 presidential campaign approached, the Democratic Party was willing to overlook JFK's lightweight congressional record and make the dashing and charismatic Jack their candidate.

He beat Richard Nixon in one of the closest races in American history, becoming the first Catholic to occupy the Oval Office and the first president to be born in the twentieth century. Though Nixon had a better command of the issues, the new medium of television made the wisecracking, handsome, easygoing Jack into something of a prime-time celebrity. Image would continue to fuel the country's love of their new president, and visions of JFK with his glamorous wife, Jackie, and their two irresistible young children flickered across TV sets and filled magazine pages.

But if presidential yacht trips dominated the gossip columns, it was

→ Kennedy had wit, charm, good looks, money, and plenty of female admirers—
   especially after he made it into the White House.

the Cold War that dominated front-page headlines. Just weeks into JFK's administration, an invasion of Fidel Castro's Cuba at the Bay of Pigs by U.S.-backed Cuban exiles ended in disaster. It was an ill-conceived scheme that didn't ease tensions between the United States and the Soviet Union, which had begun cultivating a close relationship with Cuba. Just how close would become clear when Soviet premier Nikita Khrushchev started shipping missiles to Castro's little Caribbean paradise. Faced with a nuclear threat just ninety miles from Florida, Kennedy challenged Khrushchev to remove them or face the consequences. An American naval blockade of Cuba made the Soviets back down, preventing World War III.

Though Kennedy was forced by the Soviets to remove American missiles from Turkey in exchange for the removal of Soviet missiles from Cuba, the peaceful resolution of the Cuban Missile Crisis was Jack Kennedy at his best. A lesser man might have given in to the cries from the military for an invasion of Cuba and allowed the unthinkable to occur. It also led to a groundbreaking arms limitation treaty between the two superpowers. Unfortunately, Kennedy's decisions weren't quite as sound concerning South Vietnam, where a U.S.-backed government became corrupt enough to warrant a violent coup d'état. It sent the region into a spiral of strife that would eventually compel America to commit itself to one of the most tragic wars in its history.

But Kennedy wouldn't live long enough to see the Vietnam War. On November 22, 1963, he was assassinated in Dallas, Texas, by Lee Harvey Oswald. It is this tragic moment—so vividly and horribly captured on film—that is frozen in time, the violent end to a young, vibrant life. Absent from that image is the dark side of JFK: the cocky, crooked rich kid who couldn't keep his pants zipped.

SLEPT IN THE ATTIC

In 1957, Jack Kennedy won a Pulitzer Prize for his history of leaders in action titled *Profiles in Courage*. It was mostly ghostwritten. Not that Jack couldn't write a book of his own—long before *Profiles in Courage,* he had written a book about England's lack of preparation for World War II. It was originally a thesis paper for Harvard, cobbled together while he spent time in the United Kingdom during his father's ambassadorship to that country. Joe Sr. thought it was good enough to be published and pulled some strings to get it in print. Entitled *Why England Slept*, it was poorly researched and even more poorly written. Nevertheless, it sold quite well. Why, you may ask? Because Joe Sr. immediately bought up 30,000 copies. They sat in the attic of the Kennedy household for years.

JACK'S BACK

JFK spent much of his youth in painful physical misery. Whooping cough, tonsillitis, scarlet fever, and appendicitis are among the afflictions he endured as a youth. Unfortunately, his physical burdens continued into adulthood. During the PT boat debacle, he aggravated a back injury that would plague him the rest of his life. He had two operations to remedy it: one that put a metal plate in his back and another to remove it. Both nearly killed him, and until his death, he resorted to using crutches whenever the press wasn't around. But his most serious malady was Addison's disease, which impairs the body's ability to fight infection. In addition to cortisone, JFK was regularly given shots by a doctor named Max Jacobson, popularly known as "Doctor Feelgood" by his numerous clients, many of whom were in show business. As John and Claire Whitcomb explain in their book *Real Life at the White House,* the shots were a mixture of vitamins, steroids, amphetamines, and other bizarre substances that could lead to addiction. "I don't care if it's horse piss," replied the president to his brother Bobby, who had looked into Dr. Jacobson's concoctions.

Jacobson lost his license to practice medicine in 1975 for creating and administering "adulterated drugs."

SHIP OF FOOLS

Jack Kennedy was the first navy man to make it to the White House, and he probably couldn't have done it without his dramatic experience as commander of PT *109*. PT boats were tiny wooden craft armed with torpedoes, and they depended on speed and maneuverability to survive combat with larger ships. After getting his father to pressure the navy into overlooking his physical problems, Jack became an officer and eventually weaseled his way into command of PT *109* in the Pacific. In the early morning hours of August 2, 1943, his boat was on patrol with a number of other PT boats, expecting the arrival of Japanese destroyers. They soon arrived all right, and with a bang; because visibility was so poor in the darkness, those aboard the tiny vessels never saw the Japanese coming. The lead destroyer appeared out of the mist and ran right over Kennedy's boat, slicing off part of it and sending Jack's crew into the ocean. The next day, after spending hours in the water, Jack led what remained of his crew (the collision killed two instantly) to a nearby island—saving one man's life by gripping the guy's life jacket in his teeth and swimming him to shore. On August 7, the men were rescued. In the boat were reporters sent by Jack's father to help spread the news of JFK's exploit. Joe eventually got *Reader's Digest* to publish a story about PT *109*, turning Jack into a bona fide war hero.

But wait a minute. PT *109* was the only PT boat to get rammed and sunk during all of World War II. And the navy isn't in the habit of rewarding skippers who lose their ships. In fact, the young Kennedy committed several offenses for which he could have been court-martialed: He had secretly replaced PT *109*'s only lifeboat with a heavy gun to increase the vessel's armament; he had allowed two men to sleep in the hours leading up to the collision when combat was imminent; and he had repeatedly left his men on the island to go searching for rescue boats. An inquiry was made after the incident, and many officers believed that Kennedy's career was finished. But the man responsible for writing the inquiry's report was none other than Byron White, an old friend of the Kennedys. That—and the fact that Joe Sr. had more connections in Washington than anybody dared to count—got Jack off the hook. Indeed, he was awarded a medal for saving the lives of his crewmen. And that's how a legend is born.

MOB RULE

Jack Kennedy had wit, intelligence, and personal magnetism. But he was no Washington heavyweight, and he needed all the help he could get in the 1960 presidential campaign. According to many historians, that help would come from some pretty shady characters. With the assistance of Frank Sinatra, a close Kennedy pal who rubbed shoulders with the Italian mob, Joe Sr. arranged a meeting in Chicago with none other than Sam Giancana, one of the nation's most powerful mafiosi. As Seymour Hersh explains in *The Dark Side of Camelot*, the meeting took place in a Chicago courthouse and was organized by one William Tuohy, chief judge of the Circuit Court of Cook County and another Kennedy crony. In the meeting, Giancana pledged to Joe Sr. that the mob-controlled unions would turn out in force to make sure the election went Kennedy's way. They would do it by ensuring that all their members voted Democrat and by spending money to buy votes. It is believed by many that Giancana was told that a Kennedy administration would take the heat off the Chicago crime outfit in return for the mafia's help.

In a victory with a margin of less than 120,000 votes nationwide, Giancana's help proved invaluable. Though the scheme almost certainly tipped the balance in JFK's favor in several states, nowhere was the mob's influence more vital than in Illinois, whose twenty-seven votes in the electoral college were decisive. Though accusations of vote fraud were filed after the election, they failed to result in more than a few minor indictments. After Kennedy was sworn in, the matter went nowhere—after all, the president's brother had become the new attorney general, the highest law-enforcement official in the country.

JACK IN THE BOX

If there really is life after death, one of the great mysteries that will probably be revealed to our immortal souls is the number of women Jack Kennedy slept with. No doubt it's a staggering figure. Jack learned from the best: His father, Joe, was rumored to have had numerous affairs. But Jack certainly outdid his old man—indeed, he may well have been a sex addict. As the president allegedly told Bobby Baker, secretary to the Senate Democrats, "I get a migraine headache if I don't get a strange piece of ass every day." JFK sure did get his share of ass—and most of it was strange indeed. That he had a long affair with Marilyn Monroe during his presidency is hardly a secret. That the drug-addled, neurotic Monroe could've ruined his reputation is also no secret. Among the White House emissaries sent to make sure she kept her mouth shut was Bobby Kennedy—who (rumors suggest) proceeded to boink Marilyn himself. But she was only the most infamous of Jack's women. Kennedy devoted much of his time and energy to getting the opposite sex in the sack, and his wife, Jackie, knew it. In *An Unfinished Life*, historian Robert Dallek recounts how JFK was caught on tape at his brother Ted's 1958 wedding mentioning that faithfulness wasn't required in marriage. And Jack practiced what he preached. He frolicked with naked women in the White House pool, relied on his Hollywood connections to get eager young starlets to pay him conjugal visits, and went through an army of young secretaries and prostitutes. As Dallek and other historians have pointed out, most of them were procured for Kennedy by confidants and political aides such as Dave Powers and Kenneth P. O'Donnell.

What follows is just a tiny sampling of Kennedy's profligate sex life, much of which came to light long after he'd been assassinated and, to be fair, will probably never be proven conclusively. Needless to say, they are all episodes that could have buried the glamorous president in a shitstorm of career-ruining controversy.

In 1959, Kennedy allegedly began seeing a young woman named Pamela Turnure, whose landlady—Florence Kater—snapped photos of Kennedy leaving his mistress's apartment. Kater began a crusade to discredit Senator Kennedy as a womanizing hypocrite, but to no avail. Though the Kennedys tried (unsuccessfully) to buy Kater off during the 1960 presidential election, it was the widespread public belief that she was a crazy eccentric that put the matter to rest. As for Pamela Turnure, she later became Jackie Kennedy's press secretary (and, again, JFK's sometime bedmate).

Kennedy had a long and torrid affair with a divorcée named Judith Campbell Exner—who also happened to be the girlfriend of Sam Giancana, head of the Chicago mafia. JFK stopped seeing her only after the FBI informed the president of her mob connections.

During the spring and summer of 1962, President Kennedy began seeing Ellen Rometsch, the wife of a military attaché at the West German embassy in Washington. Rometsch had two extraordinary professions: she made a great deal of money as a prostitute for exclusive D.C. clients, and—according to J. Edgar Hoover's FBI—she was a spy for the East Germans. When a Senate committee began investigating her activities, it could've spelled the end of JFK's presidency. But the investigation ran into a snag when the State Department deported Rometsch back to Europe, where she remained conveniently out of reach for questioning. Attorney General Bobby Kennedy allegedly did the rest by pulling strings and burying evidence. The issue died quietly.

SPREADING THE JOY

In the end, JFK may have carried the most tragic consequence of his sex life in his pants—specifically, in his genitalia. Throughout much of his adult life, according to doctors interviewed by Seymour Hersh, Kennedy was regularly treated for chlamydia. Indeed, while the Bay of Pigs invasion was getting under way, the commander in chief who would take responsibility for its failure was getting a giant shot of penicillin for his venereal disease. With all his womanizing, Jack kept reinfecting himself and probably took the chlamydia with him to the grave. Worst of all, he must have passed it to literally countless sexual partners.

Untreated chlamydia, incidentally, is a major cause of infertility among women.

★ ★ ★ ★ ★

LYNDON BAINES JOHNSON

BORN August 27, 1908
DIED January 22, 1973

NICKNAMES
"LBJ," "Big Daddy"

ASTROLOGICAL SIGN
Virgo

PARTY
Democratic

AGE UPON
TAKING OFFICE
55

RAN AGAINST
Barry Goldwater

VICE PRESIDENT
★ None ★
(after Kennedy assassination)
★ Hubert Humphrey ★
(elected term)

HEIGHT
6' 3"

SOUND BITE
"If you've got 'em by the balls, their hearts and minds will follow."

TERM OF
PRESIDENCY
1963
– TO –
1969

When John Kennedy was murdered in Dallas, Lyndon Baines Johnson became the first American president to be present at his predecessor's assassination. He also became the first to be sworn in with his wife holding the Bible and to take his oath of office on an airplane. His first order after assuming command was "Let's get airborne." *Air Force One* lifted off and the Johnson administration took flight.

Flying came naturally to LBJ. He was one of the most energetic politicians in American history, a man whose ceaseless efforts to get things done always kept him on the move. The business of government had been his profession since the early '30s, when he was a congressional secretary. Franklin Roosevelt made him the Texas director of the New Deal's National Youth Administration, which launched Johnson into Congress in 1937. He was a senator from 1949 to 1961 and the second youngest Senate majority leader in history.

But all that energy had nowhere to go when Johnson served as vice president under Kennedy. It wasn't just that veeps have little to do; the Kennedys never really liked Johnson very much. JFK's administration was chockablock with Ivy League–educated eggheads, and the vice president was everything they weren't: an unsophisticated, foul-mouthed, backcountry bullyboy who'd gone to school at Southwest Texas State Teacher's College—as far away from Harvard and Yale as the dark side of the moon. For all their glaring differences, however, Johnson and Kennedy shared a passionate desire to better the lot of disenfranchised Americans through the power of government. And Johnson, even more than Kennedy, achieved much toward that end.

Johnson pledged to carry through his predecessor's civil rights agenda, and he made good on that pledge with a vengeance. His "Great Society" program, interestingly enough, came through with the help of the same eastern sophisticates who'd derided their old vice president as a hillbilly—Johnson kept much of JFK's cabinet and staff. But nobody on LBJ's team worked harder than LBJ. As an ingenious legislator who spent decades on Capitol Hill, Johnson knew better than anyone how to handle—or, more accurately, manhandle—congressmen. When he wasn't schmoozing them at White House parties or charming them with his earthy Texas folk wisdom, he was threatening them in the privacy of restrooms and phoning them at all hours of the day and night. While some weren't taken in by the "Johnson treatment," enough succumbed to his efforts to pass one of the most impressive legislative programs in history. Johnson kept the momentum going after he beat the bejesus out of right-wing Republican candidate Barry Goldwater in 1964. By 1968, the president had pushed through the Civil Rights Act, the Voting Rights Act, creation of the Department of Housing and Urban Development, Medicare and Medicaid, and a slew of other laws aimed at helping minorities and the poor. Not since FDR had a liberal president achieved so much.

Halfway around the world, things weren't quite so rosy. Johnson may have inherited the Vietnam conflict from his predecessor, but he definitely made it worse by committing the United States to a giant war effort. Convinced that victory against the Communists there was only a matter of time, Johnson kept sending more and more troops until, by 1968, some half a million American soldiers were fighting for their lives in the rice paddies. That same year, Communist forces launched the Tet Offensive, decisively proving that they were anything but close to defeat. It was a catastrophe. Convinced that events had gotten away from him, LBJ declared to the nation that he would not seek reelection. Many Democrats put their hopes in Bobby Kennedy, only to see them dashed by his assassination. It was turning out to be a really bad year for the Democratic Party—a fact violently driven home at the organization's national convention in Chicago, where mobs of peace activists clashed with Mayor Richard Daley's legions of club-wielding police. Vietnam had destroyed Lyndon Johnson, divided his party, torn the nation to pieces, and—perhaps worst of all—paved the way for Richard Nixon's return from political obscurity. Oh, the humanity.

In the end, LBJ is a study in extremes. Though his legislative accomplishments continue to impress, his colossal misunderstanding of the Vietnam conflict was as unforgivable as it was fundamental to his own political destruction. And while he may have been an imperious, power-hungry ruffian, few megalomaniacs ever devoted themselves so sincerely or effectively to the cause of helping the needy. After years of eighteen-hour days, hard-driving leadership, and shameless womanizing, Johnson's health began to fail. He died on January 22, 1973—just days before the signing of the Paris Peace Accords, which marked the beginning of America's pull-out from the Vietnam War.

← At his ranch in Texas, Johnson often terrified his guests by driving ninety miles an hour—while sipping Scotch from a paper cup.

CRASS ACT

"Why do you come and ask me, the leader of the western world, a chicken-shit question like that?" replied President Johnson to a stupefied reporter. LBJ didn't exactly pay much attention to decorum during press conferences. He even exposed his appendectomy scar to impress one gathering of journalists and photographers. But his insulting language and habits weren't limited to moments with the media. Johnson was gruff and obscene virtually all of the time. He belched, swore, and scratched his privates regularly, and he even invited staffers to continue conversations with him in the bathroom while relieving himself. At his ranch in Texas, he was fond of terrifying guests by taking them on car rides down remote country roads at ninety miles an hour while he drank Scotch from a paper cup. His talent for indelicate phrases was legendary. "I never trust a man unless I've got his pecker in my pocket" summed up his political philosophy. "He doesn't have sense enough to pour piss out of a boot with the instructions written on the heel" is what he had to say about one Kennedy officeholder. And LBJ's thoughts on renewing J. Edgar Hoover's tenure at the FBI were just as colorful: "Well, it's probably better to have him inside the tent pissing out, than outside pissing in."

KEEPING THE MONOGRAMMING CHARGES DOWN

Every member of Johnson's family had the same initials: LBJ. With his wife, Lady Bird, Lyndon Baines had two daughters: Lynda Bird and Luci Baines. (Gag, retch.)

TECHNO-TEXAN

Johnson was fascinated by gadgets and gizmos that could make his life easier (or more fun). He owned a wristwatch with an alarm, which he was fond of setting off in the middle of meetings or speeches that irritated him. Obsessed with efficiency, he had televisions and phones installed in all the executive bathrooms so that he could be informed and in touch at all times. But Johnson's bizarre bathroom décor didn't stop there. He also insisted that the White House shower be installed with nozzles that sprayed water from every direction, including up from the bottom. After he found out just how incredible the new shower was, he had a similar one fashioned for his Texas ranch. The ranch also had a fire engine that Johnson received as a gift. He often impressed visitors by firing up the siren. But the ranch's featured attraction was an amphibious car—he loved to take unsuspecting guests for a ride and then head for the nearby lake while feigning panic and shouting that the brakes were shot. While the passengers freaked out and tried to open the doors, the car would plunge straight into the water—and Johnson would plunge into hysterics.

DELUGES OF GRANDEUR

Few presidents have ever reveled in the power of their office as much as Lyndon Johnson. He was almost power-mad, and he never lost an opportunity to remind people who the leader of the Free World was—especially all those Kennedy-loving Ivy Leaguers who thought Johnson was nothing but a scrub-grass-chewing pig mounter with poor breeding. In fact, his feelings of inferiority to the men who helped define JFK's brief, glamorous administration go a long way toward explaining why he felt obliged to act more like an emperor than a president. While flying aboard *Air Force One*, he was fond of conversing with reporters while his valet bathed his feet, trimmed his nails, and changed his socks. But the account of one Secret Service agent sums it up best: after being asked to shield the president while he urinated outdoors, the agent claims to have felt the moist warmth of presidential piss on his leg. When the Secret Serviceman voiced his disgust, Johnson replied, "That's all right, son. It's my prerogative."

★ ★ ★ ★ ★

37 | RICHARD M. NIXON

BORN January 9, 1913 DIED April 22, 1994	NICKNAME "Tricky Dick"

ASTROLOGICAL SIGN	PARTY	AGE UPON TAKING OFFICE
Capricorn 	Republican 	**56**

RAN AGAINST	VICE PRESIDENT
Hubert Humphrey *(first term)* George McGovern *(second term)*	★ Spiro Agnew ★ *(first term and part of second term)* ★ Gerald Ford ★ *(after Spiro Agnew resigned)*

HEIGHT	SOUND BITE	TERM OF PRESIDENCY
5′ 11″ 	*"When the president does it, that means that it is not illegal."*	**1969** – TO – **1974**

I n the fall of 1968, Richard Milhous Nixon defeated Hubert Humphrey in an election very nearly as close as the one he'd lost in 1960 to John Kennedy. It was a ruthless, filthy campaign in which dirty tricks were common on both sides. And it thrust into the White House a man who would do more to sully the office of the president than any other in American history.

Nixon's Southern California upbringing was shaped by harsh Quaker standards. His mother, whom Nixon would forever refer to as a saint, was loving but strict, and his father was angry and abusive. By the time young

Dick attended Whittier College, he had earned a reputation as an uncanny debater, a klutz, and a nerd. He scored high grades at Duke University Law School and went on to serve as a naval officer in the Pacific during World War II.

His plunge into politics was defined by personal qualities that would forever dog him: rage, paranoia, and an obsession with intrigue. In 1946, he beat Jerry Voorhis out of a seat in the House of Representatives largely by decrying his opponent's ties to communism, which were unfounded. His 1950 campaign for the Senate pitted him against Helen Gahagan Douglas, and his attempts to label her a "commie"—again, preposterously—worked. (Douglas was "pink down to her panties," Nixon charged, and it was this fight that earned him the epithet "Tricky Dick.") As his career advanced, Nixon won the support of both big business and organized crime, which filled his campaign coffers and aided him in his smear tactics.

Nixon achieved recognition during the Red Scare of the '40s and '50s, when fears of Communist infiltration swept the nation like a malarial fever. After ex-Communist Whittaker Chambers claimed that Alger Hiss, a former State Department employee, had engaged in Communist espionage, everyone's fears seemed confirmed. Nixon, then a member of the House Un-American Activities Committee, went after Hiss like a rabid dog. The performance landed him the vice presidency under Eisenhower.

Few veeps, however, have ever enjoyed less support from their bosses. And Ike wasn't alone—most people were wary of a man whose impersonal style, shadowy connections, and mean-spiritedness had become rather infamous. Though Ike sent his second-in-command on a globe-trotting itinerary that would help him become a savvy international relations expert, the trip never dispelled the belief that Tricky Dick was corrupt. In 1952, he even had to make a TV appearance before the country to kill fears that he'd received illegal contributions—it quickly became famous as the "Checkers Speech," named for a dog given to his daughters by a supporter in Texas.

By 1968, Nixon had suffered losses in a run for president against Kennedy and a run for governor of California. It looked as if his political career was finished. Unfortunately for the rest of us, he made an astonishing comeback, recasting himself as a chastened, wiser Nixon. With lavish support from the old dubious sources, he squeezed out Humphrey to achieve the title he'd wanted for so long: president of the United States.

Buried beneath the criminal activity that brought down the administration is a surprisingly liberal agenda including welfare reform and affirmative action. And Nixon's visits to China and the Soviet Union rank as some of the finest accomplishments of any chief executive.

But is that what most people remember about Richard Nixon's one and a half terms? No. And why? Because, after promising an end to the Vietnam conflict before even getting into the White House, he allowed it to drag on—and expand into neighboring countries—through five more years; because, when national opposition to the war reached a fever pitch, he responded to his critics with paranoia and brutality; because, when a group of criminals were caught breaking into the Democratic National Committee's headquarters in the Watergate building and it was discovered that their sponsors could be found in the president's circle, Nixon went out of his way to cover it all up; because, facing impeachment, he became the first American president to resign; and because he was foolish enough to capture every bit of his scheming, peevish, foul-mouthed recklessness on tape, most of which has since become available to the public.

And those are just a few of the reasons.

It's quite sad, really. Despite his titanic potential as a shaper of international peace at a time when the world needed it most, Dick Nixon threw it all away, leaving behind a heap of lies that serve as a harsh reminder to us all: unless we're vigilant, the folks we elect to high office might just get away with anything.

→   Bringing firearms into the White House is illegal—unless your name is Elvis Presley. The King brought Nixon the gift of a .45-caliber pistol.

PEACES OF HATE

The red-baiting bunk aimed at Helen Gahagan Douglas in 1950 may have won Nixon the nickname "Tricky Dick," but Dick's worst trick came almost two decades later. And it was tantamount to treason.

Nineteen sixty-eight was a banner year for the forces of chaos, what with Lyndon Johnson canceling his own reelection campaign, the assassination of Dr. Martin Luther King Jr., and Bobby Kennedy's hell-for-leather campaign for the Democratic nomination ending tragically in his own assassination. Divided and anxious, the Democratic Party descended on Chicago to nominate Vice President Hubert Humphrey after a contentious primary, only to watch the city erupt in riots. Over it all loomed the ugly spectacle of the Vietnam War.

No one wanted the war in Southeast Asia to go away more than LBJ, who rescinded his quest for a second term specifically because he knew the country was fed up with him. That year, representatives of his administration began peace talks with the North Vietnamese in Paris—a situation that played on the worst Republican fears. After all, if Johnson could make peace, it would hand his party's nominee a huge advantage in the general election. Those fears hit fever pitch in October, when the South Vietnamese signaled an interest in making major concessions in the negotiations about to get under way in Paris. Peace seemed right around the corner.

Not so fast! According to newly released tapes recorded by Johnson himself during that fateful autumn, American intelligence officials discovered a strange plot to derail the Paris Peace Talks by Nixon aide Anna Chennault. Nixon, riding a campaign promise to end the war, needed hostilities to continue until he was sitting in the Oval Office. Chennault, acting independently of official channels, told the South Vietnamese delegation that they should walk away from the proceedings and wait until Nixon was elected, at which time they'd get even better terms from the North.

The talks disintegrated, and war continued for another six and a half ghastly years. Thanks, Dick!

So why didn't this come to light for so many years? Simple: both parties come out looking compromised. After all, Nixon may have hijacked deliberations by the American government to conclude a seemingly interminable war, but Johnson was hardly clean. To learn all that he did about Nixon's shenanigans, he had directed the FBI to bug his campaign—and that's, well, illegal.

Better to let sleeping dogs lie. Or some such nonsense.

GETS BY WITH A LITTLE HELP FROM HIS FRIENDS

During Nixon's campaigns for the House of Representatives and the Senate, his camp encouraged people to answer their phones by saying, "Vote for Nixon." Should they properly do so when receiving a cold call from Nixon's headquarters, they would be rewarded with toasters, electric clocks, and other appliances.

Schemes like this one were the stock in trade of one Murray Chotiner. Having failed in politics, he became a professional conniver who devoted himself to Nixon. According to author Anthony Summers in *The Arrogance of Power*, Chotiner pulled off all sorts of nefarious deeds on behalf of his friend and master, from spying on Democratic candidates and threatening people with death to accepting laundered cash and securing the release from prison of Teamsters leader Jimmy Hoffa in return for money. He even represented Nixon in negotiations for large—and suspect—cash contributions from eccentric, maniacal rich guy Howard Hughes, who bent over backward to buy influence. Hughes even "lent" some $205,000 to Nixon's inept brother Donald, who was experiencing business troubles in a dubious transaction that would repeatedly dog Nixon right through the Watergate investigations.

MR. TOUCHY-FEELY

Few people ever achieved anything like a close relationship with Nixon, who was notoriously aloof and impersonal. Even his wife, Pat, endured a distant marriage; Nixon was fond of communicating with her and their daughters through memos signed "The President." Chief of Staff H. R. Haldeman, who went to jail for attempting to shield his boss from the administration's lawlessness, maintained that Nixon never asked him a thing about his family. The one time they shook hands in the seventeen years they knew each other was when Nixon was forced to sack him during Watergate.

DIZZY DICK

If you've studied the previous chapters closely, you've probably noticed that running the country and drinking booze often go hand in hand. The Nixon White House was no exception. The problem with Nixon, however, was his tolerance—he had none. Henry Kissinger, who served Nixon as national security advisor and as secretary of state, once said, "Two glasses of wine were quite enough to make him boisterous, just one more to grow bellicose or sentimental with slurred speech." Historian Anthony Summers even claims that Nixon sometimes mixed his alcohol with sleeping pills.

Nixon's weakness for drink first alarmed administration members in 1969, when an American intelligence-gathering aircraft was shot down by a North Korean fighter in international waters. That Nixon actually contemplated using nuclear weapons in retaliation is shocking enough—but, as Seymour Hersh relates in *The Price of Power*, the new president was blitzed when the crisis broke.

The president's poor timing was repeated several times, according to Summers, most notably when Palestinian terrorists hijacked a TWA jetliner and forced it to land at Damascus until their demands were met. When Henry Kissinger phoned Nixon to inform him of the situation, Dick—who was sloshed—replied, "Bomb the airport of Damascus." Nothing came of it, as Kissinger and other administration officials knew enough not to act on an alcohol-inspired presidential edict.

POMP GOES THE WEASEL

"Don't you dare call me Dick," Nixon said to a longtime associate after being elected president. "I am the president of the United States. When you speak to me, you call me Mr. President." Nixon, no doubt, had delusions of grandeur, and he did all sorts of things to imbue his White House with an imperious air. He commissioned new uniforms to adorn the White House police force, complete with epaulets, gold embroidery, and tall military caps. But when the press made them the subject of scornful ridicule, Nixon sold them to a high school band in Iowa.

EVERYBODY LOVES NIXON!

And you can, too. Just listen to what these folks had to say about him:

Dwight Eisenhower: *"This man will never be president. The people don't like him."*

Henry Kissinger: *"The most dangerous, of all the men running, to have as president."*

Harry Truman: *"Nixon is a shifty, goddamn liar, and people know it."*

John Kennedy (upon becoming president in 1960): *"If I've done nothing for this country, I've saved them from Dick Nixon."*

Averell Harriman (upon discovering that Nixon was a fellow guest at a dinner party): *"I will not break bread with that man!"*

DICK SHTICK

Nixon's opinions on all manner of things might have been lost to posterity were it not for the library of taped conversations he left behind (and which were subpoenaed by the government to build a case for impeachment). A voice-activated system captured everything spoken in the Oval Office, ostensibly for his memoirs. Now, thanks to his assiduous self-bugging—as well as numerous off-the-cuff remarks made to people throughout his career—we can gain insight into his wisdom on such topics as:

Italians: *"Difference is they smell different, they look different, they act different . . . trouble is, you can't find one that's honest."*

Affirmative action: *"With blacks you can usually settle for an incompetent, because there are just not enough competent ones."*

Reporters: *"I wouldn't give them the sweat off my balls."*

Leadership: *"You're never going to make it in politics. You just don't know how to lie."*

TWO KINGS

Someone had once told Elvis Presley, who collected sheriff's badges, that he'd have to go to the president of the United States if he wanted to add a federal narcotics badge to his collection. So the King did just that, and he came bearing the gift of a gold-plated .45-caliber pistol (security, anyone?!). The weapon remains on display in the White House. Nixon and Presley embraced each other for the cameras in a photo that remains one of the most famous in presidential history.

THE BIG W

No discussion of Nixon would be complete without at least a cursory mention of Watergate. Nixon was fond of gathering information about the swarms of people he considered enemies, so he recruited a cadre of supporters who hired men to do the dirty work (e.g., Gordon Liddy, an ex-FBI agent who enjoyed listening to military music and conjuring new ways of killing people). Originally called the Plumbers (they plugged leaks, see), they focused their criminal activities—burglaries, wiretapping, and such—on digging up anything that could be used against opponents. It wasn't long before the Democratic National Headquarters, located in the Watergate building, became a prime target.

The extent to which Nixon knew of the Plumbers' activities is open to question. But when the Watergate burglars were caught, Nixon did quite a bit to cover up their connection to the Oval Office, including a ploy to get the CIA to intervene in the FBI's investigation. It took months, but Congress eventually built up a case for impeachment that convinced Tricky Dick that he had only one option: resign.

LINCOLN LOG

"Have you ever been to the Lincoln Memorial?" Nixon asked his valet, Manolo Sanchez. It was before dawn on May 9, 1971, the day when protesters gathered in Washington in remembrance of the May 4 Kent State shootings, in which four students died from National Guard bullets. "No," replied Sanchez. And so they went.

After a brief tour, Nixon walked over to some student protesters. He engaged in a listless conversation (and posed for a picture), then climbed back into the car. Before taking off, a student walked up and gave him the finger.

Nixon gave it back. "That S.O.B. will go through the rest of his life telling everybody that the president of the United States gave him the finger," said Nixon. "And nobody will believe him!"

PRESIDENTIAL PETS

Chickens and lizards and bears, oh my! All kinds of strange creatures have resided in the White House over the years; here are just a few of our favorite presidential pets:

THOMAS JEFFERSON had a mockingbird that would take food from the president's mouth.

ZACHARY TAYLOR's beloved horse Old Whitey could often be seen munching on the White House lawn. He was included in his master's funeral procession, marching right behind the coffin.

ABRAHAM LINCOLN gave his sons two goats, Nanny and Nanko, which little Tad Lincoln harnessed to an overturned chair to fashion a chariot. Lincoln also adopted a litter of kittens that appeared one day in the War Department's telegraph office, insisting that the officers who staffed the wire take care of them when he was not present.

RUTHERFORD B. HAYES's wife, Lucy, had a Siamese cat—purportedly the first in the country—sent to her by the American consul in Bangkok.

GROVER CLEVELAND owned a house on the outskirts of Washington that he and his wife used as a sanctuary from the press. It was also home to an impressive menagerie that included canaries, rabbits, foxes, and rats.

WILLIAM MCKINLEY had a parrot that could whistle "Yankee Doodle."

THEODORE ROOSEVELT presided over a veritable barnyard White House. Among the innumerable nonhuman residents were chickens, bears, lizards, a blue macaw named Eli, and a pig named Maude.

CALVIN COOLIDGE was the owner of a raccoon that he would walk on a leash around the White House grounds.

FRANKLIN ROOSEVELT's Scottish terrier Fala was present aboard the USS *Augusta* when his master and Winston Churchill signed the Atlantic Charter in 1941.

JOHN F. KENNEDY's White House was the home of ponies, lovebirds, hamsters, and (a gift from Nikita Krushchev) Pushinka, daughter of Strelka, the Russian dog sent into space.

LYNDON JOHNSON got into trouble with the media when he picked up his beagles, Him and Her, by the ears in front of a gaggle of reporters.

And while everyone remembers Chelsea Clinton's cat, Socks, let's not forget that **BILL CLINTON** had a pet of his own (no, not Monica—shame on you): Buddy, a chocolate lab.

GERALD R. FORD

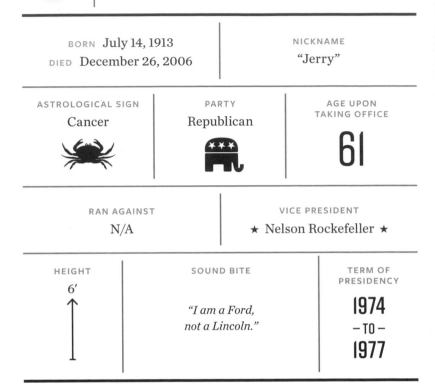

BORN July 14, 1913	NICKNAME
DIED December 26, 2006	"Jerry"

ASTROLOGICAL SIGN	PARTY	AGE UPON TAKING OFFICE
Cancer	Republican	61

RAN AGAINST	VICE PRESIDENT
N/A	★ Nelson Rockefeller ★

HEIGHT	SOUND BITE	TERM OF PRESIDENCY
6′	*"I am a Ford, not a Lincoln."*	1974 – TO – 1977

Gerald Ford became vice president and then president without ever receiving a single vote from American citizens. He is the only man in American history to have been foisted on the nation by circumstances—twice.

The first time was when Richard Nixon's vice president, Spiro Agnew, was forced to resign in 1973 amidst accusations of graft. The mostly Democratic Congress told Nixon that the only Republican replacement they'd approve was Gerald Ford, whose bland, happy-go-lucky style made him virtually the only man in Washington who had no enemies. Watergate thrust the new vice president into the Oval Office on August 9, 1974, after Nixon gave in to national and congressional disgust and bailed out.

President Ford's first priority was rebuilding the American people's trust in their chief executive, and he was the perfect guy for the job. Born Leslie Lynch King Jr., in Omaha, Nebraska, he became Gerald Ford after his mother divorced her abusive husband and married again, this time to a paint store owner named Gerald Ford. After taking his stepfather's name, the young Ford became every parent's dream: a good student and athlete who even found time to make Eagle Scout. He got a football scholarship to the University of Michigan, where he played center and was voted most valuable player. After graduating in 1935 with a degree in economics, he was offered contracts to play pro ball by the Green Bay Packers and the Detroit Lions but turned them down to go to Yale, where he studied law while coaching football and boxing. He fought the Japanese as a navy officer in World War II, opened a law practice in Michigan, and went on to beat the local Republican politician for a seat in Congress in 1948. He would remain in the House of Representatives for the next twenty-five years, ever hopeful that he'd achieve his dream of becoming speaker.

His dream never came true. But then, he never thought he stood a chance at becoming president. Once he took office, however, the nation embraced him as a breath of fresh air after years of Nixonite stench. Ford was laid-back, self-deprecating, friendly, and eager to answer questions from the press—everything his imperious, paranoid predecessor was not. The man even cleaned up after his own dog. Americans cooed when he beat a staffer to a fresh coil left by the presidential pooch, Liberty, at a ski lodge in Vail, Colorado. The new chief could do no wrong, and his approval ratings shot up. Oh, happy day.

Then he did the one thing that could ruin the honeymoon: after only a month in office, he pardoned Nixon. It was intended as a way to put the "national nightmare," as he called it, to rest. But people across the nation saw it as a cop-out. Ford even appeared before a House committee to answer charges that he'd made a deal with Nixon. Overnight, Ford's approval ratings plummeted. So much for winning the people's trust.

Things never really improved. It was bad enough that a 1973 oil embargo by OPEC sent the country into a recession the likes of which hadn't been seen since the Great Depression, but Ford's attempts to solve the problem ran up against a hostile Congress. The 1974 midterm elections

packed both houses with Democrats still having nightmares about Tricky Dick, and Ford seemed like so much residue from the bad old days. Oil shortages crippled the country, and inflation continued apace.

Congress didn't even let Ford conduct his own foreign policy. You wanna continue sending arms to Turkey in exchange for the security of American military bases there? Sorry. Aid for a beleaguered South Vietnam? Ha! And so it went until, after announcing his bid for reelection in 1976, he had to fight for the Republican nomination against a very popular Ronald Reagan. Ford won that race, but he went on to lose a close one with the Democratic opponent, Jimmy Carter.

Ford was crushed by the loss. But it freed him to do the things he truly excelled at: touring the lecture circuit, serving on corporate boards, taking ski vacations, and playing endless hours of golf. Sure beats getting bitched at by Congress.

BEEFY CHIEF

Gerald Ford wasn't just one of the most athletic presidents in history, he was also a darn good-looking man (in his younger days, anyway). In 1939, he and his girlfriend appeared in a *Look* magazine pictorial that gave readers a peek at how the "beautiful people" live. His modeling career went into high gear three years later when he appeared on the cover of *Cosmopolitan*. Ford remains the only president to have worked as a model.

CRITICAL DUNCITY

Though he graduated in the top third of his class at Yale and had an extraordinary grasp of economic issues, Ford earned a reputation as a clod. As Lyndon Johnson once said, Ford had "played football too long without

← Every klutzy thing Ford did ended up in the news—like the night he locked himself out of the White House while walking his dog.

a helmet." In 1975, while descending the stairs from *Air Force One* in Salzburg, Austria, Ford lost his footing and tumbled onto the tarmac below. His presidency was never the same again. Chevy Chase performed scathing impressions of him on *Saturday Night Live*, the press jumped on every remotely klutzy thing Ford did, and the country began to believe that the president was a buffoon. Ford even got locked out of the White House one night while walking his dog.

PUBLIC SPEAKING 101

Ford did nothing to dispel his thick-headed image with his pronouncements, some of which bordered on the moronic. While speaking at Iowa State University, he referred to the audience's institution as Ohio State University. He declared at a party celebrating Lincoln's birthday that "if Lincoln were alive today, he'd roll over in his grave." But nothing damaged his reputation so much as a remark he made during a televised debate with Jimmy Carter. In response to a foreign relations question about the Communist bloc in Eastern Europe, Ford proclaimed, "There is no Soviet domination in Eastern Europe, and there never will be during a Ford administration." Anyone with a map knew this wasn't the case, and the president was met with a firestorm of criticism. He only made things worse by trying to explain what he had meant with such crystalline statements as, "We are going to make certain to the best of our ability that any allegation of domination is not a fact." Oh, my.

BRAWN WITH THE WIND

Lyndon Johnson once claimed that Gerald Ford was too dumb "to walk and fart at the same time." Perhaps. But Ford could definitely fart while standing still, which he apparently did with alarming frequency and abandon. According to his Secret Service detail, the president would loudly let one rip and then always attempt to put the blame on one of them with indignant remarks like, "Jesus, did you do that? Show a little class."

HOW TO GIVE A GUY A COMPLEX

On September 5, 1975, while walking to the California capitol building in Sacramento, President Ford saw a group of well-wishers and went over to press the flesh. Unfortunately, not everyone in the group was wishing him well—particularly Lynette "Squeaky" Fromme. An old member of the Charles Manson "family," Fromme took the opportunity to express her hatred of the American status quo by producing a pistol and aiming it at her president. Secret Service agents wrestled the weapon from her hand and took her into custody. In San Francisco just seventeen days later, Ford was met with a similarly warm reception—this time by Sara Jane Moore, who, unlike Squeaky Fromme, managed to squeeze off a shot at her target. Ford's security shoved him into his limousine, jumped on top of him, and got him back to *Air Force One* without harm. Moore's bullet struck a nearby taxi driver.

In 1976, just as Ford was getting over his fear of California, a fellow named Chester Plummer managed to get over the White House fence and advanced on the White House with a metal pipe in his hand. He was shot on the lawn by guards.

★ ★ ★ ★ ★

39 | JAMES EARL CARTER

BORN October 1, 1924

NICKNAME
"Jimmy"

ASTROLOGICAL SIGN
Libra

PARTY
Democratic

AGE UPON TAKING OFFICE
52

RAN AGAINST
Gerald Ford

VICE PRESIDENT
★ Walter Mondale ★

HEIGHT
5′ 10″

SOUND BITE

*"In a very Christian way,
as far as I'm concerned,
he can go to hell."*
(referring to the Reverend
Jerry Falwell)

TERM OF PRESIDENCY
1977
– TO –
1981

O n his inauguration day in 1977, James "Jimmy" Carter took his wife, Rosalynn, and young daughter, Amy, in hand and walked the mile and a half to the White House rather than ride in a bulletproof limo. It drove the Secret Service crazy, but it was vintage Carter all the way. He'd won the election against Gerald Ford by claiming to be one of the people, an ordinary guy from an ordinary place with ordinary values. Unfortunately, the issues he had to confront as president required an extraordinary man.

Americans were ready for a Washington outsider in 1977, and that's exactly what they got. Jimmy Carter was an extremely intelligent man who graduated 59th in a class of 820 from Annapolis and then studied nuclear physics while training for the navy's prestigious submarine pro-gram. He had intended to pursue a lifelong career in the navy, but he end-ed up taking over his family's extensive peanut farm in Plains, Georgia, an operation that would eventually make him rich. By the time he an-nounced his candidacy for president, the most impressive political cre-dentials on his résumé were one term as governor of Georgia. But after years of getting screwed by professional politicians who were schooled in every dark secret of Washington power brokering, the nation welcomed this D.C. newbie who spoke of returning power to the people. That he was a soft-spoken, painfully sincere, born-again Christian who seemed about as likely to lie as take the Lord's name in vain didn't hurt, either.

But the very quality that got Carter elected in the first place—his "outsiderness"—was precisely the thing that most bedeviled his presi-dency. He not only failed to grasp how Washington worked, he seemed determined not to learn. The vast majority of those appointed to his staff were also outsiders, and the administration butted heads with Congress over every bit of the presidential agenda. From government reorganiza-tion to immigration reform, Carter's ideas were stymied by members of Congress—including those in his own party—who didn't think the presi-dent had any concept of give-and-take. The president's folksy manner, as exemplified by the televised "fireside chat" he gave dressed in a cardigan sweater, was increasingly viewed by the rest of the government as political naiveté. Though he managed to get through some laws that protected the environment and helped ease the plight of the poor, much of his agenda either fell by the wayside or attracted widespread disdain (as was the case with his treaty to return control of the Panama Canal to Panama).

The ailing economy wasn't helping the president's situation. In addi-tion to double-digit inflation, the nation stooped beneath the burden of a severe oil shortage that resulted in skyrocketing prices at the gas pump. Carter urged his fellow Americans to conserve energy and personally kept the White House thermostat turned down to a temperature that required staff members to type with gloves. As lines at gas stations grew longer across the country, the oil shortage got even worse when Iranians stormed the American embassy in Tehran in November 1979. The result-ing shock to the world's oil market was severe, but Carter now had much more than an energy shortage to worry about. Close to seventy people, the majority Americans, were taken prisoner by Iranians enraged that Carter had allowed Iran's deposed shah to receive life-saving surgery in the United States. Later that same year, the Soviets celebrated Christmas by invading Afghanistan. America had truly lost its ability to shape the course of international events.

Though Carter seemed incapable of enforcing his nation's interests abroad, he scored his greatest victory with international diplomacy. In 1978, he managed to get Israel's Menachem Begin and Egypt's Anwar Sadat to come to Camp David to settle their differences. The result was the Camp David Accords, which ended thirty years of conflict and promised hope for a peaceful Middle East.

But a peaceful resolution to the hostage crisis in Iran proved elusive. After a disastrous military rescue attempt that left the charred remains of American helicopters and servicemen in the desert, Carter continued to negotiate with the Iranians, but to no avail. The stalemate ultimately destroyed his chances of winning reelection against Republican candidate Ronald Reagan, whose cheery, nationalistic rhetoric seemed so appealing after Carter's tired ineffectiveness. After losing in a landslide, Carter endured the humiliation of seeing the hostages released on Reagan's inaugural day.

Virtually none of Carter's original campaign promises came true, a fact the press drove home with ruthless glee. But if Carter was something of a dud as America's chief executive, he has evolved into the greatest living former president in recent memory. He turned his presidential library into the Carter Center, a sort of think tank devoted to the pursuit of peace around the world, and—when not helping to build homes for the poor with Habitat for Humanity—he has gone on to negotiate peaceful resolutions to several international conflicts. No wonder he won a Nobel Peace Prize in 2002. He is perhaps the greatest man ever to be a lousy president.

→ Jimmy Carter remains the only president to have reported sighting a UFO.

JIMMY WHO?

Jimmy Carter wasn't just a Washington outsider—when he began his campaign for the White House, he was a virtual unknown. Even his mother didn't believe he had it in him. After hearing her son's intentions to run for president, her first words were "president of what?" Just three years before the 1976 presidential election, the then-governor of Georgia appeared on an episode of *What's My Line?* The panel came very close to not guessing his identity.

THE GOSPEL ACCORDING TO JIMMY

A born-again Christian since 1966, Jimmy Carter was one of our most religious presidents. He juggled his duties as chief executive with a Bible class he insisted on teaching regularly at the First Baptist Church in Washington, D.C. In a 1976 interview with *Playboy* magazine, the president admitted to having "lusted in [his] heart"—i.e., he felt attracted to women he'd seen from time to time, which, for him, was as bad as cheating on his wife, Rosalynn. Unfortunately, he sometimes attempted to hold his staff members to the same high standard. He is known to have told several federal employees to get married to their significant others and stop "living in sin."

WHITE HOUSE WEED

Willie Nelson once performed at the Carter White House, after which he enjoyed the first family's hospitality by staying over. That night, the country crooner climbed up on the roof, took in a little star-gazing, and—while marveling at the way in which the city's streets converged on the executive mansion—lit up what he called a "fat Austin torpedo." Security agents were nowhere to be found. As Nelson insightfully recalled after the experience, "The roof of the White House is the safest place I can think of to smoke dope."

THE TRUTH IS OUT THERE

According to Jimmy Carter, while attending a 1969 Lion's Club meeting in Georgia, he and several others saw a genuine UFO. His official report to the International UFO Bureau described a noiseless object "as bright as the moon" that came to within 900 yards of him and his party. Carter is the only president to have admitted to a UFO sighting.

DROPPING THE BALL

Jimmy Carter was a micromanager who insisted on personally handling duties that most presidents would have delegated, from line-editing detailed reports for grammar to overseeing White House plumbing. Staffers who wanted to use the White House tennis courts had to get his personal approval.

Carter wasn't nearly as fussy when it came to matters of national security, however. During the first family's vacations in Plains, Georgia, military personnel who carried the "football"—the portable case holding codes for releasing the nation's missiles in case of nuclear attack—were forbidden to stay on the president's property. As a result, they had to stay in the town of Americus, ten miles away. Because the "football" can only be utilized by the president in person, any response to a Soviet strike while Carter relaxed in his Plains home would've required that he get into a car and drive the ten miles to Americus. One wonders if there would've been anything left of the country by the time he got there.

40 | # RONALD REAGAN

BORN **February 6, 1911** DIED **June 5, 2004**	NICKNAMES "Dutch," "The Gipper," "Ronnie," "The Great Communicator"

ASTROLOGICAL SIGN Aquarius 	PARTY Republican 	AGE UPON TAKING OFFICE **69**

RAN AGAINST Jimmy Carter *(first term)* Walter Mondale *(second term)*	VICE PRESIDENT ★ George Bush ★

HEIGHT 6′1″ ↑	SOUND BITE *"It's true hard work never killed anybody, but I figure, why take the chance?"*	TERM OF PRESIDENCY **1981** – TO – **1989**

As President Ronald Reagan once admitted, "I don't know if I could do this job if I weren't an actor." And therein lies the central issue with our fortieth president. After a career starring in B movies with monkeys and military hardware, he finally got the lead of a lifetime: leader of the Free World. To him, it was another acting part, and he played it to the hilt.

Ronald Wilson Reagan graduated from Eureka College in Illinois and got his start in showbiz as one of the Midwest's most popular radio sports announcers. After breaking into movies in the 1930s, he secured supporting roles in such films as *Brother Rat*, *King's Row*, and *Knute Rockne, All American* (featuring Reagan as terminally ill football player George Gipp, who inspired Notre Dame to win one "for the Gipper"). After World War II broke out, Reagan joined the army, but the only shooting he did was on the sets of propaganda films. Such hokey roles irrevocably damaged his career, and by 1951 he found himself sharing the camera with a chimpanzee in the irritatingly insipid *Bedtime for Bonzo*. He made the switch to television, hosting the weekly *General Electric Theater* and introducing *Death Valley Days*. By 1964, despite having fifty-three films to his credit, Reagan's most interesting Hollywood accomplishments were being married to starlet Jane Wyman (who divorced him in 1948) and arousing the ire of Errol Flynn (who, upon discovering at a movie shoot that Reagan was the only actor to show up sober, told him to "go fuck himself").

So Reagan decided to give politics a try. As leader of the Screen Actors Guild from 1947 to 1952, he had been a dyed-in-the-wool New Deal Democrat. But the 1960s witnessed a dramatic change of heart in Reagan, and in 1964 he gave a rousing television appearance on behalf of Republican candidate Barry Goldwater. The party loved it, and Reagan was on his way. He served two terms as governor of California, came close to stealing the Republican nomination from Gerald Ford in 1976, and then beat Jimmy Carter in 1980 with a campaign based on right-wing rhetoric about love of country and economic hope. Reagan had become the first actor in American history to make it to the White House.

He was also the oldest man to become president, a fact that gave the nation pause when Reagan was shot just weeks into his first term by John Hinckley, Jr. Reagan made an impressive recovery, all the while keeping the hospital staff in stitches with his good humor and off-the-cuff remarks. Wisecracking optimism was the new president's modus operandi, an artifice he used to keep everybody smiling while he drove home an economic agenda that many thought was mired in hopeless absurdity. To undo the recession he inherited from Jimmy Carter, Reagan wanted to push through drastic tax cuts and take on the national debt. To hold the Soviet Union (the "Evil Empire") to ultimate account, he intended to make an outrageous increase in military spending. Even his old simian costar from *Bedtime for Bonzo* could've seen the impossibility of marrying the two. But Reagan just plowed ahead, duping Congress, the press, and the American people with his polished actor's panache. Even those

FLORIDA
NEVADA
ILLINOIS
President
IDAHO
CALIFORNIA
NEWYORK
ALASKA
President
OKLAHOMA
President
IOWA

who criticized the president's policies found him irresistible.

The results were mixed. The economy showed signs of recovery, enough to give Reagan a 1984 victory against Walter Mondale in the biggest electoral landslide in presidential history. And America's willingness to spend lavishly on arms brought Mikhail Gorbachev's Soviet Union to the point of making unprecedented conciliations. The two superpower leaders developed a closeness that ultimately helped end the Cold War and bring down the Soviet Union. But the Reagan administration's cut-and-spend policies saddled America with a gigantic national debt and trade deficit. Add to that an increase in bold terrorist activity around the world, the explosion of the space shuttle *Challenger* in 1986, a growing gap between rich and poor, a stock market crash in 1987, and Reagan's own struggle with prostate cancer, and you have the makings of a troubled presidency.

Military adventures in Grenada and Libya couldn't diffuse the growing fear that Ronald Reagan was losing his grip on the reins. When it came to light that the administration was selling arms to Iran in exchange for hostages, then using the profits to illegally fund the Contra rebels in Nicaragua, it spelled doom for Ronald Reagan. But the Great Communicator's hold on the populace, combined with his subordinates' willingness to take much of the blame, saved him from the sort of disgrace that had befallen Richard Nixon. Reagan claimed not to know a thing about the Iran-Contra scandal—and as he blithely smiled his way through the congressional hearings, the majority of Americans decided to let him off as an aging, doddering delegator. If that isn't the performance of a lifetime, what is?

Did Reagan really know what his White House was doing in the Iran-Contra mess? We will probably never know, especially since Reagan eventually descended into Alzheimer's disease. Whether you admire him or not, the fact remains that Ronald Reagan is one of the most beloved presidents in history. He is also one of the most loathed. One thing is certain—

← Acting in movies with a chimpanzee named Bonzo didn't hurt Reagan's chances of becoming president.

few presidents have ever been able to get voters to pay more attention to image than to substance. In that capacity, Reagan was certainly an actor to the end.

DADDY'S LITTLE BOY

Reagan's father was an alcoholic who once had to be dragged inside the house by his son after passing out on the front lawn. But the elder Reagan did make one contribution to his son's future. When he observed his infant son screaming his head off one day, the man remarked, "For such a little bit of a fat Dutchman, he sure makes a hell of a lot of noise." The name "Dutch" stuck and would be one of the future president's frequent nicknames.

GO FIGURE

In 1940, Reagan was voted "Most Nearly Perfect Male Figure" by the University of California. As a result, he had the honor of posing, nearly naked, for art students attempting to sculpt the human physique.

HIS RIGHT FROM HIS LEFT

Long before Ronald Reagan got swept into the White House for being an outspoken neoconservative, he was a devoted liberal. How left-wing was he? The man who would one day devote so much of his nation's resources toward outspending what he called the Evil Empire may have come close to joining the Communist Party. According to one account, he approached the organization in the late 1930s and was turned down because he didn't seem ardent enough in his devotion to the cause. It's intriguing, in light of Reagan's future efforts on behalf of the right wing, but we shall probably never know for sure whether it really occurred.

LIFE IMITATING ART

When asked whether he was nervous during a televised debate with candidate Jimmy Carter in 1980, Ronald Reagan replied, "No, not at all. I've been on the same stage with John Wayne!" A longtime fan of Wayne's, Reagan approached nearly every crisis with the question, "What would the Duke do?" This sort of fusion between Reagan's politics and his Hollywood mindset pervaded his eight-year presidency and could often be a trifle unnerving to those around him. While visiting the office of House Speaker Tip O'Neill, the newly elected president made an admiring remark about the large oak desk that dominated the room. O'Neill said that it had been used by President Grover Cleveland, to which Reagan replied, "You know, I played Grover Cleveland in the movies." As the speaker was quick to point out, Reagan had done no such thing—he had, however, played Grover Cleveland Alexander, a baseball player, in *The Winning Team.*

Both Reagan and his wife, Nancy—another actor—were avid filmgoers and spent some part of almost every day watching movies either on television or in the White House screening room. Colin Powell once remarked that Reagan's plan to exchange defense technology with the Soviets was inspired by the famous sci-fi film *The Day the Earth Stood Still.* And when Chief of Staff James Baker showed up at the White House only to discover that the president hadn't even opened a large and important briefing Baker had given him the day before, Reagan merely shrugged. "Well, Jim," explained the president, "*The Sound of Music* was on last night."

BEDTIME FOR RON-ZO

Ronald Reagan was the oldest president in American history, and he often acted like it. His habit of dozing off in meetings became the butt of jokes, including his own. "As soon as I get home to California," he quipped near the end of his second term, "I plan to lean back, kick up my feet, and take a long nap. Come to think of it, things won't be that different after all." Reagan may have been snoring his way through the White House, but his strange behavior and cluelessness led many to think that he still wasn't getting enough sleep. How else can you explain his distressing pronouncement that trees caused 80 percent of the country's air pollution? He once called Oklahoma Senator Don Nickles "Don Rickles" and even had difficulty remembering who his top officials were. When Samuel Pierce Jr., Reagan's secretary of housing and urban development (and the only African American in the cabinet), attended a conference of the nation's mayors, Reagan strode up to him and greeted him with "How are you, Mr. Mayor? How are things in your city?" At a White House dinner honoring François Mitterand, the French president, Reagan was supposed to escort Mrs. Mitterand to her place at the table. When she refused to move, Reagan reminded her that it was time to proceed, only to be told by the interpreter that he was standing on her gown.

STARSTRUCK

Both Ronald and Nancy Reagan were superstitious people. But for Nancy, the belief in the mysterious powers of the universe achieved a new urgency after her husband was shot in 1981. Shortly after the assassination attempt, she began consulting San Francisco astrologer Joan Quigley in the hopes of avoiding future calamities. With time, Quigley's advice—based on the president's star charts—was shaping the conduct of the administration as much as any of its cabinet members. White House Chief of Staff Donald Regan took to color-coding his boss's schedule based on Quigley's directives as sent through the first lady: red for potentially negative days, green for potentially good days, and so on. Even *Air Force One* take-offs and landings were dictated by the astrologer, often to the second.

★ ★ ★ ★ ★

BORN June 12, 1924	NICKNAME "Poppy"

ASTROLOGICAL SIGN	PARTY	AGE UPON TAKING OFFICE
Gemini	Republican	**64**

RAN AGAINST	VICE PRESIDENT
Michael Dukakis	★ Danforth Quayle ★

HEIGHT	SOUND BITE	TERM OF PRESIDENCY
6′ 2″	*"I have opinions of my own, strong opinions, but I don't always agree with them."*	**1989** – TO – **1993**

W hen George H. W. Bush made his run for president in 1988, no sitting vice president had been voted into the White House since Martin Van Buren in 1837. But Bush had two things going for him: Ronald Reagan's blessing and the fact that he was running against a liberal named Michael Dukakis in an age when *liberal* had become a four-letter word.

The Republicans played up Dukakis's Eastern urban elitism, contrasting it to Bush's beer-drinking Texas simplicity. Ironically, it was Bush who had the truly privileged pedigree. Born in Massachusetts and raised in Connecticut, George grew up in the backseats of limousines. He was preppy all the way: the son of financier and Republican senator

Prescott Bush and a graduate of the Phillips Academy in Andover, Massachusetts. After serving as the youngest pilot in the navy during World War II, he graduated from Yale and decided to strike out on his own by making a go of the Texas oil industry. Texas may have become his adopted state, but he never lost his Yankee patrician ways, no matter how much he tried to pass himself off as a good ol' boy.

His identity crisis notwithstanding, Bush had an impressive résumé: congressman from 1966 to 1970, ambassador to the United Nations, chairman of the Republican National Committee, envoy to Beijing, CIA director, and Reagan's vice president. But he'd always been merely an agreeable administrator with a gift for taking direction from willful superiors such as Richard Nixon and Ronald Reagan. (Bush was pro-choice until he joined the Reagan ticket in 1980.) Such a background didn't lend itself to taking an active role as leader of the Free World, and when Bush admitted in 1988 to having trouble with "the vision thing," he as much as admitted his intention to become a caretaker president.

Foremost among those policies was the dismantling of Eastern Europe's Communist regimes. One by one, the nations of the Eastern Bloc dumped the old order, until even the Soviet Union gave in under Boris Yeltsin. Bush, a man whose every political office had been shaped by the Cold War, soon found himself baffled by its absence. He had shepherded one of the century's most impressive accomplishments to completion but lacked the vision required to create a new world order in its place.

Back home, his agenda was hampered by ugly confirmation squabbles over secretary of defense candidate John Tower and Supreme Court justice appointee Clarence Thomas. In 1988, Bush had said, "Read my lips: no new taxes," then went back on his word in 1990. And aside from pushing the Clean Air Act and the Americans with Disabilities Act through Congress, he failed to initiate much legislation. That "vision thing" was biting him in the ass.

Circumstances abroad would come to the rescue. Bush invaded Pan-

→ After Bush vomited on the Japanese prime minister, a new word entered the Japanese language. *Bushusuru*—literally, "to do the Bush thing"—is slang for vomiting.

ama in 1989, kidnapping Manuel Noriega to stand trial for drug charges back in the United States. But real martial glory was afforded the commander in chief thousands of miles away in the Middle East. After Iraqi leader Saddam Hussein invaded Kuwait in 1990, Bush showed his strength in international affairs by organizing an unprecedented coalition to throw back Iraqi aggression.

Unfortunately, nothing is that simple. Bush went a little overboard by comparing Saddam Hussein to Adolf Hitler, and people the world over couldn't help feeling that the whole bloody affair was really over oil—a fact driven home when the coalition smashed Iraqi forces only to leave Saddam in power to wreak murderous havoc on his own people. As a result, Bush was incapable of turning Operation Desert Storm into a reelection victory. Economic issues only made things worse—the brief resurgence brought on by "Reaganomics" had fizzled, and Americans were already wondering what a Democratic candidate like Bill Clinton could do to put more money in their wallets.

And so George Bush was denied a second term, freeing him to do the sort of things that presidents should avoid, like parachuting out of an airplane, which he did in 1997.

BEST LITTLE WHOREHOUSE IN TEXAS

After Bush decided to go west in 1948, he took his wife, Barbara, and two-year-old son George W. and relocated to the little town of Odessa, Texas. Once there, they moved into an apartment building, where they had to share a bathroom with a mother-daughter duo of prostitutes.

??????

George Bush wasn't exactly the most eloquent of chief executives. The press took to calling his bizarre pronouncements Bushspeak, some of which was downright nonsensical. "I stand for anti-bigotry, anti-Semitism, and anti-racism," he proclaimed in a 1988 campaign speech. His attempt at describing his "New England values" during a 1992 speech came out as "Remember Lincoln, going to his knees in times of trial and the Civil War and all that stuff. You can't be. And we are blessed. So don't feel sorry for—don't cry for me, Argentina." He explained the significance of an upcoming meeting with Mikhail Gorbachev as "Grandkids. All of that. Very important," and he once replied to a journalist's question with "I'm glad you asked it because then I vented a spleen here." But perhaps his greatest inanity was the response he gave to a question about how his presidency would differ from Reagan's: "Like the old advice from Jackman—you remember, the guy that came out—character. He says, 'And then I had some advice. Be yourself!' That proved to be the worst advice I could possibly have. And I'm going to be myself. Do it that way." If you can figure out what the hell that means, *you* should be president.

SKIRTING THE ISSUE

"I'm not going to take any sleazy questions like that from CNN. I am very disappointed that you would ask such a question of me, and I will not respond to it." So said President Bush to Mary Tillotson's inquiry about Bush's alleged affair with his secretary, Jennifer Fitzgerald. Tillotson was one of the first journalists ever to ask a sitting president such a question. Bush may not have bothered to answer it, but plenty of those who knew him did—and they claim that Bush did in fact cheat on his wife with Fitzgerald and plenty of other women. No solid evidence, however, has ever been found to substantiate the relationships.

GEORGE DISGORGE

If President Bush wanted to make a splash during his visit to Japan in 1992, he succeeded—and with flying colors. In the middle of a state dinner in Tokyo, the president turned white as a sheet and threw up into the lap of Japanese Prime Minister Kiichi Miyazawa, then slid out of his chair until he was nearly under the table. The Japanese haven't forgotten the incident; to this day, the word *Bushusuru*—literally "to do the Bush thing"—is slang for vomiting.

42 | WILLIAM JEFFERSON CLINTON

BORN August 19, 1946	NICKNAMES "Bill," "Bubba," "Slick Willie," "Comeback Kid"

ASTROLOGICAL SIGN	PARTY	AGE UPON TAKING OFFICE
Leo 	Democratic 	46

RAN AGAINST	VICE PRESIDENT
George H. W. Bush *(first term)* Robert Dole *(second term)*	★ Al Gore ★

HEIGHT	SOUND BITE	TERM OF PRESIDENCY
6′2″ 	*"I want you to listen to me. . . .* *I did not have sexual* *relations with that woman,* *Miss Lewinsky."*	1993 – TO – 2001

A s a young man, William Jefferson Clinton was a gifted saxophone player who won contests in his home state of Arkansas, organized his own jazz bands, and received music scholarships from several colleges. He also had three other passions: politics, lying, and sex.

Bill Clinton's father died before he was born, and his mother, Virginia, married a man who spent virtually all his time drinking and abusing his wife, son, and stepson. Bill rose from these humble beginnings to become a brilliant student who joined every club in sight and made friends through his remarkable sincerity and compassion. After graduating from Georgetown University, he was awarded a Rhodes scholarship and studied at Oxford for two years before returning to study law at Yale. He married fellow law student Hillary Rodham, returned to Arkansas, served as the state attorney general, and ran for governor. Though he won and became the youngest governor in the country, his policy of raising car license fees to pay for badly needed road construction got him voted out after only one term. Rather than give in, Clinton earned his nickname "Comeback Kid" by running again and winning another four terms.

Winning the White House was a little tougher. Independent candidate Ross Perot managed to grab a significant number of votes in the 1992 presidential election, meaning that Clinton, though victorious, couldn't claim a mandate from the people—he'd received only 43.5 percent of the popular vote, just 5 percent more than George H. W. Bush. Nevertheless, Clinton seemed full of potential; the first president born after World War II, he had terrific rapport with people of all ages and conveyed the image of a youthful, keenly intelligent, and confident leader.

He also conveyed the image of a man whose marriage was at least a little troubled. Gennifer Flowers, a TV reporter turned nightclub singer from Arkansas, had upset Clinton's 1992 campaign by claiming she'd had a twelve-year affair with him. After she produced audiotapes suggesting Clinton had told her to deny everything, the presidential candidate went on *60 Minutes* with his wife. While denying the Flowers allegations, he did admit to causing "pain" in his marriage. The ploy worked—but Clinton's past had begun to haunt him, and questions about his sexual shenanigans were now on everyone's radar.

Once he was president, Clinton's agenda ran into resistance from congressional leaders who thought his ideas were too ambitious, too complicated, or both. First Lady Hillary was made leader of an effort to overhaul the health-care system, producing a report that proved too byzantine for anyone on Capitol Hill to read, much less vote on. The issue petered out. And Clinton had to back off on one of his central campaign promises, a big tax cut for the middle class. Nevertheless, he worked with Congress to pass the North American Free Trade Agreement, the Family and Medical Leave Act, gun-purchasing legislation under the Brady Bill, and other accomplishments. In addition, higher taxes on the wealthy helped cut the deficit, and economic recovery started accelerating.

Then the 1994 midterm elections spoiled Clinton's fun, and in a big way. Republicans swept into Congress in what most considered a severe indictment of the presidency. But when GOP leaders, led by the snide and rapacious Newt Gingrich, started acting like right-wing revolutionaries who'd all but forgotten about the executive branch of government, Clinton was afforded the opportunity to look like a force for moderation. He reinvented himself as a New Democrat—a centrist who stood for traditional Democratic ideas (such as education and social programs) as well as Republican priorities (crime bills, for example). The result was yet another comeback and a victory against hapless Bob Dole in 1996.

By the time Clinton's second term was well under way, the deficit had vanished and the economy was roaring. But the president's foreign policy was another matter entirely. Clinton wasn't exactly a towering commander in chief. One of the many issues on which he was forced to compromise early in his first term was persecution of gays in the military. The solution—"Don't ask, don't tell"—meant that gays shouldn't admit to their sexual orientation, and nobody should pester them about it. It pleased no one, including Clinton. His actions overseas were similarly hazy. From Haiti to Bosnia, Somalia to Iraq, the administration reacted to events rather than shaping them. He did manage to stop Serbian leader Slobodan Milosevic's ethnic cleansing in Kosovo through NATO-sponsored bombing in 1999, but Clinton's legacy in foreign policy has continued to be a sore spot with critics.

But who remembers all that? Or the booming economy over which he presided? Or his eloquent and persuasive speaking ability? For all the political events of Clinton's eight years in office, most people can recall only two words: Monica Lewinsky. As virtually everybody knows by now, she was the White House intern with whom Clinton did all sorts of lewd things except have intercourse, which he believed gave him the right to deny having "sexual relations" with her. Of course, Monica Lewinsky was

← For all the political events of Clinton's eight years in office, most people can only recall two words: Monica Lewinsky.

asked about her relationship with the president only because investigator Kenneth Starr was interested in building a case against Clinton in the Paula Jones case. Through a series of scandals, "Slick Willie" managed to dodge the bullets fired at him by what his wife called "a vast right-wing conspiracy." In fact, his approval ratings remained high throughout his presidency, despite widespread horror at his personal conduct. But the evidence in the Monica Lewinsky affair was irrefutable, forcing us all to realize that he was not only brilliant and charming but also disgusting and deceitful. Perhaps he should've stuck to music after all.

FEEL A DRAFT?

In May 1969, during the Vietnam War, Bill Clinton received his draft notice and joined an ROTC unit out of the University of Arkansas. Rather than report to his unit in the fall, he went back to Oxford, where he had been studying as a Rhodes scholar. It was a move he claims to have been given permission to do by the ROTC. No letter to that effect has ever been found, however. In October, he told the draft board to end his deferment, but by then the Nixon administration had made it clear that fewer men were going to be called up, and it seemed as if Clinton's chances of being drafted were slim to none. As if all this weren't a little suspicious to begin with, Clinton wrote a letter to his colonel expressing his interest in getting back into the draft. According to the letter, he did it "for one reason only: to maintain my political viability within the system."

SLICK WILLIE'S SLICK WILLIE

Bill Clinton often expressed his admiration for Jack Kennedy. Indeed, young Bill traveled to Washington in 1963 as a member of the youth group Boy's Nation, meeting JFK and shaking his hand. But Clinton had more in common with his idol than just politics. Like Kennedy, Clinton seemed to be a reckless, no-holds-barred, let's-hope-my-wife-doesn't-catch-me sex addict.

According to Christopher Andersen, author of *Bill and Hillary: The*

Marriage, Clinton is rumored to have fondled a woman in the bathroom during the reception at his own wedding; two former Miss Arkansas winners have claimed to have had sex with him; and a woman named Juanita Broaddrick claimed that she'd been raped by Clinton in 1978. (Broaddrick's husband made a scene at a 1980 campaign party, threatening to kill Clinton if he ever came near Juanita again.) He allegedly had a twenty-five-year affair with fellow lawyer Dolly Kyle and a fifteen-year affair with Susan McDougal. Arkansas trooper Larry Douglas Brown, who was engaged to the nanny of the Clintons' daughter, Chelsea, swore in a deposition that he was charged with personally contacting hundreds of women to have sex with Governor Clinton. Brown also testified that Clinton showed a passion for having sex in locales that could easily be discovered. Such dangerous behavior was apparently part of the thrill.

STARR-STRUCK

From the moment he appeared on *60 Minutes* in 1992 with his wife to answer the charge of infidelity before a gawking nation, Bill Clinton's life as a national figure was riddled with scandal. Whitewater, Travelgate, Filegate, Vince Foster, Paula Jones, Monica Lewinsky. The list of alleged crimes, missteps, and cover-ups was enough to give even the most ardent Clinton supporter a bleeding ulcer.

Not everyone was gulping Tums, however. Of the many foes Bill Clinton seemed to collect as easily as a cistern captures rain, none proved more implacable than Kenneth Starr. And if all these various threads of Clintonian ugliness have a connection, it's Starr's effort to investigate and topple the president.

Just six months into Clinton's first term, a friend of the first family turned up dead just outside D.C. with a gunshot wound to the head. The poor fellow's name was Vince Foster, and he had been a deputy White House counsel responsible for handling the administration's issues regarding the longstanding allegations that the Clintons had been involved in illegal financial dealings with a failed Arkansas real estate scheme called the Whitewater Development Corporation. Could Foster have been murdered to take his secrets to the grave? Actually, no. So said an independent counsel named Jim Fiske, appointed the following year by the attorney general to investigate the whole Whitewater mess. Foster, it was ruled, had committed suicide. Undeterred, Republicans wrangled a replacement for Fiske and got Starr, a veritable bloodhound who would not rest until something, anything, shook out about the Clintons.

The independent counsel's dragnet of the Whitewater skullduggery bagged a handful of scam artists and little else. Nothing, it seemed, could indict the Clintons of anything worse than a decade-old case of bad judgment. Even unsought opportunities that popped up in the course of the investigation proved unrewarding. In 1993, it was found, the president had sacked the employees of the White House travel office and began using the services of an Arkansas-based travel company operated by an old friend. But "Travelgate" proved a tempest in a teapot, as did "Filegate," in which a White House official improperly acquired FBI background reports on Republican Party members.

But if Starr couldn't hang Clinton on fraud, murder, corruption, or privacy violations, he could hang him by his pants—er, at least the lack of them. Starr's relentless quest (for other things) in Arkansas turned up Paula Jones, who filed a lawsuit in 1994 contending that Bill had exposed himself to her three years earlier in a Little Rock hotel. Following that trail in search of a pattern of sexual licentiousness led Starr to one Monica Lewinsky, a White House intern rumored to have had sexual dalliances with the president.

Lewinsky's friend Linda Tripp produced a taped conversation in which Lewinsky admitted to having an affair with the president. Clinton, who had denied the accusation, was forced to renege. He was also accused of coaching his secretary to mislead prosecutors and of using his influence to get Lewinsky a job in New York to get her out of D.C.

The upshot of Starr's sleuthing? Clinton became the first president since Andrew Johnson to be impeached by the House of Representatives. The Senate, however, failed to reach the two-thirds majority needed to remove him from office.

The best estimate to date puts the cost of the Whitewater investigations at $70 million. Now *that's* bang for your buck.

WHAT'S IN A DRESS?

In November 1997, Monica Lewinsky admitted to her friend Linda Tripp that she possessed a blue Gap dress still adorned with the president's semen from one of their sexual encounters. This, by the way, is one of those conversations that people do not encounter every day. Or...well, ever. Tripp managed to dissuade her confidante from having the garment dry-cleaned and, lo and behold, it became the most notorious dress in American history.

Eventually Lewinsky turned the shifty shift over to the Starr investigation team, and it was subjected to lab tests that confirmed her story: William Jefferson Clinton was clearly the originator of the semen whose stains adorned one of the Gap's finest.

In 2015, an organization known as the Las Vegas Erotic Heritage Museum offered to purchase the garment from Lewinsky for $1 million, but she sensibly declined the offer, eager to move on from the whole debacle.

WAIT PROBLEM

On his inauguration day, Bill Clinton was twenty-seven minutes late for his customary courtesy call on the Bushes. It was a sign of things to come. The new president seemed almost incapable of keeping his appointments on time. He once kept Supreme Court Justice William Rehnquist waiting forty-five minutes and even showed up late for his formal greeting of the king of Spain. It wasn't just those in government who found themselves remaking their schedules around the president's sloppy timekeeping. *Air Force One* once held up air traffic at the Los Angeles airport while Clinton got a $200 haircut from famed stylist Christophe.

★ ★ ★ ★ ★

43 | GEORGE W. BUSH

BORN July 6, 1946

NICKNAMES
"Junior," "Dubya"

ASTROLOGICAL SIGN
Cancer

PARTY
Republican

AGE UPON
TAKING OFFICE
54

RAN AGAINST
Al Gore

VICE PRESIDENT
★ Richard Cheney ★

HEIGHT
5′11″

SOUND BITE

*"A key to foreign
policy is to rely
on reliance."*

TERM OF
PRESIDENCY
2001
– TO –
2009

O n September 11, 2001, militant Islamic terrorists succeeded in crashing two jets into the World Trade Center and another into the Pentagon. It was the most tragic day in modern American history and one that would come to define the administration of George W. Bush. But if it was Osama bin Laden's Al Qaeda organization that made Americans realize how vulnerable they were at home, it was, by a controversial turn of events, Saddam Hussein's Iraq that would become the focus of George W. Bush's administration—a fact that ultimately divided his country and the world.

George Walker Bush was raised in Texas but followed in his father's footsteps by attending some of the most prestigious schools in the North-east. After graduating from Andover, Bush partied his way through Yale, then joined the Texas Air National Guard, which spared him from service in Vietnam. Despite his below-average grades and binge drinking, he managed to get into Harvard and graduated in 1975 with an M.B.A. Then it was back to Texas, where Bush founded an oil and gas exploration firm, made an unsuccessful run for Congress, and became a managing partner in the Texas Rangers baseball team. Bush's most valued asset seems to have been his father: those willing to curry favor with the elder Bush did business with the younger one, and George W. soon became a rich man. He was elected governor of Texas in 1994, won a second term in 1998, and announced his bid for the presidency the following year.

Bush was a political lightweight whose Democratic opponent in the 2000 presidential race, Al Gore, was light-years ahead of him intellectually. But Gore had two strikes against him: his vice presidency under Bill Clinton, whose scandalous administration had exhausted the nation's patience, and his stiff public persona, which made him appear like a talking two-by-four. Such failings were enough to damn Gore in many voters' eyes, despite his opponent's empty-headed campaign errors. (For example, Bush made a point of speaking at the preposterously conservative Bob Jones University, an anachronistic institution that banned interracial dating.)

In the end, more Americans voted for Gore, but not enough to offset the shenanigans that resulted in an electoral college victory for Bush. When it looked as if voting machines in Florida were improperly processing voting cards and that the voting cards in some counties were confusing, Gore insisted on a hand count to ensure accuracy. After Florida's secretary of state certified Bush the winner, the issue went to the Florida Supreme Court, which ruled in favor of an extension. As the new deadline approached, Bush—despite being an avowed states' rights man—went over Florida's head and appealed to the Supreme Court of the United States. With most of the judges in the Republican camp, they sided with Bush, who then became the forty-third president.

George W. is the second son of a previous president to also become president. And like the first one to do it, John Quincy Adams, Bush secured his office without a mandate from the people. His problems didn't stop there: the "tech wreck" of 2000 had sent the economy into a tailspin, and

Bush's appointment to the cabinet of such ultraconservatives as Attorney General John Ashcroft offended more than a few Americans. Then came the attacks of September 11. Americans rallied around the president as he attempted to lead the nation out of horror and disillusionment. While the scandals of Enron and WorldCom racked the people's confidence in national corporate institutions, the Bush administration ramped up the war on terror with the creation of a Homeland Security Department and a mostly successful war against militant Islamic forces in Afghanistan.

As Bush's relatively high approval ratings reflected confidence in his willingness to confront terrorism, his administration felt compelled to expand the conflict. Ever since the Gulf War of 1991, Saddam Hussein's Iraq had repeatedly defied United Nations resolutions to account for weapons of mass destruction, and Bush felt it was time to do something about it. Insisting on a connection between Iraq and Al Qaeda, Bush—citing Saddam Hussein's appalling record of invasion, murder, and chemical weapons programs—pushed for a disarmament of Iraq or else. This was all well and good; anybody with more than seven brain cells could see that Saddam was a world-class sadistic douchebag. But skeptics in the U.S. and abroad raised plenty of important questions: Wasn't Al Qaeda the real threat? Didn't it take precedence? Was Dubya merely settling an old score, one that his pop had failed to finish? And where was the irrefutable evidence of complicity between Iraq and Al Qaeda? As U.N.-sponsored weapons inspectors combed Iraq for evidence of biological, chemical, and nuclear threats, U.N. members such as France, Germany, Russia, and China began to fear the reckless flexing of American muscle at least as much as anything Iraq might try. As Bush's saber-rattling got louder, the world only became more and more wary of an America that seemed heedless of other nations' desire to proceed cautiously.

Despite all the opposition, Bush and his British ally launched the military option against Iraq, and with predictable results. The Iraqi military

→   In January 2002, George W. Bush experienced a brief period of unconsciousness while choking on a pretzel.

was swept aside, leaving the world to decide how a democratic government should be created in a place that has known nothing but ruthless autocracy for decades. And not surprisingly, Dubya's approval ratings went back up. But as the 2004 campaign loomed, he faced a dilemma uncannily similar to the one his father faced at reelection: how to leverage military success abroad into political victory at home despite an economy that couldn't seem to pull itself out of the toilet. Oh, and there's still that Al Qaeda problem. Remember those guys?

Bush lucked out when the Democrats found perhaps the only major political figure capable of losing a debate to W. and then made him their 2004 presidential candidate. John Kerry had served for nearly two decades as a Massachusetts senator and won numerous military honors serving his country in Vietnam. But he was a stiff on the stump who seemed to be forever searching for the right thing to say. Kerry proved so unlikable that the Bush campaign even managed to turn the three Purple Heart medals Kerry had received in Vietnam against him, making claims through surrogates that he may have deserved only two of them.

Things went from bad to worse during Bush's second term, with many calling him the least effective president in U.S. history. The big turning point came in the summer of 2005, when Hurricane Katrina slammed into New Orleans. The city's overmatched levees failed and floodwaters raged through its downtown. Images of stranded refugees and dead bodies floating through a major American city appalled the nation and the world. As did W.'s response—or lack thereof. Because while New Orleans and several other Gulf Coast communities drowned, Bush fiddled away on another long vacation at his Crawford ranch. When a few days later he finally showed up in New Orleans searching for a heroic photo op, it was too little too late.

With the economy faltering, gas prices skyrocketing (along with profits for oil companies), Osama bin Laden still on the loose, and U.S. troops fully entrenched in a WMD-free Iraq, W. ended his term with record low job-approval ratings. By the last year of his term, 80 percent of Americans believed the country had headed in the wrong direction during his presidency. In the 2006 midterm elections Republicans had lost control of both houses of Congress, and Bush served out the rest of his term as the lamest of lame ducks.

ONE MORE FOR THE ROAD

Though the widespread rumors of Dubya's alleged cocaine usage have remained unproven, there is no doubt that he was an avowed drinker in his younger days—and he has the police record to prove it. While driving (swerving, actually) near his family's compound in Kennebunkport, Maine, on Labor Day weekend 1976, Bush was pulled over and arrested for driving under the influence. He was taken into custody and fined $150, and his driving privileges were suspended. Years later, Bush put his drinking days behind him: he became a teetotaler after his fortieth birthday in 1986.

OFF HE GOES, INTO THE WILD BLUE YONDER . . .

During the course of the Vietnam War, many young men joined the National Guard as a way of avoiding service in Southeast Asia. Guard units were far more likely to stay home than get shipped overseas. With this in mind, Dubya took some tests to join the Texas Air National Guard in 1968—and scored in the 25th percentile. Despite his low marks and a waiting list of five hundred, Bush got into flight school. How? According to author Paul Begala in *Is Our Children Learning?*, Texas House Speaker Ben Barnes pulled some strings on Dubya's behalf at the request of Sid Adger, a friend of the Bush dynasty.

Once in uniform, however, Bush seems not to have taken his duties all that seriously. In 1972, he decided to help Alabama Republican Winton Blount in a race for the Senate and requested a transfer to the Alabama National Guard. But after getting his transfer approved, Bush—according to the records—failed to report to his new command. In fact, not a single person or sheet of paper can attest to Bush's service in Alabama. It's as if he spent all his time working on Blount's behalf and shirked his military responsibilities. When he was pressed on the issue, Dubya's response wasn't exactly encouraging: "I can't remember what I did." Hmmm.

GIVING 'EM THE BUSINESS

George W. Bush is the first president to have an M.B.A. Even though he's a rich man, his business dealings seem rather unimpressive, if not downright suspicious. Dubya founded Arbusto, his Texas oil and gas exploration firm, in 1977. The start-up money came from some very wealthy guys who apparently wanted to get in tight with Dubya's father, the other George Bush, who was by now a Washington bigwig. But despite some serious cash injections, Arbusto nearly went el-busto, and Dubya was forced to sell the firm (now called Bush Exploration) to a firm called Spectrum 7—which, in turn, was bought by Harken Energy. Throughout the series of transitions, Bush exhibited a conspicuous lack of business sense or managerial skill. He did, however, leverage his family's name, which always persuaded companies like Spectrum 7 and Harken Energy to keep him on. When you're the son of a vice president turned president, you don't need to make decisions—you just have to impress investors, which Dubya always did. His connections raised the cash.

Apparently not enough, however. Harken's creditors eventually threatened to foreclose, and Bush—who was a director of the firm—sold two-thirds of his stock in Harken in June 1990, making a titanic profit before the company bottomed out. Did he know that Harken was in trouble? Did he profit from the debacle? We may never know. But Bush failed to report his stock sale when it happened, waiting eight months after the legal deadline to file it.

TWISTED

On January 13, 2002, George W. Bush sat watching a football game. Suddenly, he slumped off the couch, his head thumping upon the floor, giving him an abrasion. A pretzel had become lodged in his throat, choking him and causing a brief period of unconsciousness. Times are tough indeed when the Secret Service has to start paying close attention to the White House snack food.

??????, TAKE 2

Like his father, George W. Bush has vocalized plenty of brain farts that are truly astonishing. Consider these examples:

"I understand small business growth. I was one."

"If you're sick and tired of the politics of cynicism and polls and principles, come and join this campaign."

"Reading is the basics for all learning."

"Governor Bush will not stand for the subsidation of failure."

"We ought to make the pie higher."

"I know how hard it is for you to put food on your families."

"Keep good relations with the Grecians."

"There is madmen in the world, and there are terror."

"My education message will resignate among all parents."

"There's an old saying in Tennessee—I know it's in Texas, probably in Tennessee—that says, fool me once, shame on—shame on you. Fool me—you can't get fooled again."

"There's no doubt in my mind that we should allow the world's worst leaders to hold America hostage, to threaten our peace, to threaten our friends and allies with the world's worst weapons."

"I promise you I will listen to what has been said here, even though I wasn't here."

"Do you have blacks, too?" (to the president of Brazil).

★ ★ ★ ★ ★

BORN **August 4, 1961**	NICKNAMES "Barry," "'Bama," "Obamber"

ASTROLOGICAL SIGN Leo 	PARTY Democrat 	AGE UPON TAKING OFFICE **47**

RAN AGAINST John McCain	VICE PRESIDENT ★ Joe Biden ★

HEIGHT 6′ 2″ ↑	SOUND BITE *"I can sum up my foreign policy in one phrase: Don't do stupid shit."*	TERM OF PRESIDENCY **2009** – TO – **2017**

B arack Obama is a great orator. Consider this: he entered the White House less than five years removed from life as an obscure state senator and law school professor in Illinois. To become the first president who was black, the first born outside the continental United States, and the first born to an African Muslim, Obama overcame the considerable Clinton political machine and the almost-as-considerable appeal of bona fide war hero John McCain. What else could possibly account for this victory except his inspiring message of hope and the public-speaking skills he employed?

Obama's first presidential campaign was one of the most aspirational in modern history. But once he was in office, his aspirations collided head-on with the mess his administration inherited: two unpopular wars and the worst economic crisis since the Great Depression. In the effort to grapple with these nightmares and still find time to tackle the stuff that made him want to be president in the first place, Obama exhibited coolness and grace under pressure; he would also become, by virtue of his own idiosyncrasies and the era in which he rose to high office, one of the most polarizing figures in American history.

Barack Obama Jr. was born in Hawaii to Ann Dunham, a white woman from Kansas who had met and married Barack Obama Sr. while studying at the University of Hawai'i at Mānoa. The couple separated when Junior was two years old and later divorced. Obama Sr. returned to his home country of Kenya, seeing his son only once more before dying in a car accident in 1982. Dunham then married another college classmate, Lolo Soetoro. In 1967 she and her son moved with Soetoro to his native Indonesia, where young Barack attended grade school. He returned to his home state at age ten to live with his mother's parents and attend Punahou, a prestigious private preparatory school. Next it was off to Occidental College in Los Angeles, Columbia University, and—after a three-year stint as a community organizer in Chicago—Harvard, where Obama received national publicity for being selected the first African American editor of the *Harvard Law Review*. After graduating with honors he returned to Chicago, where he practiced and taught law.

Obama's political career had been relatively undistinguished when he announced that he would run for president. He'd served for eight years as an Illinois state legislator, lost a bid to become the Democratic nominee for a U.S. House of Representatives race in 2000, and won a U.S. Senate seat in 2004. That year, he took the leap into national prominence with a stirring, widely lauded keynote address at the Democratic National Convention, showing off the public-speaking chops that would get him to the Oval Office.

Yet many were surprised when, in 2007, he announced his intention to become the party's presidential nominee. Obama was young, eloquent, and charismatic, but the facts were plain: he had few accomplishments to show for his two years of Senate service. Even he questioned his viability, telling a New Hampshire crowd, "The fact that my fifteen minutes of fame

has extended a little longer than fifteen minutes is somewhat surprising to me and completely baffling to my wife."

But if Hillary Clinton had a huge campaign bank account, endorsements from top Democrats and powerful interest groups, and a fifteen-year head start, Obama had his oratory. Throughout the campaign, he drew enthusiastic crowds more befitting of a rock concert than a political speech. After beating the odds in the primary, Obama maintained momentum against Republican challenger John McCain, who elevated an obscure governor of Alaska to become his running mate. Sarah Palin—a gun-toting, plainspoken, intellectual featherweight with virtually nothing to offer the ticket but her gender—proved the Democrats' greatest weapon, comitting one embarrassing gaffe after another. The notion of placing the likes of Palin a heartbeat away from the presidency was enough to drag the ticket down.

As president, Obama promised to lead the nation out of what had become an interminable cycle of wasteful military ventures that robbed attention and effort from worsening domestic issues. Obama had inherited a house on fire, and so the first piece of legislation to receive his signature had nothing to do with expanding healthcare (we'll get to that) or closing the controversial prison camp for terrorists at Guantanamo Bay (what's the hurry?). It was the American Recovery and Reinvestment Act, which threw $800 billion of public stimulus spending at an economy still in freefall.

And it worked . . . mostly. As significant as the stimulus plan was to saving the republic from what could have been the next Great Depression, it also set a precedent: seemingly everything Obama did became a lightning rod, highlighting how polarized America had become in the age of social media. Free-market advocates wondered why the stimulus had to happen at all. Why not let the banks and automakers fail? Wasn't that what markets were supposed to do? By contrast, Keynesian economists

← Fortunately for Barack Obama, "bowling" is entirely absent from the official presidential job description.

and those on the left criticized the plan for being too small, stunting the pace of a rebounding economy.

The same divisiveness surrounded the passage of 2010's Dodd-Frank Wall Street Reform and Consumer Protection Act, intended to prevent a recurrence of the financial skullduggery that produced the Great Recession in the first place. And then, of course, there was the Affordable Care Act. Popularly dubbed (or derided as) "Obamacare," the ACA represented the culmination of decades of aspirations by various policymakers on both the left and the right to extend affordable health care to (nearly) every American. Republicans, who viewed it as a descent into the bowels of hell, voted against it with vitriolic unanimity.

Just months after Dodd-Frank and the ACA, the 2010 midterm elections gave the GOP control of Congress. And so, in addition to a skein of foreign-policy nightmares and a still-flagging economy, the president now had to contend with a Republican-controlled legislative branch whose avowed policy was to avoid even a single act of cooperation with a president they viewed as the closest actual approximation of a hobgoblin. Obama persevered, always with the cool—some say aloof—demeanor that put foreign heads of state at ease but made critics detest him as emotionally inert.

In 2012, a few months before winning reelection, Obama made what is probably his worst mistake as president. Responding to the unfolding civil war in Syria, he publicly delivered a message to Syrian president Bashar al-Assad to stop the slaughtering of his own people—or else. Roughly a year later, Assad crossed the line, killing over a thousand Syrians with sarin gas in a suburb of Damascus. The ramifications were clear: Assad's forces needed to be struck with American military might. The entire Obama administration moved toward that end—all except its chief. Obama balked, talking himself out of a military response and throwing the decision to Congress. Although Obama saved face somewhat by joining with the Russians to pressure Assad to surrender his chemical arsenal, the damage was done.

If Obama had erred in judgment, it was in making the declaration in the first place. His decision not to punish Assad was at least consistent with his wider doctrine, which many have called "realist." Unless a foreign-aggression matter directly affected U.S. national security, Obama would resist the decades-long tradition of resorting to force. However dreadful Assad's crimes, they posed no existential threat to the United States, a superpower whose political capital had been spent in two expansive, unpopular wars. Knee-jerk air strikes in far-flung crisis points were, for the first time in decades, open to question. Indeed, when the president threw the option to Congress, lawmakers showed little stomach for it.

Realism characterized the foreign policy of a president who wanted, almost more than anything, to avoid walking in George W. Bush's footsteps. As in Afghanistan, where Obama believed a continued American presence could avert disaster, decisions abroad became situational. If Vladimir Putin acts aggressively in Eastern Europe, the responses should be, "How does the future of Ukraine impact America's safety?" and "Is a hard-line stance worth the escalation and cost in lives?" When Libya's dictator, Muammar Qaddafi, threatens to bulldoze his rebel adversaries into the Mediterranean en masse, shouldn't the best response be to goad powers with a greater investment in Libya's future to act and back them in a coalition? Drones, Obama's weapon of choice, prowl the skies and take out bad guys at a fraction of the cost of sending troops into harm's way.

Meanwhile, Americans wage a war of their own, firing opinions about their former president like bullets flying at the speed of the Internet. For every citizen who thinks drones are a nifty way to keep the nation safe from enemies, at least one thinks the indiscriminate slaughter from the skies has only radicalized a frustrated, terrified people. In a nation where denial of anthropogenic climate change has become a badge to those on the right, plenty of people on the left believe Obama didn't do enough for the environment, conveniently forgetting that, after the 2010 midterms, there was nothing he could do short of issuing executive orders (and how popular *those* can be . . .). Googling Obama's name turns up hits insisting that the man who ordered the assassination of Osama bin Laden is *himself* a Muslim terrorist. Go figure.

SEX SYMBOL

Obama is believed by many to be a natural charmer who brought "cool" back to the White House. But as a young man he had little luck attracting women. His wife, Michelle, turned him down the first several times he asked her out, when he was a summer intern at a Chicago law firm and she his supervisor. She believed he was not particularly charming or attractive and later described him as "a slob." She began to warm to her future husband's advances after—what else?—hearing him deliver a speech to a local community group. Works every time.

PRIME DIRECTIVE

If it weren't for Obama's 2004 U.S. Senate win, he may never have found the national forum required for a presidential run. Yet that win came only after the spectacular fall of Republican Jack Ryan, an early favorite who withdrew from the race after the release of embarrassing documents detailing his divorce from actress Jeri Ryan (the alien "Seven of Nine" on the *Star Trek: Voyager* TV series). During the legal proceedings, Jeri accused Jack of forcing her to go to sex clubs and urging her to have sex in public. Obama demanded that Ryan release the divorce records but then changed his position, saying that Ryan's private life should not be a campaign issue—though he did so only after a judge had already ordered the records to be released. Less than three months from the election, Illinois Republicans were forced to enlist Alan Keyes to run in Ryan's place. Keyes, a Maryland resident, scrambled to acquire legal residency in the state in time to get on the ballot. Obama won the election handily.

BIGFOOT

According to journalist Jeffrey Goldberg, not long after becoming president Obama was scandalized to learn just how much it took to move the president, along with his massive entourage and security detail, wherever they went. Taking in the huge armada of vehicles, he remarked, "I have the world's largest carbon footprint."

IN THE GUTTER

During the 2008 primary campaign, Obama traveled to a Pennsylvania bowling alley to be videotaped playing a game popular with the white, working-class males he was having trouble winning over for the state's upcoming presidential primary. He rolled a gutter ball in his first frame and went on to bowl a 37, a score that would disappoint a clumsy child. Pundits, Clinton supporters, Republicans, radio talk show hosts, and late-night comedians all mocked Obama's hapless display.

WAFFLING

During his first presidential campaign, Obama's greatest rhetorical gift seemed to be his ability to say very little, but to say it in a particularly thoughtful and stirring manner. If he did take a stand on an issue—the war in Iraq, offshore drilling, free trade, unions, campaign finance reform, healthcare, immigration, even whether he was running for president—he was almost certain to state the opposite during a subsequent speech. Pressed by a reporter at a 2008 campaign stop in Pennsylvania to clarify his position on a key foreign policy issue, Obama responded, "Can't I just eat my waffle?"

ANOTHER TRIUMPH FOR THE LEFT

Obama is just the sixth confirmed left-hander to serve as U.S. president (not counting the ambidextrous James Garfield) and the fourth to occupy the White House since 1981, following Bill Clinton, George H. W. Bush, and Ronald Reagan.

AW, NUTS

When Sam Kass, the White House chef, relayed to the *New York Times* that he and the first lady teased the president about his habit of enjoying a late-night snack of exactly seven almonds, it confirmed Obama's image as abstemious and a little uptight. But Obama later set the record straight during an interview on the *Today* show, insisting that he did indeed snack on almonds, but didn't always count out exactly seven. "But, you know, almonds are a good snack," he went on. "I strongly recommend them."

LAUGH IT OFF

It's telling indeed that one of the contenders to replace Obama in 2017 once made a virtual career out of insisting that the forty-fourth president was not a natural-born citizen of the United States. The fact is, many of Obama's worst critics hated him so much that they'd believe almost anything about him.

Being president in an age of virulent, deeply entrenched polarization couldn't have been easy. But through his time in office, Obama largely remained cool as a cucumber. He also had a secret weapon: a killer sense of humor. "Who is Barack Obama?" the future president asked his audience at the 2008 Al Smith dinner. "Contrary to the rumors you have heard, I was not born in a manger. I was actually born on Krypton and sent here by my father Jor-El to save the planet Earth."

Granted, he had speechwriters, just like every other president. But Obama, who often shaped and tweaked the jokes given to him by writers, also had *delivery*—that vague but vital skill that encapsulates elements of timing and intelligence to make good material even better. He also had the rare gift of conveying self-awareness and making it work. Professional entertainers recognized him as one of their own, a rare thing for a high-profile politician. In addition to being a frequent guest on the late-night circuit (when Jimmy Fallon asked him if he thought the GOP was happy with Trump as their candidate, the president responded, "Uh . . . *we* are"), he joked with Zach Galifianakis on *Between Two Ferns* and rode shotgun with Jerry Seinfeld in *Comedians in Cars Getting Coffee*.

More than any other venue, the yearly White House Correspondents' Dinner, at which the president is allowed to show a playful side, turned the spotlight on Obama's wry sarcasm. Some highlights: "The Jonas Brothers are here, they're out there somewhere," he quipped in 2010. "Sasha and Malia are huge fans, but boys, don't get any ideas. Two words for you:

predator drones. You will never see it coming. You think I'm joking?" And this, from 2012: "Despite many obstacles, much has changed during my time in office. Four years ago, I was locked in a brutal primary battle with Hillary Clinton. Four years later, she won't stop drunk-texting me from Cartagena." And in 2013: "Some folks still don't think I spend enough time with Congress. 'Why don't you get a drink with Mitch McConnell?' they ask. Really? Why don't you get a drink with Mitch McConnell?" Perhaps his best material played on the "birther" movement, which alleged that Obama was born in Kenya, not Hawaii. In 2011 he announced to fellow dinner-goers that he was releasing, for the first time in fifty years, his actual "birth video." When the audience turned to watch the large screen, they were treated to the scene from *The Lion King* showing the birth of the lion cub Simba. As funny as that was, the follow-up—delivered deadpan—was pure Obama: "I wanna make clear to the Fox News table, that was a joke. That was not my real birth video. That was a children's cartoon. Call Disney if you don't believe me. They have the original long-form version."

45 | DONALD TRUMP

BORN June 14, 1946	NICKNAMES "The Donald," "Donald Drumpf"

ASTROLOGICAL SIGN	PARTY	AGE UPON TAKING OFFICE
Gemini	Republican	70

RAN AGAINST	VICE PRESIDENT
Hillary Clinton	★ Mike Pence ★

HEIGHT	SOUND BITE	TERM OF PRESIDENCY
6′ 3″	*"Oh, look at my African American over here. Look at him."*	2017–

D onald Trump's behavior during the 2016 presidential campaign was so outrageous and unprecedented that many pundits questioned his desire to win. In a year that turned seemingly everything on its ear, nothing stood out quite as much as "The Donald," blasting through one prediction of defeat after another, channeling his hatred of scripted speaking and nuanced thought and illegal immigrants and Hillary Clinton and "losers" and Muslim terrorists and consistency and uncooperative journalists and uncooperative Republicans and lengthy briefings and the Obama administration and Mexico and … and … and … His was stumping that looked more like shoddy comedic theater than a run for the White House. Trump was unrestrained, provocative, vulgar, juvenile, inflammatory, haughty, and relentlessly contemptuous of facts.

And he won.

Donald Trump was born and raised in the unlikeliest of places for a future crusader for ordinary white folk in rural heartland America: the borough of Queens, New York. He attended Kew Forest preparatory school in Forest Hills, where he displayed erratic and abusive behavior. Fred Trump, a wealthy real estate developer, hoped to sort out his son's disciplinary issues by sending him to the New York Military Academy, from which Trump graduated high school.

As a student from 1964 at Fordham University and then the Wharton School at the University of Pennsylvania, Trump skipped Vietnam with a series of student deferments. He also got a medical deferment owing to "heel spurs," which must have been more harrowing than the jungle warfare he was spared in Southeast Asia.

Even more greatness awaited him—this time in the rental markets of Queens, Brooklyn, and Staten Island. Even before graduating from college, Trump began working for his father's real estate company. He took it over in 1971 and, in the very first instance of what would become a long string of unimaginative christenings, named it . . . the Trump Organization.

Yes, Donald Trump soon developed a keen love of seeing his name on things. There's Trump Plaza, Trump Tower, Trump Taj Mahal, Trump Shuttle (jets!), *Trump Princess* (his yacht, don't you know), Trump Plaza Hotel and Casino, Trump World Tower, Trump Towers Istanbul, Trump Ocean Club International Hotel and Tower, the Trump Building, Trump Place, Trump International Hotel and Tower Chicago, Trump Hotel Las Vegas, Trump Park Avenue, Trump Winery, Trump Steaks . . . well, you got the idea.

After all, nothing says "Success!" quite like forcing people all over the world to see your name splashed on stuff they have to walk past on their way to work. But our hero didn't limit his noble endeavors to real estate, gambling, merchandise, and beef; no, he went into the greatest calling of all of America's most aspirational leaders—show business. Most famously, he starred in a reality television show called *The Apprentice*, in which ordinary people fought one another for the privilege of becoming an employee of Trump's vast empire. The show did well, not least because

Americans love watching people grovel before megalomaniacs, especially on TV.

But that's nothing compared to Trump's love affair with the prince of sports, World Wrestling Entertainment, that fine organization in which violent theatrics combine with bovine spectator reactions to create a spectacle too terrible to resist. If proof is needed of Trump's extraordinary marketing skills, it's this: he managed to sell his brand in real estate, clothing, and other things as "high class" (no, seriously) while engaging closely with the most ridiculous of low-class indulgences, professional wrestling.

Oh, to be leader of the free world! Our hero thought about it, again and again, and again. And again. He changed political affiliations, again and again. And again. A supporter of Ronald Reagan, Trump started out as a Republican. Then he was a member of the Reform Party. Before long he was a Democrat, until 2008. In 2011 he was an independent, for less than half a year. Then he became a Republican. Again.

Throughout these cognitively turbulent years, Trump contemplated runs for the presidency, some of which were little more than publicity stunts. Then, in 2015, he actually committed to running for the White House. For real.

But how could a real estate mogul from New York City with several divorces under his belt and a Queens accent win over the Republican Party? And against such stiff competition! Jeb Bush had his family's name, too, and none of the abject political failure that tarnished his brother Dubya. Ted Cruz was brilliant, highly educated, and evidently backed by the fell powers of Satan. But Trump did the one thing that none of his opponents could: he went all-in on unscripted speaking. It became the quintessential Trump MO, a kind of calling card. While everyone else in the GOP primary attempted to outline policy proposals for ending Obamacare, dealing with ISIS, cutting taxes, and expanding the military, the Donald

→   Prior to being elected President of the United States, Donald Trump was seen
tackling and assaulting Vince McMahon at Wrestlemania XXIII.

simply ranted and raved. He showed a gift for playing to crowds, a phenomenon that also worked well on the twenty-four-hour TV news cycle. Soon people across the country began to warm to a guy who was as fed up and impatient for change as they were. It was bold, rash even—he was laughed off as a clown and a narcissist by both the left and the right. But what nobody seemed to understand was the power of tapping into the national undercurrent of anxiety and staying on message. Few Americans wanted proposals that sounded tired and bound to go nowhere in a federal government that didn't seem to care. They wanted to bitch and moan and feel justified in their hatred and resentments. And Trump bitched and moaned right along with them.

"They're bringing drugs," Trump famously grumbled about illegal Mexican immigrants, "they're bringing crime. They're rapists." He even had the temerity to call out John McCain's ironclad status as a hero who had endured the unendurable in Vietnam: "He's not a war hero. He's a war hero because he got captured. I like people that weren't captured." Come again? While we're on the subject of prisoners, Trump had this to say about the treatment of those we capture in the ongoing war on terror: "I would bring back waterboarding, and I'd bring back a hell of a lot worse than waterboarding."

Nothing, however, drew as much attention—both negative and ecstatic—as his pledge to call for "a total and complete shutdown of Muslims entering the United States." The most inflammatory of declarations, it invited a firestorm of criticism, not least for its unconstitutionality.

Almost no one predicted that Trump would earn the GOP nomination for president, a fact that served to vindicate Trump's radical approach. His message was that the establishment—the very people who dismissed his candidacy as a bad joke in the first place—was out of touch. By winning, he proved it.

But to do so he had stunned the world with a performance that was, to say the least, controversial. Too many Republicans considered him a boor and a bigot who had hijacked the party. Not a few believed he was going to destroy it. During the Republican convention, Ted Cruz did the unthinkable, refusing to endorse the candidate during his primetime speech. Those Republicans who hoped Trump would somehow civilize his approach or at least grow up a little during the general election campaign against "Crooked Hillary" were disappointed. By the end of the summer, just two months before the election, more than a hundred prominent Republican leaders and luminaries had publicly declared their intention not to vote for their own party's nominee, including former New Jersey governor Christine Todd Whitman, Mitt Romney, Jeb Bush, and Senator Lindsey Graham.

How, in a general election, could such a person pull off a victory against an overqualified candidate like Hillary Clinton when he had a brushfire in his own backyard?

Clearly, 2016 was an election year like no other. Three things conspired to shatter public faith in government: first, widely reported statistics pointing to a growing and seemingly unstoppable income gap between the rich and everyone else; second, the related perception that, especially in the wake of the Supreme Court's Citizens United decision, the rich were transforming their mounting wealth into influence at every level of government, gaming the system and thwarting the will of ordinary people; and third, the very uneven recovery from the Great Recession that left large swaths of the population behind.

All of this played to Trump's advantage: he postured himself as the alternative to the ultimate "business-as-usual" candidate, a woman who had been in politics for over twenty-five years. Then there were voters who honestly believed that Trump's colossal wealth and business acumen made him a natural choice to lead a nation stuck in perpetual recovery. When you throw in all the racists and white supremacists who thrilled to Trump's anti-Mexican, anti-immigrant, anti-Muslim rhetoric, you have a very odd but large coalition—one aided by all the Americans too distrustful of Clinton to vote for her.

One of the unlikeliest victories in all of presidential politics (a mere two and a half months before the election, the *New York Times* gave Trump a mere 10 percent chance of winning), the elevation of Donald Trump to the White House represents a true sea change in the dynamic of Washington politics. For one thing, he's the richest man ever to be elected U.S. president, and by a country mile—although just *how* rich is a matter of conjecture, since his wealth is the product of a kaleidoscopic mélange of debt, real estate ownership, rentals, sales, and other stuff that keeps journalists at *Forbes* up at night sorting it out. And for another thing, the country now has a president whom many legislators in both parties loathe and may well refuse to work with.

But something even deeper has occurred. Donald Trump, whatever his appeal to the millions who voted for him, got where he is by being spectacularly nonpresidential. No candidate in American history has so perfectly or loudly broadcast his lack of qualifications for the office. That, apparently, is what the nation wanted: a rejection not just of the political status quo but of decorum, probity, vision, decency, forbearance, and wisdom.

What could go wrong?

BULLY PULPIT

"So if you see somebody getting ready to throw a tomato," quipped Donald Trump at a February 2016 rally, "knock the crap out of them, would you?" It was the sort of casual reference to violence at public appearances that occasionally made headlines during Trump's candidacy. Many of his supporters reacted atavistically to his messages, and when things got rough between them and protesters, the candidate happily fanned the flames. During another public-speaking event, he used a jeering tone while jerking his arms about to mock Serge Kovaleski, a *New York Times* reporter who happens to have arthrogryposis, a condition that limits the use of the arms and legs. "Now this poor guy, you ought to see this guy," said Trump contemptuously.

It was the bully from Kew Forest prep school all grown up. From a young age, Trump had a reputation for acting out, causing trouble, and picking on classmates. According the *Washington Post*, Donny got into trouble so often that his initials "DT" became shorthand for the punishment of going to detention. According to his memoir, *The Art of the Deal*, Trump slugged his second-grade music teacher in the eye and "almost got expelled." (Way to go, Junior.)

If there's any question that Donny hasn't changed since those early days, just ask him: "When I look at myself in the first grade and I look at myself now, I'm basically the same," he once said in an interview. "The temperament is not that different."

GETTING SKIN IN THE GAME

In August 2016, then-candidate Trump made a speech before an over-whelmingly white crowd in Ohio and asked a question: "What do you have to lose?" It was directed at African Americans, whose votes he desperately needed. He went on to say, "You're living in poverty, your schools are no good, you have no jobs, 58 percent of your youth is unemployed. What the hell do you have to lose? And at the end of four years, I guarantee you, I will get over 95 percent of the African American vote, I promise you." That Trump didn't see this type of message as offensive and demeaning is worse than the speech itself. But then, the Donald's issues with race go back quite a ways.

"My legacy has its roots in my father's legacy," Trump said in 2015. And those legacies include the plausible accusations of racism that surrounded the Trump real estate dynasty during the 1960s and 1970s. In 1973, responding to years of complaints from civil rights groups, local activists, and plenty of prospective tenants, the federal government charged Fred Trump and his son Donald with violating the Fair Housing Act, which prohibited racial discrimination in housing. Donald took the remarkable step of responding in kind: he hired Roy Cohn, the lawyer who had spearheaded Senator Joseph McCarthy's anticommunist crusade, to direct a countersuit against the government. After the two-year struggle, during which witness testimonials supported the claim that the Trumps systematically denied vacancies to black prospective tenants, the real estate company was compelled to sign a consent decree obliging them to desegregate their properties. However, because the ruling did not include an admission of guilt, Donald Trump, er, trumpeted it as a victory.

ATTENTION, ATTENTION!

According to *Trump Revealed*, by Michael Kranish and Marc Fisher, Trump dislikes extensive reading material. A typical example: during his campaign, a CEO bearing news that China was taking advantage of America offered to send Trump a full report. "Send me, like, three pages," came the reply. "I want it short." As he grew closer to his own nomination, Trump even considered reading a biography of a president, something he'd never done. Alas, he couldn't find the time.

The most damning evidence of Trump's short attention span comes from none other than Tony Schwartz, the man who ghostwrote *The Art of the Deal*, the monumental best seller that turned Donald Trump from a powerful real estate mogul into a huge celebrity. In his interview with the *New Yorker*, Schwartz painted a picture of a grown man who acted during interviews "like a kindergartner who can't sit still in a classroom." Schwartz, who has since regretted his role in paving the way for a Trump presidency, continued: "Trump has been written about a thousand ways from Sunday, but this fundamental aspect of who he is doesn't seem to be fully understood.... It's impossible to keep him focused on any topic, other than his own self-aggrandizement, for more than a few minutes.... If he had to be briefed on a crisis in the Situation Room, it's impossible to imagine him paying attention over a long period of time."

LYING LIKE A RUG

One of the great ironies of the 2016 presidential race was how Hillary Clinton was pegged as untrustworthy, though if anyone made a habit of lying, it was the Republican candidate whose nose wouldn't stop growing. First, let us recall that it was Trump who made a cottage industry out of denying that then-president Barack Obama had been born in the United States.

Trump continued spewing falsehoods, including a few in the speech announcing his candidacy. "Last quarter, it was just announced, our gross domestic product ... was below zero. Who ever heard of this? It's never below zero." As Pulitzer Prize–winning Politifact points out, this statement is wrong on two levels, the first involving Trump's misuse of the phrase "gross domestic product," or GDP. What he meant was *growth* in GDP, which has often been zero or less, especially during recoveries from recession.

Though plenty of organizations tracked the authenticity and verisimilitude of Trump's speeches, average Americans did not. Trump and his camp almost certainly knew this; truth was a casualty of hysterical messaging. Here are more falsehoods Trump spread, usually repeatedly despite being debunked:

- The United States has a $500 billion trade deficit with China.

- Thousands of Jersey City, NJ, Muslims cheered when the World Trade Center collapsed.

- 81% of murdered whites are killed by blacks; 16% are killed by other whites.

- Christian Syrian refugees cannot enter the United States, but Muslim Syrian refugees can.

- The U.S. has a trade deficit with Japan of over $100 billion.

- Healthcare premiums are going up 35, 45, 55 percent.

TEFLON DON

The nation's forty-fifth commander-in-chief has a history of espousing, saying, and even funding things that would have caused serious trouble for candidates of an earlier age.

Take, for example, the outrageous boondoggle of Trump University. Pestered for years by the state of New York to change its name (because it was not an accredited university with a charter), the outfit was renamed "Trump Entrepreneur Initiative." Its playbook and instruction material, along with unsealed affidavits from court cases against the defunct organization, paint an alarming picture of just what went on there. Selling the idea as a means of learning Donald Trump's secrets in wealth creation, the institute promised all kinds of things that it didn't actually deliver,

like access to Trump (according to one piece in the *New Yorker*, "The closest that the attendees at the seminars got to Trump was when they were
encouraged to have their picture taken with a life-size photo of him"), a
curriculum overseen by Trump (he had nothing to do with the courses),
and instructors hand-picked by Trump (he didn't hand-pick anyone). All
this values education cost a hefty sum and was sold to prospective students through an elaborate bait-and-switch program aimed at building
trust and getting buyers to invest in ever-more-expensive instruction
packages. "Based upon my personal experience and employment," wrote
a former salesman for the group, "I believe that Trump University was a
fraudulent scheme, and that it preyed upon the elderly and uneducated to
separate them from their money."

SELECT BIBLIOGRAPHY

Andersen, Christopher. *Bill and Hillary: The Marriage.* New York: William Morrow and Company, 1999.

Anderson, Fred. *Crucible of War: The Seven Years' War and the Fate of Empire in British North America, 1754–1766.* New York: Alfred A. Knopf, 2000.

Ayres, Alex. *The Wit and Wisdom of Abraham Lincoln.* New York: Meridian, 1992.

Begala, Paul. *"Is Our Children Learning?": The Case Against George W. Bush.* New York: Simon and Schuster, 2000.

Bernstein, Carl. *A Woman in Charge: The Life of Hillary Rodham Clinton.* New York: Vintage Books, 2008.

Boller, Paul F., Jr. *Presidential Anecdotes.* Rev. ed. New York: Oxford University Press, 1996.

Brallier, Jess, and Sally Chabert. *Presidential Wit and Wisdom: Maxims, Mottoes, Sound Bites, Speeches, and Asides—Memorable Quotes from America's Presidents.* New York: Penguin Books, 1996.

Brands, H. W. *TR: The Last Romantic.* New York: BasicBooks, 1997.

Brinkley, Alan, and Davis Dyer, eds. *The Reader's Companion to the American Presidency.* New York: Houghton Mifflin, 2000.

Clinton, Hillary Rodham. *Living History.* New York: Scribner, 2004.

Cunningham, Noble E., Jr. *In Pursuit of Reason: The Life of Thomas Jefferson.* New York: Ballantine Books, 1987.

Dallek, Robert. *An Unfinished Life: John F. Kennedy, 1917–1963.* New York: Little, Brown and Comany, 2003.

Donald, David Herbert. *Lincoln.* New York: Simon and Schuster, 1995.

Dumbauld, Edward. *Thomas Jefferson, American Tourist.* Norman: University of Oklahoma Press, 1946.

Ellis, Joseph J. *American Sphinx: The Character of Thomas Jefferson.* New York: Vintage Books, 1996.

———. *Founding Brothers: The Revolutionary Generation.* New York: Alfred A. Knopf, 2000.

Freidel, Frank Burt. *Franklin D. Roosevelt: A Rendezvous with Destiny.* New York: Little, Brown and Company, 1990.

Green, Mark, and Gail MacColl. *There He Goes Again: Ronald Reagan's Reign of Error.* New York: Pantheon Books, 1983.

Halliday, E. M. *Understanding Thomas Jefferson.* New York: HarperCollins, 2001.

Hamilton, Neil A. *Presidents: A Biographical Dictionary.* New York: Checkmark Books (Facts on File), 2001.

Hannah, Mark, and Bob Staake. *The Best "Worst President": What the Right Gets Wrong About Barack Obama.* New York: Dey Street, 2016.

Hersh, Seymour M. *The Dark Side of Camelot*. New York: Little, Brown and Company, 1997.

———. *The Price of Power: Kissinger in the Nixon White House*. New York: Summit Books, 1983.

Ivins, Molly, and Lou Dubose. *Shrub: The Short but Happy Political Life of George W. Bush*. New York: Alfred A. Knopf, 2000.

Kessler, Ronald. *Inside the White House: The Hidden Lives of the Modern Presidents and the Secrets of the World's Most Powerful Institution*. New York: Pocket Books, 1995.

Ketcham, Ralph. *James Madison: A Biography*. New York: Macmillan Company, 1971.

Klein, Philip S. *President James Buchanan: A Biography*. University Park: Pennsylvania State University Press, 1962.

Kranish, Michael, and Marc Fisher. *Trump Revealed: An American Journey of Ambition, Ego, Money, and Power*. New York: Scribner, 2016.

Landler, Mark. *Altar Egos: Hillary Clinton, Barack Obama, and the Twilight Struggle Over American Power*. New York: Random House, 2016.

Lewis, Thomas A. *For King and Country: The Maturing of George Washington, 1748–1760*. New York: HarperCollins, 1993.

Maraniss, David. *Barack Obama: The Story*. New York: Simon and Schuster, 2013.

McCullough, David. *John Adams*. New York: Simon and Schuster, 2001.

Morris, Edmund. *Dutch: A Memoir of Ronald Reagan.* New York: Random House, 1999.

Nagel, Paul C. *John Quincy Adams: A Public Life, a Private Life.* New York: Alfred A. Knopf, 1997.

Randall, Willard Sterne. *George Washington: A Life.* New York: Henry Holt and Company, 1997.

———. *Thomas Jefferson: A Life.* New York: Henry Holt and Company, 1993.

Remini, Robert V. *The Life of Andrew Jackson.* New York: Harper and Row, 1988.

Seager, Robert II. *And Tyler Too: A Biography of John and Julia Gardiner Tyler.* New York: McGraw-Hill Book Company, Inc., 1963.

Smith, Jean Edward. *Grant.* New York: Simon and Schuster, 2001.

Smith, Richard Norton. *Patriarch: George Washington and the New American Nation.* New York: Houghton Mifflin, 1993.

Stebben, Gregg, and Jim Morris. *White House Confidential: The Little Book of Weird Presidential History.* Nashville, Tenn.: Cumberland House Publishing, 1998.

Summers, Anthony. *The Arrogance of Power: The Secret World of Richard Nixon.* New York: Viking Penguin, 2000.

Whitcomb, John, and Claire Whitcomb. *Real Life at the White House: Two Hundred Years of Daily Life at America's Most Famous Residence.* New York: Routledge, 2000.

INDEX

William McKinley, 152, 187
assaults, 57–58, 59, 60, 92, 115
Atzerodt, George, 114

B

Babcock, Orville, 122
bachelors, 98
Baer, Jacob, 98
Baker, Bobby, 221
Baker, James, 259
Bankhead, William, 199
banks and banking, 55, 57, 62, 71, 171. *See also* recessions
Barkley, Alben W., 202
Barnes, Ben, 279
Bay of Pigs, 218, 223
Begin, Menachem, 250
Belknap, William, 122
Biden, Joe, 282
bin Laden, Osama, 274, 278, 287
Blaine, James G., 128, 130, 140
bodyguards, *see* security
Booth, John Wilkes, 109, 114
Boss Tweed, 125
Boutwell, George, 122
Boxer Rebellion, 152
Brandegee, Frank, 179
Breckenridge, John C., 95, 101
bribery, 23, 32, 130, 135, 149
Britton, Nan, 178, 179
Broaddrick, Juanita, 271
Brown, Larry Douglas, 271
Bryan, William Jennings, 150, 152, 164
Bryant, Joseph, 145
Buchanan, James, 93, 94, 95–100

bullies, 298
Burr, Aaron, 22, 27, 53
Bush, Barbara, 189, 264
Bush, George Herbert Walker, 254, 261–65, 266, 289
Bush, George W., 264, 274–81
Bush, Jeb, 294, 297
Butt, Archie, 168
Butterfield, Daniel, 121–22

C

Calhoun, John C., 46, 54, 80
Callender, James Thomson, 32
card players, 48, 176, 178, 213
Carow, Edith Kermit, 159
Carter, James Earl, 245, 246, 248–53, 254, 255
Carter, Rosalynn, 189, 248, 252
Cass, Lewis, 79, 80
Cermack, Anton, 200
Chambers, Whittaker, 231
Chase, Chevy, 246
Checkers Speech, 231
Cheney, Richard, 274
Chennault, Anna, 234
Chotiner, Murray, 235
Christian, Elizabeth Ann, 178
Churchill, Winston, 198, 199, 203, 241
citizenship, 291
Citizens United, 297
Civil War, 101–102, 104, 106, 111, 117, 126, 135–36, 142, 150, 154
Clay, Henry, 46–48, 54, 67, 71, 75, 80, 85
Clemenceau, Georges, 160

ACKNOWLEDGMENTS

Of all the sources used in researching this book, five were indispensable. *The Reader's Companion to the American Presidency*, edited by Alan Brinkley and Davis Dyer, and Neil A. Hamilton's *Presidents: A Biographical Dictionary* are excellent overviews of the men and their times. Paul F. Boller's *Presidential Anecdotes* remains a classic chronicle of White House folklore, while *Real Life at the White House: Two Hundred Years of Daily Life at America's Most Famous Residence*, by John Whitcomb and Claire Whitcomb, is a veritable treasure trove of information about presidential families and their struggles with everyday existence. For a look at the presidents in their own words, I found *Presidential Wit and Wisdom: Maxims, Mottoes, Sound Bites, Speeches, and Asides—Memorable Quotes from America's Presidents*, by Jess Brallier and Sally Chabert, to be extremely helpful.

I would also like to thank my editor, Jason Rekulak, who believed in me from the start and whose comments helped create a better book; Erin Slonaker, whose assiduous reading of the manuscript held me to the highest of standards; Eugene Smith, whose inspired illustrations are as entertaining as anything I've written; designer Andie Reid, who whipped an unwieldy project into a beautiful book; and Lauren Beck, without whose love, support, and input this whole thing would literally have been impossible.